FASCISM

PAST, PRESENT, FUTURE

FAS

Walter Laqueur

OXFORD UNIVERSITY PRESS

New York   Oxford

Oxford University Press

Oxford   New York
Athens   Auckland   Bangkok   Bogotá   Bombay
Buenos Aires   Calcutta   Cape Town   Dar es Salaam
Delhi   Florence   Hong Kong   Istanbul   Karachi
Kuala Lumpur   Madras   Madrid   Melbourne
Mexico City   Nairobi   Paris   Singapore
Taipei   Tokyo   Toronto   Warsaw

and associated companies in
Berlin   Ibadan

Copyright © 1996 by Walter Laqueur

First published by Oxford University Press, Inc., 1996

First issued as an Oxford University Press paperback, 1997

Oxford is a registered trademark of Oxford University Press

Library of Congress Cataloging-in-Publication Data
Laqueur, Walter, 1921–
Fascism: past, present, future / Walter Laqueur.
p.   cm.   Includes bibliographical references and index.
ISBN 0-19-509245-7
ISBN 0-19-511793-x (Pbk.)
1. Fascism—History.   2. Fascism.   I. Title.
JC481.L34   1996
320.5′33′09—dc20   95-17612

1 3 5 7 9 10 8 6 4 2

Printed in the United States of America

To the memory of Naomi

Her ways were ways of pleasantness
and all her paths were peace.

Contents

3   Postfascism

FASCISM

Introduction

In an introduction, the author should state what his subject is and also perhaps why he thinks it of some importance. In regard to this book, the second part of the question is easier to answer than the first. Although fascism seems to be dead, it could have a second coming in different forms. If the history of art is a history of revivals, so, mutatis mutandis, is political history.

In the preface to *Fascism, a Reader's Guide*, which I edited in 1976, I wrote:

> Fascism remains a subject of much heated argument. In daily usage it is hurled as an invective against political enemies. It is frequently invoked in the media; in the university it attracts more students of history and political science than almost any other subject; and on the loftiest level it has become the topic of metaphysical speculation. It also continues to be the subject of controversy, partly because it collides with so many preconceived ideological notions, partly because generalizations are made difficult by the fact there was not one fascism but several fascisms.

Today one could not stop there. Communism has collapsed; there has been an upsurge of the extreme Right; and events outside Europe affect both our interpretation of historical fascism and the prospect of its successor movements.

This book is divided into three parts. The first deals with historical fascism, its ideology, its specific features, the reasons that it received the support of many millions, and how it came to power. This section also describes, albeit briefly, the way in which various nations coped with their fascist past after the defeat of the Axis.

Part 2 deals with the emergence since World War II of fascist, neofascist, right-wing extremist, and radical nationalist populist movements; they can be described by many terms. I try to single out the characteristics that they share with the fascism of Hitler and Mussolini, as well as those that make them different. Even though such groups were marginal fifteen years ago, today some of them can no longer be dismissed as inconsequential.

Part 3 deals with clerical fascism—that is, radical Islam and similar trends in other religions, and the appearance of extremist groups in the former Soviet Union and Eastern Europe. Although ultranationalism and religious fundamentalism are movements quite distinct from the fascism of Hitler and Mussolini, they also have much in common with fascism.

The Conclusion sums up the facts and the interpretations and briefly discusses the prospects of these movements.

With the end of World War II and the defeat of the Axis powers, it was generally assumed that the era of fascism had ended. This belief prevailed for several decades after 1945, and to some extent there is no reason even now, half a century later, to revise this judgment. Italian Fascism, German National Socialism, and the other movements of the 1920s and 1930s fashioning themselves after their example arose in certain historical conditions that no longer exist. Small groups in various parts of the world continue trying to revive the old Nazism and Fascism, embracing their emblems and slogans and, of course, their ideas and political programs. But even if these corpses could be resurrected, they would still be irrelevant to today's world. Just as Communism in its Leninist–Stalinist incarnation cannot be resurrected, historical fascism cannot have a second coming, either.

But does this means that the fascist genus no longer exists, that there is no longer a fascist impulse, that the fascist tradition is no longer relevant? Few people can give a categorical answer. How can we identify the movements and regimes that have appeared in parts of the world such as the former Soviet Empire and the Middle East, in which fascism had no foothold at the time? Few of these movements refer to themselves as *neofascist*, preferring instead such labels as "National Front," "Republican," or even "Liberal." Academic writers now refer to them as right-wing extremists or right-wing populists, national revolutionaries, national socialists, or some other such term.

Such movements all have a strongly nationalist orientation and oppose liberalism and Communism. But with the demise of the Soviet bloc, Communism is no longer a major enemy, and so the antiliberal and anticapitalist component in their ideology has taken pride of place, together with the hatred of foreigners in their midst. The adherents of these groups see the parliamentary system as breaking down, and so they favor a strong government and law and order. Moreover, they believe that some of the experience of Nazism and Fascism was positive and should be adapted to modern conditions.

The movements that have gathered strength inside and outside Europe since the early 1980s belong to a tradition that in one form or another can be traced back a century or even longer. The emergence of these movements should not come as a great surprise, as without them the political spectrum would be incomplete. As one observer put it, this is the normal pathology of modern society.

Among Marxists it was at one time fashionable to consider the advent of fascism as a punishment for the weakness, incompetence, and political mistakes of the revolutionary working-class movement. But it was precisely the revolutionism (often merely verbal) of the extreme Left that antagonized wide sections of the population and enabled the fascists to attract a mass base. Indeed, with greater justification it could be argued that the strengthening of fascism, then and now, was the result of the failure of democratic systems to resolve the problems facing them. The breakdown of democratic institutions—the failure of the democratic spirit—opened the doors to fascism. This generalization should not however, be pushed too far, for even though it may apply to much of Europe, it is not valid in countries that never knew democracy.

In France, Russia, Italy, and Austria, the parties of the extreme Right are among the strongest. By adopting certain aspects of contemporary youth culture (such as the skinheads), neofascist groups have been able to gain a foothold in most European countries and beyond. In addition, the presence of millions of foreign workers (and foreign unemployed) and the resulting tensions have become a major political issue, and this xenophobia has become a breeding ground of neofascism.

In new guises the ghost of fascism also has surfaced in parts of the world where few expected it. The former Soviet Union and the countries of Eastern Europe face enormous difficulties in the transition to a new social and political order. Although Communism has been overthrown, it is by no means dead: It merely has reappeared as national Communism or national socialism; the "Red–Brown alliance" is its new look.

In the Middle East, radical Islam is a rising force and has a striking overlap with fascism. But this *clerical fascism* is not a new phenomenon, as the term was used in Italy as far back as 1921 to describe those advocating a symbiosis between Catholicism and the dynamic new political movement headed by Benito Mussolini. During World War II, clerical fascist regimes ruled Slovakia and Croatia. Slovakia may have been more conservative, but the Ustasha state in Croatia was radical by any standard. Today the phenomenon is of greater political importance than it was in the past.

Clerical fascism is part of a wider movement in the Third World. The possibility and likelihood of fascism outside Europe and North America was discussed during the years before and after World War II, and most observers argued that this was a "false fascism." Such an appraisal was true at the time but no longer seems to be correct. That is, being a modern mass movement, fascism was feasible only once a country had reached a certain level of modernization. This was not the case in the 1930s, but it does apply to an increasing number of countries today. But would not Third World fascism be more Third World than fascist? This could well be the case, as it certainly was correct with regard to Third World Communism. But fascism always had much more room for variation than Communism did, even in Europe. Therefore, the composition of the fascist synthesis must be examined and may be different in each case.

Hundreds of books and thousands of articles have been written on a theory of fascism, but even as they clarified a few issues, they obfuscated others. For example, the author of a recent study on right-wing extremism that provided a survey of its present state concluded that we are only at the beginning of finding a theory.[1] There is reason to assume that we shall stay at the beginning for a long time to come. The purpose of a theory is not to find the broadest general denominator but to clarify a particular phenomenon. If the theory fails to do this, it might still be of interest on an abstract level, but equally, it may be disregarded without much risk.

There is a widespread misconception that one cannot begin to study a subject if it does not have an exact definition and a good theory. Unfortunately, however, the real world is very complicated and one usually must do research and describe events without the benefit of a theory, which, in any case, should come at the end rather than the beginning.

Fascism resembles pornography in that it is difficult—perhaps impossible—to define in an operational, legally valid way, but those with experience know it when they see it. Does such a subjective, "impressionistic" approach open the door to all kinds of arbitrary judgments and incorrect interpretations? Not necessarily. President Franklin Roosevelt was called a fascist at one time (by the Communists), and so were the Social Democrats (by Stalin) and Stalin (by the anti-Communists). But Roosevelt, Stalin, and the Social Democrats were not fascists, and there is no good reason to take seriously every eccentric allegation.

According to the purists, the use of the generic term *fascist* has been problematic even with regard to historical fascism. I have some sympathy with this point of view, for the term *fascism* tends to gloss over the important differences between Germany and Italy. Hitler would have strongly denied that he was a fascist, just as Mussolini would have rejected the Nazi label. Aleksandr Barkashov, leader of one of the most militant neofascist groups in Moscow, is a karate instructor, not an ideologist. But when he asserted in an interview that he was a National Socialist and not a fascist, he was correct.

Nonetheless, the generic term *fascism* has continued to be used, mainly for practical reasons: A single word is needed rather than several paragraphs. However, the systematic use of the term *fascism* in regard to Nazi Germany was also politically motivated. Many on the Left had an instinctive horror of applying the term (*national*) *socialism* to an abomination such as the Nazi Party. The use of the term *fascism* with regard to Nazi Germany also obliterates the important differences between the two regimes and the fact that leading authorities on the subject, such as K. D. Bracher and Renzo de Felice, were among the most outspoken opponents of the use of the generic term *fascism* provides, at the very least, food for thought.

The use of the term *neofascism* is even more problematical. *Neo* makes it clear that it is not identical with historical fascism, but *fascist* is the stronger part of the definition. Fascism conjures up visions of hundreds of thousands of brown and black shirts marching in the streets of Europe, of civil violence and aggressive war, of terror and relentless propaganda, of millions of victims. This, of course, is no longer true with regard to the postwar period, certainly not with regard to the 1990s. Furthermore, the term has been discredited as the result of its overuse and misuse in the political discourse. It has been used as a synonym for racialism, xenophobia, sexism, right-wing conservative and reactionary views, Stalinism, and so on. But not everyone who opposes further immigration is a fascist; not every anti-Semite is a fascist; and not every ultranationalist is a fascist. There is a "fascist minimum," and those who do not qualify may still sympathize with certain aspects of fascism or even share certain basic tenets, even though they are not full-fledged fascists or neofascists.

Present-day European realities, the welfare state, the greater rootedness of democratic institutions, the collapse of Communism, and, above all, Europe's diminished status on the world scene impose restrictions on those enthralled by the dictatorships of the 1930s. The slogan of the 1930s, "Fascism means war," certainly does not make sense today. Although some neofascists may want war, it just is no longer possible except in the Caucasus or Yugoslavia. What kind of fascism is this, without violence, without threats to exterminate the enemy? Why use the term *neofascism* in the first place if the neofascists observe the democratic rules of the game? But it could be a little too early to take their commitment to democracy for granted. Outside western Europe, in Russia and the Middle East, such democratic claims are not even made. For the time being, fascist parties in Western Europe are relatively weak and so must move cautiously. No one knows, however, how democratically they would act if they were in power.

More important yet, what alternative terms could be used? Several have been suggested, as we mentioned earlier, terms such as *right-wing extremism, right-wing radicalism, radical right-wing populism, national populism,* and *national revolutionaries*. But it is generally agreed that these terms also are unsatisfactory. To some people, but not others, they may be more or less correct. According to accepted belief, the Right is the party of privilege and of conservative, antisocialist views. But the political support for the "extreme Right" now comes mainly from the lower classes, and they are not particularly eager to conserve the present social and political order. Many favor some form of state socialism (or capitalism).

The use of the term *right, extreme,* or *radical* makes sense only if one assumes the coexistence of two or more rights, one conservative and the other radical, and this introduces a new element of confusion. The law-and-order label may partially fit the far Right in France and Germany and perhaps also in Italy. However, the newcomers among the *radical Right*, such as the skinheads (almost entirely a working-class phenomenon), the Zhirinovsky movement, the dictatorship of the mullahs in Iran, and fundamentalism in general, cut across the right–left typology.

In the 1930s, Nazis and Fascists took great pride in belonging to their respective movements. Today, however, this is no longer so, and not just because it would be politically unwise or because fascism is illegal in some countries. Nor is the *populist* label of much use. Although it seems to offer a way out of taxonomic difficulties, it is only at the price of great fuzziness. In turn, this leads inevitably to the discovery of subcategories, such as left or right (or radical and moderate) populists following different, and indeed conflicting, policies. One writer defined populism as a "movement of the propertied middle class that mobilizes the lower class, especially the urban poor, with radical rhetoric, directed against imperialism, foreign capitalism and the political establishment."[2]

Khomeinism, a recent extremist movement in Iran, is not merely a religious crusade but also an expression of socioeconomic grievances. But attempts to reduce complex political movements (such as fascism or populism) to their "class character" are never completely successful and often are misleading. Even if they were successful, they could only explain, at most, why such movements initially receive mass support and become powerful. Over time, they invariably break away from their socioeconomic base, although once the genie is out of the bottle, the "propertied middle class" cannot put it back in again.

Political parties, furthermore, tend to change over the years; even the Italian MSI is not what it was in 1980, and so its change of name did not come as a surprise. Likewise, the Republican Party of Ruritania contains neofascist elements as well as conservative antirevolutionaries. Some of its leaders and followers are staunch anticapitalists, whereas others take a dim view of socialism in any form. Furthermore, parties usually split or merge with another within a year or two, which affects their political orientation.

In sum, few of the parties mentioned in this book are pure, unalloyed neofascism or right-wing extremism, but all contain certain such elements, some more, others less.

I am not happy with my own choice of terms and definitions, but I am not aware of better ones. Should I focus instead on underlying motives and social and psychological origins, rather than aims? It has been suggested that extreme right-wing and neofascist parties consist of the "losers of modernity," that is, those who have suffered as the result of modernization or those who have not yet been affected but fear that such a fate is in store for them. This might be true for some movements in some countries, but it does not explain France's Le Pen or Italy's neofascism or, in retrospect, Hitler or Mussolini.

Alternatively, it has been argued that in every society, people with an "authoritarian personality" tend to join groups of the extreme Right. If this were true, it would be tantamount to singling out only one aspect of a multifaceted phenomenon, usually to the detriment of others. Until the demise of Communism, some people maintained that despite all the similarities between fascist (or neofascist) and Communist movements, their attitudes toward the economy were diametrically opposed: the market and private enterprise versus nationalization of the means of production. It is a matter of dispute whether this division was really ever as fundamental as some wanted to have it. But whatever the historical record, more recently Communism has moved away from the old Soviet model, whereas the extreme Right, always uneasy about capitalism, has moved toward a "third way." Whatever the differences that survive, they are certainly not basic.

The terms *right* and *left*, although not altogether useless, become more problematical as one moves away in time and space from nineteenth-century Europe. They can still be used with caution in regard to Western Europe and North America, but elsewhere they are quite misleading. Those Russians who voted for Zhirinovsky do not see themselves as belonging to the extreme Right or Left; likewise, radical Islam (or the Nation of Islam) is neither leftist nor rightist.

Although one could quarrel endlessly about terms and definitions, such purism is not helpful and might even be dangerous. It is not helpful because an ideal generic definition covering every aspect of the phenomenon does not exist. According to a recent definition, fascism is a "genus of political ideology whose mythic core in its various permutations is a palingenetic form of popular ultra nationalism" (Roger Griffin). ("Palingenetic" refers to a renaissance of the national spirit.) Even though it might be difficult to improve on this statement, it still covers movements that are not really fascist and omits others that are.

The quandary facing students of history and politics is similar to that of physicians having to deal with a disease about which they have insufficient knowledge: Each case may be a little different; none corresponds entirely to the textbooks; and its similarities to other diseases may create confusion. But all this does not exempt the doctor from making a diagnosis, even if imperfect, and to take appropriate action. In the real world, as distinct from the world of abstraction and theory building, absolute exactitude is always lacking. This conclusion is unsatisfactory but, in practice, usually not very important, and in any case we must live with it.

The quandary facing contemporary observers is similar to that facing Tocqueville when writing 150 years ago about the coming dangers:

> I think . . . that the species of oppression by which democratic nations are menaced is unlike anything that ever before existed in the world. Our contemporaries will find no prototype in their memories. I seek in vain for an expression that will accurately convey the whole of the idea I have formed of it. The old words despotism and tyranny are inappropriate; the thing itself is new, and since I cannot name it, I must attempt to define it.

The search for definition and formulas belongs to the postfascist age. Those who lived under fascism knew (and know) in their bones in what way this regime differed from others. Such practical experience with fascism is difficult to bequeath, however; hence the preoccupation with the theory of fascism.

In the meantime, those not preoccupied with taxonomy—that is, the great majority—watch with fascination the emergence of new species of fascism outside Europe. These newcomers feel no guilt and no urge to apologize. Some are open and brazen about their doctrines and politics, whereas others are not even aware of their heritage: They are instinctive fascists. Fascism originated in the early years of this century. As this century draws to a close, these powerful impulses still exist, but the scenery surrounding them has changed.

Writing about the enduring relevance of the totalitarian temptation, Karl Dietrich Bracher noted several years ago that modern technological developments have perfected the techniques of surveillance and manipulation and that the mass media and information technology are a potential threat to liberty. "All ideas and movements with an absolute, unilateral objective are today potentially totalitarian, if the goal is seen to justify the means and if the movements spread the belief that there is one key to solving all problems here on earth."[3]

When Bracher wrote these words, the Communist system still existed. Although this particular danger has now disappeared, it has been replaced by new threats in Eastern Europe and the former Soviet Union, which I discuss in this book. In brief, the nightmare is not over yet.

1

FASCISM

The Essence of Fascism

The question of what fascism is has been debated for many decades but frequently has produced more heat than light. It has intensely preoccupied political scientists in their search for a "generic model" covering all varieties of fascism. For the wider public these exercises have not been of much interest. One can endlessly discuss whether Nazism was the highest, most accomplished form of fascism and Mussolini's regime was therefore a mere halfway house, or whether Italian Fascism—perhaps because it was the first on the scene—should be the yardstick by which all other fascisms should be measured. In this case, Nazism seems in retrospect a hyperradical, exaggerated version of a new idea relentlessly pursued to its logical conclusions. One can debate forever whether Nazism and Italian Fascism were modernizing movements by intention or despite their intention or whether they were reactionary. Fascism did not belong to the extreme Left, yet defining it as part of the extreme Right is not very illuminating either. In many respects, fascism was not conservative at all in inspiration but was aimed at creating a new society with a new kind of human beings.

One would hope that there would be no need to define once again the essence of fascism. But it is necessary because in popular parlance it is used quite indiscriminately. Writers and speakers tend to denounce their political foes as fascists (or at least semi- or parafascists); that is, it has become a synonym for a dozen or more phenomena, usually negative in character. It therefore is easier to define what fascism is not. Twentieth-century dictatorships may be detestable, but they are not necessarily fascist. Japan in the 1930s was not a fascist country, nor was Atatürk's Turkey, nor Poland under Pilsudski, nor Spain under Franco. Likewise, the military dictatorships after World War II such as Chile under Pinochet and Greece under the colonels were not fascist.

When fascism first appeared on the political scene, it should have been clear that it contained certain essentially new factors, that it belonged to a new breed. But this was not widely realized at the time. Everyone agreed that Nazism and fascism were extremely nationalistic in orientation and that they were antidemocratic. Beyond this, however, there was no unanimity, and since it is only natural to interpret new phenomena in the light of old ones, some analysts referred to the Bonapartist model (the great Napoleon as well as his descendant Napoleon III). Others saw fascism in the tradition of the extreme right-wing, antiliberal groups of the late nineteenth century. Defining fascism was difficult because only two countries ever became fascist. During World War II, the Vichy-style regimes under Axis tutelage cannot truly be considered fully fledged fascist, even though some, such as Croatia, tried hard to move in that direction.

Fascism was also not a static phenomenon. During its early period, Italian Fascism was radical in it orientation, but once it seized power it became more moderate in essential respects. Then in its last stage, it again returned to its radical beginnings.

Italian Fascism meant something different in the cities and in the countryside. Only six years passed from the time the Nazi regime came into power until it unleashed the war, when all domestic concerns were subordinated to the war effort. We can only speculate what Nazi policy would have been if Germany had won the war, whether, for instance, the economic system would have been changed, whether it would have turned against the church, whether those people considered racially inferior would have been killed or expelled, whether the regime would have moderated its policies, or whether, in sociological terms, *routinization* and *normalization* would have taken over.

One of the few issues on which there was a consensus at the time was the assumption that fascism was a European phenomenon. This seems true even now in regard to "historical" fascism. At that time, fascism in very backward countries was technically impossible because the masses could not be mobilized and propaganda and terror were not yet sufficiently effective. Whether this is still true today is less certain, because with the spread of modern technologies the preconditions for non-European varieties of fascism do exist now in many parts of the world.

What made fascism different from earlier dictatorships was the presence of a mass party that monopolized power through its security services and the army and that eliminated all other parties, using considerable violence in the process. This new style of party was headed by a leader who had virtually unlimited power, was adulated by his followers, and was the focus of a quasi-religious cult. The party's doctrine became an obligatory article of faith for not only its members but all other citizens and was constantly projected by means of a powerful propaganda machinery. Such a party—and, later, a state apparatus—would not have been feasible earlier in history because it would have been impossible to impose similar political, social, and cultural controls and to influence masses of people so intensively.

What we have said so far also applies to the Communist regimes. True, the interference of the fascist state in the economy was much less far reaching than under Communism. Soviet ideology stressed the class character of the regime or, rather, the gradual abolition of (antagonistic) classes. Conversely, in fascist doctrine, solidarity of the classes was the supreme aim. Communism was strictly atheistic, whereas fascism was vaguely deistic, striving for an accommodation with organized religion on condition that the church accept the state as its political overlord and support it. Whereas fascism was overtly nationalistic, militaristic, and expansionist, Communism was theoretically internationalist and antimilitarist and had no dreams of territorial expansion. But in reality the differences, especially from the 1930s onward, were not always visible to the naked eye.[1]

The two systems were quite similar, almost identical, in some respects but different in others, so they were bound to collide once fascism prevailed in Germany. Hitler had persuaded himself that unless Germany acquired new *Lebensraum* in his lifetime, it would collapse, because it did not have sufficient raw materials to provide a decent standard of living for its citizens and also to maintain its status as a great power.

The Soviet regime was under no such immediate pressure, although in the long term it could feel secure only if Soviet-style Communism prevailed at least in Europe and contingent parts of Asia. But Stalin did not have the same desperate urgency to expand right away.

What conditions favored the rise of these new types of mass parties, and in what circumstances did fascism find it impossible to progress? Although "conditions" are only one of the factors in this equation, they are an important one. "Conditions" alone, however, would not have brought about the triumph of Hitler and Mussolini. On the other hand, in the absence of a favorable political constellation, even the greatest political genius would have failed to make headway.

In both Germany and Italy, the Nazi and Fascist seizure of power was greatly facilitated by the leading figures of the old order: in Germany by the Conservatives and Hindenburg's entourage and in Italy by the Conservatives and the monarchy. Hitler was the leader of the strongest parliamentary faction, and based on the constitution, a case could be made in favor of inviting him to be the next chancellor. Aware of their own weakness, the Conservatives assumed that it would be possible to rein in the Nazis and make them behave "reasonably." The pressures in Italy eleven years earlier that had brought about the Fascist takeover had been similar.

It is impossible, even with the benefit of hindsight, to say with any certainty whether Hitler and Mussolini would have dared to seize power without such legal sanction. And even if they had dared it, there is no certainty that they would have been successful. Elsewhere, violent fascist coups did fail, but this is not conclusive evidence, since Nazism and Italian Fascism were stronger than those who were defeated, and the resistance against them was weaker.

Why did strong fascist movements develop in some countries but not in others, and what attracted men and women and generated an enthusiasm much greater than that among the democratic parties? Observers from Britain and France visiting Germany and Italy in the 1930s expressed admiration and even envy when reporting the new spirit of optimism in the fascist regimes. Fascism prevailed in countries in which the old order seemed no longer to work, in which democracy was not deeply rooted, in which the waves of nationalist resentment were running high, and which felt threatened by economic breakdown and social disorder. Without World War I and the postwar crises, fascism would have remained a small sect if it had emerged at all. Therefore, large segments of the population in these countries were ready to support a movement that, unlike other parties, professed not to pursue narrow partisan or class interests but, rather, announced that it stood for the values of the whole community, that it strove for unity and order, and that this was the only way to save the country from chaos.

Such explanations can be contested on various grounds. One could argue, for instance, that the postwar crisis in Italy had been more acute in 1920 than in 1921, and more acute in 1921 than in 1922 when the march on Rome took place. By 1922 the immediate crisis was passing and the revolutionary challenge had been defeated. Mussolini's assessment, in any case, was unambiguous: "To maintain that the Bolshevik danger still exists in Italy is to mistake fear for reality" (*Popolo d'Italia*, July 2, 1921).

Or one could argue that the German economic crisis of 1923 was as grave as that in 1933 but that in 1923 Nazism was a mere local phenomenon that was easily defeated. The German crisis reached its nadir in 1932, and so if the center–right government had been able to stay in power for one more year, the situation might have improved. Indeed, some of the "chains of Versailles" (referring to the hated World War I peace treaty) had been broken even before Hitler became chancellor. But the economic recovery and the concessions by the Allies came too late: The crisis had a cumulative effect, and too many people in Germany had lost hope. The system was not corrupt, however, even though Nazis and Communists were forever claiming that it was. If anything, the regime was too honest—

and too devoid of imagination. The German people saw only too clearly that the government was baffled by the depth of the crisis and the failure of the medicines it had administered. For its part, the government made no secret of the fact that it was at the end of its tether, that it did not know how to cope. Such governments are bound to fall in the face of a determined challenger.

Whereas Germany had been the great loser of World War I, Italy had been among the victors. But Italy had not come close to receiving the spoils of victory it had hoped for. Furthermore, nationalist passions were running as high as they were in Germany; only two generations had passed since the nation had unified, and the people did not yet feel that their country was secure, a self-evident fact.

The depth of the economic crisis cannot serve as the only clue to the advent of Nazism or Fascism. The United States and Britain were as much affected as Germany was by the Great Depression. Indeed, the impact on America was probably even greater, simply because Americans were altogether unprepared for the disaster; they had taken constant progress for granted. Germans on the other hand, had already had such traumatic experiences. Despite major unemployment and economic decline, fascism in England remained a marginal phenomenon, even though its leader, Sir Oswald Mosley, had at least as much popular appeal as the continental fascist leaders did. In the United States there were all kinds of fascist or parafascist organizations, but they never achieved a political breakthrough. Spanish fascism had attractive popular leaders, and Jacques Doriot, a Communist, had been one of the most popular figures in France before he became a fascist. But in neither Spain nor France was personal popularity of decisive importance.

Instead, the postwar crisis was a moral and cultural crisis. Before 1914, European societies had been far from democratic in many respects, but despite all their imperfections, they were more civilized than ever before. Human rights were increasingly respected, and few dared dismiss them as of no consequence. Moreover, the false accusations against an obscure French officer of Jewish origin had turned into a major European scandal.

World War I, with its hecatombs of victims and its enormous destruction, changed all this and had lasting consequences. The chauvinist orgies led to a brutalization of public life. The sanctity of human life no longer counted after millions had been killed. Although there had been cases of political murder in the world before 1914, in civilized countries it would have been unthinkable to advocate or justify it, let alone establish extermination camps for whole groups of people. Tsarist Russia had been the most backward and cruel regime in Europe, but the murder of its victims was only a microscopic fraction of the millions put to death by its successor regime. In addition, the moral breakdown after World War I was more profound even than the economic crisis.

The cultural crisis coincided with the eclipse of state power, the increasing lack of confidence among the ruling stratum, and the reluctance to deal forcefully with fascist street violence. The forces of order could have stamped out armed attacks (as they had in Munich in 1923), but instead they took only halfhearted measures, too few and too late. As the result of such hesitation and weakness, the fascist paramilitary units received fresh impetus. They became more aggressive, and once their number had swollen, dealing with them became more risky.

The historical record shows that fascism (like terrorism) could succeed only in a liberal democratic system. It had a chance only where it could freely agitate. When competing with a military dictatorship (Romania or Spain)—let alone a Communist regime—it invariably suffered defeat. Even in a mildly authoritarian regime such as that in Austria, it failed in 1934. Fascists despised, rather than hated, the democratic institutions: They regarded the parliament as a *Schwatzbude*, a place where unending inconclusive debates took place and where politicians were held in contempt because of their weakness. This mood could be found not only in the extreme Left and Right but also among many who did not consider themselves radicals. In the end, democracy collapsed because not enough democrats were willing to defend it.

What sections of the population were attracted to fascism? They varied from country to country, according to political tradition and social conditions. In general, the lower middle class showed the greatest affinity to fascism, particularly those who had suffered the most from the Great Depression. The Nazis made inroads among the peasantry, which was hard hit, and also among the middle class, which had lost its savings during the inflation and now faced further losses. Italian Fascism found support among war veterans who could not be reintegrated into civilian life and among students who were unable to find employment upon graduation.

A closer examination shows that there was no rigid pro-Nazi pattern according to class, generation, or gender. Before 1933 there was no significant difference in Germany between male and female voters or among voters of different age groups. Although the Nazi leaders were younger than their rivals, their voters were not. Up to 1931 the Nazis were, to a significant extent, a part of the lower middle class, but after 1931 they gained support from both the lower and upper social classes.

All that can be said with certainty is that the Nazis were stronger in Protestant than in Catholic regions; they did not make significant inroads on the positions of the Catholic Center Party. Fascism faced similar difficulties in other countries, except in Croatia and Slovakia, where the church supported the local fascists.

There was an interesting difference between the votes in big cities and small towns. If the Nazi vote was 37 percent on average, nationwide, in the July 1932 elections, the small town vote was 42 percent, whereas in the big cities such as Berlin and Hamburg it was closer to 33 percent. The working class was not immune to the Nazi upsurge; in fact, more workers and unemployed voted for the Nazis in 1932 than for the Social Democrats and Communists together. Both Nazism and Italian Fascism mobilized sections of the population that had previously been inactive.

The situation in Italy was different inasmuch as the *fasci* originally appeared in northern Italy and only gradually spread to the south. Subsequently, however, the south became a stronger bulwark of Fascism than the north, and this is true also with regard to neofascism in the postwar era. Agrarian fascism was also a significant factor in Italy—a reaction of the big landholders in the Po Valley and also of the smallholders in Emilia Romagna against the growing strength of the landless farmworkers. In Western Europe, fascism did not gain a foothold in the countryside in either France or the Netherlands, and in Britain it was hardly found outside London.

In Romania and Hungary, on the other hand, the fascists had support in the countryside, and the Finnish Lapua was predominantly agrarian. White-collar workers were fairly strongly represented in most fascist movements, whereas working-class representation varied greatly: It was initially strong in France and relatively strong in Spain, but less so in Eastern Europe, except in Hungary. The reason was largely accidental—a popular local leader who joined the fascists would bring with him his followers.

Students were strong supporters of the fascist movements in Spain and Romania, and so in these countries fascism was in the early years a phenomenon confined mainly to particular universities. Likewise, the Nazis emerged victorious in Germany's university elections well before they became a major political factor nationwide. Nonetheless, there were few university graduates in the higher echelons of the Nazi Party; Goebbels, Hans Frank, and Ley were rare exceptions. Whereas the last Weimar governments were made up largely of members of the free professions, there were considerably fewer such persons in the Nazi and Fascist governments. Only five of the Nazi *Gauleiter* were university or technical school graduates; the seventeen *Reichsleiter* had a more elitist background. Primary school teachers were strongly represented in the Nazi elite, even though on various occasions Hitler expressed contempt for a profession that, he claimed, attracted only people of limited intelligence.

The general mood in the Nazi and Fascist leaderships was anti-intellectual. Academics were regarded with distrust, suspected of conceit, of *Standesdünkel*, for which there was no room in the Nazi community. In the Third Reich, the number of students graduating declined markedly, and as a matter of principle, Hitler refused to accept honorary doctorates.

Fascists believed in hierarchical structures but aimed at transcending class divisions. Nazism and fascism preached that the class struggle had to be replaced by national unity, that ideals and values were more important than material possessions, and that the Führer, the party, and the state were the supreme arbiters. This message was quite effective, as reflected in the enthusiasm generated by fascism. Even his enemies acknowledged Hitler's personal popularity. After the Nazis seized power, they scored very high in honest elections. Indeed, Hitler gave instructions not to interfere with the voting, and no documentary evidence has ever been found that the results were forged. The Nazi leaders were certain that they had popular backing.

Although fascism had, of course, a monopoly on the media after the Nazis seized power, this was not so before 1933. They had no access to the radio, and before their electoral breakthrough in 1930, they had fewer newspapers than the other parties did. The written word played a minor role in the spectacular rise of the Nazis between 1930 and 1933, and it is doubtful whether anyone ever became a Nazi because of having read *Mein Kampf*. The situation in Italy was different, inasmuch as Mussolini was an accomplished journalist and had an influential newspaper at his disposal.

The Nazis relied on the speeches of their key leaders and many party orators of the second and third rank. But this does not offer a satisfactory clue to their rise to power, because only Hitler and Goebbels (and Mussolini) were gifted speakers. Since these two were not omnipresent, this leads to the conclusion that the message rather than the medium must have been of decisive importance. The Nazis' propaganda was always intense, but so was the Communists'. Yet the latter was not remotely as successful. Although the Nazi propaganda was too crude to command great respect among the intelligentsia, it was gradually accepted after the seizure of power. There had been associations of Nazi lawyers and physicians even before 1933, but they did not amount to much. Leading thinkers such as Martin Heidegger and the jurist Carl Schmitt paid their tribute; Giovanni Gentile was a pillar of Mussolini's regime. The reasoning of these profascist intellectuals was that genius and success in politics could not be measured by normal ethical (and aesthetic) standards. Hitler, as they saw it, was an enormous improvement over their previous impotent leaders. The Nazis succeeded where others had failed, and despite their imperfections— considered transitory—they were Germany's great and only hope. This positive assessment was also shared at one time or another by leading writers and thinkers outside Germany. Even most of the leading foreign statesmen had some good words for Mussolini in the early days, whereas Hitler never found the same acclaim outside his own country.

Few Western intellectuals became full-fledged fascists. Nonetheless, many thought that although fascism was unsuitable for their own country, it might well be suitable for Germany and Italy, just as Communism was for the Soviet Union. From time to time, they even argued that a dynamic leader such as Mussolini could do some good in France or Britain, by abolishing the excesses of parliamentarism and getting things done.

Fascism meant various things to various people, and likewise, it attracted them for a variety of reasons. To discuss all of them would, however, lead to a definition both vague and unhelpful. Looking back fifty years after the demise of fascism, the oldest explanation still has much to recommend it: Fascism was the manifestation of a moral and cultural crisis, in which traditional values, religious as well as humanist, no longer counted for much. Fascism developed out of the delirium generated by World War I, out of insecurity and political immaturity, and out of a revolt against reason and a reaction against the atomization of society.

These moods had existed to some extent well before the war, in all European countries: Nationalism was turning into imperialism, corporationist and racialist theories, social Darwinism, the revolt against reason, and the cult of youth. It needed however a major political, social, and economic upheaval to open the floodgates. For the apostles of extreme nationalism, of "life" and "power" (in contrast to reason and peace), to obtain a mass following it was not sufficient that people be spiritually uprooted, they also had to be socially and economically uprooted. Like pathogenic bacilli, fascism could be found in every organism. But it could prevail only if the organism was weakened or in some other way predisposed.

Fascist Doctrine

Fascism in Europe rose and spread quickly because of the ravages of World War I and the political and spiritual vacuum they had left behind. The Continent had been shaken by violent political and economic convulsions, and in half of Europe the old conservative order had disappeared but a new one had not been accepted. The moral certainties of the world of yesterday had vanished, and the middle classes had become impoverished. To some, the last vestiges of civilization seemed threatened by a new, mysterious, highly contagious phenomenon—Bolshevism. Those who believed that a strong leadership and a new order were needed but who found

Communism unacceptable in view of its internationalism and egalitarianism (the main pillars of Communist ideology in those early days) craved a
political alternative.

Many basic tenets of fascism were not new, as their antecedents can be
traced back well before World War I. No serious study of fascism can ignore
them, but it is also true that the search for precursors is not without danger.
Such a search should not ignore or belittle the important differences between the ideas of the prewar apostles preaching an antiliberal and antidemocratic gospel and the novel elements inherent in postwar fascism. References
to Nietzsche or Sorel are of only limited help in understanding fascist
politics, just as the debates of the Second International in the 1890s between
the reformists and the revolutionaries are not sufficient to explain events in
the Soviet Union after 1917. The prewar writings were expressions of a
cultural and also a political malaise, of dissatisfaction with the heritage of the
Enlightenment; they were manifestations of a new irrationalism.

No direct thread, however, leads from the nineteenth-century thinkers
to fascism. At all times, all kinds of ideas—good, bad, indifferent, sensible,
and lunatic—emanate from the studies of professors and from literary
coffeehouses, but they tend to influence politics only in certain constella-
tions. For instance, much has been written about the reactionary tradition
in German intellectual life from Luther to the late-nineteenth-century
chauvinist and racialist thinkers. There is no denying that this tradition
existed and that it contributed to a climate of opinion in which Nazism
developed and prospered. But even though there also was such an intellectual heritage in Britain and France, its political impact remained marginal.
In Italy, on the other hand, the antiliberal, antidemocratic impulses were
quite strong after the turn of the century, and it was precisely there that
fascism first prevailed.

Fascism was, above all, nationalist, elitist, and antiliberal. It was militarist, and whenever the country it occupied was sufficiently strong, it advocated imperialism and territorial expansion. Nationalism, however, was a
dominant force in many countries before 1914, and its appeal was by no
means limited to the Right and the Center. Nor was elitism an innovation.
Few political parties admitted to subscribing to it, though all practiced it.
Antiliberalism was rampant among the Catholic Church and the right
wing. Advocates of imperialism could be found among liberals as well as
conservatives, and sometimes even among socialists.

The difference between fascism and its predecessors is partly one of
degree, the consequence of the general radicalization caused by World
War I. Before 1914, political parties were dominated by small groups, but
unlike the fascist movement, they were not based theoretically and practi-
cally on the *Führerprinzip*. Racialism was preached before 1914 by both

German conservatives and the Action française. But this was not an extreme racialism, except perhaps in the writings of some exalted litterateurs and other outsiders who did not count for much. Many conservatives felt unhappy about the growing influence of the Left, and there was a great deal of muttering about firm action to prevent this danger. Some young Italian intellectuals wrote about the right of proletarian peoples to acquire new territories to obtain raw materials and relieve the population pressure. But in fact there were no coups d'état and little expansion between 1890 and 1914.

There was, however, a basic difference between fascism and prewar parties on the Right: Whereas fascism stood for far-reaching, even revolutionary, changes, the Conservatives—despite their criticism of parliamentary democracy—had accepted the principle of power sharing. The fascists wanted absolute power, and they knew that a wholly different, nonparliamentary approach was needed to achieve this aim. The Conservatives were the party of the preservation of the status quo and of order. Fascism wanted a new order, and for this reason it had to destroy the old one. Mussolini was certainly familiar with the writings of the Action française and was influenced by them. But he was even more influenced by Sorel, who was not a conservative. The break between Hitler and the old German conservative, antidemocratic tradition was even more pronounced, and it was not just a matter of a new tactical approach. There is a link between the Nazi doctrine and the "ideas of 1914" that in turn was a somewhat streamlined version of some of the ideas of the 1890s. But we cannot stress too often that it was only as a result of the world war, the political unrest, and the economic crisis that these ideas—simplified and popularized—acquired a power that they had not possessed before.

These sentiments and ideas varied from country to country, but they all originated in a feeling of discontent with the general state of affairs, of the *Kulturpessimismus* that spread widely in the last quarter of the nineteenth century. The enemy in France and Italy was "liberalism." In Wilhelmian Germany, the reaction was primarily directed against "destructive rationalism" and excessive individualism.

The German critics complained about the growth of materialism, as both a philosophy and a way of life; about the decline of spiritual values; about the effects of industrialization on one hand and of laissez-faire capitalism on the other; and about the fragmentation of society and the breakdown of old social ties. They noted with sorrow the growing cultural sterility and predicted that without a revival of the national community (the *Volk*), the general decadence that had already set in would continue inexorably, gather momentum, and eventually lead to total ruin.

Such dire forebodings were exaggerated but not altogether baseless, for all these evils did in fact exist. They also were observed by Leftist writers, who interpreted them as the inevitable consequences of the bankruptcy of capitalism, which would be overcome once the old social order had been overthrown. They pointed as well to cultural decline, to the alienation and atomization of society. But their cure—revolution—was not acceptable to the right-wing critics of capitalism. Socialism, as the rightists saw it, was materialist, had no higher ideals, and was totally preoccupied with restructuring the economy. They could not share the hope that socialism would somehow lead to a better society. In their eyes, socialism simply meant more of the same, replacing the present elite by a new and even more inferior hierarchy. It meant *Vermassung*, not the elevation of the standard of the masses but their further moral and cultural decline, to the detriment of all the value that had been established over many centuries.

The cultural revolution envisaged by the right-wing precursors of national socialism was to be based on a regeneration of the *Volk*, a return to traditional values, and the restoration of a community in which a natural hierarchy would exist, an aristocracy of prophets and warriors. The German concept of community (*Gemeinschaft*) was juxtaposed to the Western idea of society: High German culture was contrasted with inferior Western civilization. In France and Italy, the emphasis was on the nation rather than the *Volk*, and although racialism was not absent from French right-wing thought, it was in Germany that it found more fertile ground.

According to this doctrine, the German people, though inherently superior to others, were in mortal danger of disintegration. Therefore, the purity of their blood had to be preserved, which meant, above all, the elimination of Jewish influence, of the protagonists of liberalism, of Marxist socialism, and of all supernational forces. It also meant that to fulfill its historical mission, the German race needed more *Lebensraum*. These ideas were developed and popularized by various thinkers, some of whom had originally been men of the Left (Wilhelm Marr and Eugen Duehring), whereas others had come from abroad (Houston Stewart Chamberlain). Not everyone believed that the superiority of the German race could be scientifically proved. But in the end, it did not really matter whether this conclusion was reached on the basis of pseudoscientific reasoning or an article of faith of extreme nationalism.

The myth of the *Volk* and the emphasis on racialism were particularly strong in Germany. Elsewhere, as in Italy, the stress was on the nation and even more on the role of the state. D'Annunzio wrote that he gloried in the fact that he was a Latin, and he considered every non-Latin a barbarian. But D'Annunzio was not a representative of mainstream fascism. According to Mussolini, it was not the nation that had given rise to the state; rather, this was an antiquated "naturalistic concept" that afforded a basis for nineteenth-century nationalism. Instead, it was the state that had created the nation, conferring volition and therefore real life on a people made aware of its moral unity. Or as a British fascist and admirer of Mussolini wrote: "Racism is a materialist illusion, contrary to natural law and destructive of civilization, and truly logical application would be farcical and impractical."

Thus on the philosophical level, there was a sharp conflict between Nazi ideology and Fascist doctrine, but this was more apparent than real. The mythos of the *Volk* by no means excluded the mythos of the Reich. In any case, the Nazis were at least as strongly committed as the Italians were to the rehabilitation of strong state power, in contrast to the impotent liberal state. As the Nazis envisaged it, the assignment of the state was not to safeguard the greater happiness of the greatest number. On the contrary, the interest of the state always took precedence over the right of the individual. State power was to be based on leadership, and the legitimacy of this leadership was provided by the very fact that the people followed the leaders. Seen in this light, the leader embodied the will of the people, and fascism was true democracy.

According to Nazi and fascist doctrine, the supreme aim and value was greatness, not equality and humanism, the false idols of the Age of Enlightenment. Right is what helps the state and the nation. One nation is the others' natural enemy, according to *Mein Kampf*, and those with the greatest willpower, the most fanatic and brutal, will prevail. There is a racial hierarchy both within each nation and among nations. The higher master races are called to rule, the inferior to obey, and the progress of humankind will be achieved by the preservation of pure blood (race). German imperial leadership answers an universal need; it is the natural order of things. Thus any war led by Germany is, by definition, a just war. Germany and France are eternal enemies, and the Slavs constitute an inferior race. Inside Germany, power should be in the hands of a leader, and a new nobility born from blood and soil. But if the Führer and the new nobility are not up to their job, will there be a way to remove them? In Nazi doctrine, this question was left unanswered.

Italian Fascism based its ideology on the central role of the nations in the natural order of things. Fascists were indeed aware that the nation was a myth, not a reality. As Mussolini put it shortly before the march on Rome: "We have created our myth. The myth is a faith, it is a passion, in our myth is the nation, and to this myth, to this grandeur we subordinate all the rest." Such a doctrine had no time for the niceties of democracy. Humanitarianism was a mere irrelevancy. The main aim was to work for the greatness of the nation. The instrument toward this end was the state, which should control all political, moral, and economic forces.

The state was not a mere arbiter, working to resolve conflicting interests. Rather, it had a will of its own; outside the state no human or spiritual
values existed. This then was the ideal, and from a philosophical point of
view it is not important that fascist reality never really approximated fascist
doctrine.

Fascism was rooted to a decisive extent in a pre-1914 strand of thought
that was antiliberal, antidemocratic, and anti-Enlightenment and went
well beyond the official nationalist ideology. This kind of ideological
ambience, again, provided the breeding ground for fascism. It was bourgeois and at the same time antibourgeois; it rejected the rationalism and
individualism of liberal society and the self-satisfaction of conservatism.
Its supreme value was not the pursuit of happiness but fighting and
adventure; appropriately, its slogan later became: "To live dangerously."
Fascism admired nature (as it understood it), physical strength, brutality,
and barbarism. This was a rebellion of youth against philistinism, a revolt
against mediocrity, caution, tolerance, big-city life. It wanted to create a
new human being and a new civilization (or, as the Germans put it, a new
Kultur). Some of fascism was not more than posturing and the effusions of
minor philosophers hoping to gain a wider audience by making extreme
statements, or of decadent writers who had turned into men of action—
such as Barrès or D'Annunzio. But there was also a general feeling of
dissatisfaction and boredom. The old order had somehow functioned
over the years, but it provided little spiritual guidance and not much
satisfaction. Young writers in various European countries on the eve of
World War I described a feeling of suffocation and a feeling of deliver-
ance when the war broke out: At long last, everything was bound to
change!

If it had not been for the cataclysm that followed, this mood would have
remained no more than an interesting chapter in intellectual history, like
that of symbolism or naturalism. But a clear message was needed in the
uncertainties of the postwar period, as well as strong leadership to cope
with the many dangers engulfing countries such as Italy and Germany.
Liberal democracy often seemed—and indeed was—weak and irresolute.
In such conditions there was a growing readiness to support political
movements, however antidemocratic, provided only that they seemed capable to cope with the crises. In addition, there was a new psychological
readiness to accept violence that had not existed before the war.

Two questions remain to be answered. It is a far cry from the longings
for a new closely knit community, from the dreams about greatness and
heroism, to the crimes committed by fascism. The discrepancy between
the ideas of the late-nineteenth-century *Kultur Kritiker* and the reality of
fascism is as great as the distance between the likes of a Hitler, a Goebbels,

or a Streicher and the aesthetic ideal of a Nordic race. An expansionist and militarist doctrine was bound to lead to conflict. But it cannot be said with certainty that the specific radicalism of fascism was foreordained and, with it, its total debacle.

The ideas of the philosophical precursors of fascism were not wrong in every detail. They appealed to both base instincts and strong idealist elements, for they were based partly on noble dreams and visions. For this reason, fascism attracted many young idealists, not just careerists, adventurers, and the dregs of society. But to what extent did the fascist leaders believe in their own doctrine, or did they use it cynically to manipulate the people in order to seize power and to keep it? Even Hitler did not believe all the obscurantist nonsense of the early racialist thinkers about blood and soil, and he was often contemptuous of their fantasies. He had never read Rosenberg's *Myth of the Twentieth Century* and once said in conversation that "only our enemies have read this book." Fascists in power had to compromise: They achieved neither the total social revolution they had promised nor even the "return to the soil" that had figured so prominently in Nazi thought. Nazi "pragmatism" was equally evident in its alliance with such non-Nordic nations as Italy and Japan, which could hardly be justified with reference to the Nazis' race doctrine.

In other respects the fascist leaders remained faithful to their principles: They acted according to the nationalist "sacro egoismo"; they practiced the Führer principle; and they certainly were not converted to tolerance and humanism. They were not nihilists, as some believed. Nazi and fascist policy cannot be understood unless one accepts that the fascist leaders had a cause, however perverted, in which they firmly believed. Their myths were both a propagandistic device and, as they saw it, part of a higher order of reality, bound to come true. As one of the racialist thinkers once disarmingly put it: "Perhaps the higher race we constantly invoke does not really exist. But we shall create it anyway." The fanaticism of the true believers was more striking in German National Socialism than in Italian Fascism, but it did exist to some extent in every fascist movement. Fascism was possible only if based on genuine belief.

The Leaders

Without Hitler and Mussolini, National Socialism and Fascism might not have prevailed. In any case, a Nazi regime under, say, Goering and a fascist party headed by Grandi or Balbo would have followed a less radical course. It seems improbable that such regimes would have deliberately provoked war. The German Right and the Italian Ultras were revisionists and revanchists, who stood for the revision of the World War I peace treaties. But they would have been reluctant to accept the risk of a second world war, the price of which was likely to be too high and the outcome too uncertain.

In Italy in 1922 and in Germany ten years later there was much support for a dictatorship of the Right. The emergence of antidemocratic regimes was favored by Italy's postwar social crisis and by Germany's economic and political crisis. However, this opportunity might well have passed if it had not been for the presence of leaders absolutely convinced of their mission and capability of infusing the masses with their own ambitions and enthusiasm. In a similar way, the chance for the Bolsheviks to seize power in 1917 might well have passed if Lenin had not been standing in the wings. The presence of such charismatic figures is a historical accident, and for this reason it is futile to try to understand the Nazi phenomenon solely or mainly in "objective circumstances." That the Nazis would not have had their opportunity if the world's economic depression and mass unemployment had not made such a great impact in Germany goes without saying. But it explains only the psychological readiness of the masses to embrace the Fascist and Nazi message. It does not explain why the Berlin–Rome Axis came close to victory in 1941/1942. At the time, many prophets offered similar nationalist and militarist messages, but there was only one Hitler and one Mussolini able to make full use of such opportunities.

At the very beginning of his political career Hitler was greatly underrated, and Mussolini also was not taken seriously. Hitler was considered little more than a provincial demagogue, a clown in the beer-hall tradition, a rabble-rouser devoid of education, consistency, and rational thought. In the early days, Hitler's ideas were thought to be conventional, typical of the populist Right. As he became more radical during the 1920s, it was widely believed that his ideas were far fetched and nonsensical, that they stood no chance of gaining mass support. Even Hitler's allies on the Right talked of him as a "drummer" who would help mobilize the masses; they would discard him once the establishment Right no longer needed him. "We shall push him into the corner," Franz von Papen, Hitler's predecessor, explained. Those on the Left thought of him as Hugenberg's Golem, that is, the tool of the conservatives and the reactionaries.

Those who misjudged Hitler were liberal intellectuals who were impervious to his mass appeal or traditional politicians who understood much less well than he did the mass psychology and the mass politics of the twentieth century. Hitler's appeal to the masses was rooted in the nationalist resentment, the fanaticism, and, of course, his promise to solve the immediate economic and political problems and to lead Germany to a secure and happy future.

After the Third Reich ended, all kind of myths surfaced about the reasons for Hitler's great attraction. One of the most persistent and most mistaken version concerned Hitler's alleged all-consuming passion—anti-Communism—and his fear of the Soviet Union. His harping on this theme struck a certain chord in the hearts and minds of the middle classes, but how important a political factor was this?

That Hitler loathed Communism is obvious, and it is equally certain that for a majority of Germans, Communism was beyond the pale. But was it an issue of life and death? In Hitler's magnum opus (*Mein Kampf*), Marx appears just once and Lenin not at all. In the same book Hitler wrote that the "giant empire in the East is ripe for collapse"—so much for his panic fear of Bolshevism. True, Hitler made countless references in his speeches to "Marxism," but he made it clear that he did not mean the Communist Party but the social democrats and the nonsocialist parties of the center. On most occasions, he used "Marxism" as a synonym for the "November criminals," the (bourgeois) parties that constituted the government coalition before 1933 and that were, in reality, not less anti-Communist than he was.

The key issue was the shock of the Great Depression, the feeling that the system did not work, that facing unprecedented internal and external enemies, Germany would go under unless strong and purposeful leadership was restored. For this purpose, a majority of Germans were willing to sacrifice their unloved Weimar Republic, with its human rights and democratic institutions, which were not, in any case, deeply rooted in German political tradition.

Hitler satisfied this longing for a savior admirably. He brought to the political game a new substance and a new style: simple nationalist and populist slogans and the demand to give him a few years to carry out his program. Aside from Mussolini, he was the first leader in Europe to use the new means of mass communication, and assisted by Goebbels and others, he did it with an unprecedented intensity and dynamism. Whereas the leaders of the Weimar Republic were prematurely aged and cautious people, lacking self-confidence and persuasive power, he and the other Nazi leaders symbolized the advent of a dynamic new generation.

Nazism, like Italian Fascism, appeared as the movement of youth; to wit, the Italian anthem was "Giovinezza" (Youth). Most Nazi leaders were in their late twenties and thirties. Goebbels was made head of the Nazi organization in Berlin at age twenty-eight and became minister of propaganda at thirty-six. Himmler became head of the SS at twenty-nine, and other key figures in the Nazi leadership were equally young. In Italy, Balbo became a minister at thirty-three; Grandi, at thirty-four.

A great deal of effort has been invested in psychological speculations about Hitler's personality, but it has not resulted in many new and deeper insights. The importance of the sadomasochistic streak in his mental makeup and whether he had one testicle or two seem to have had no bearing on his political decisions. Hitler was certainly not the "great mediocrity" that his early enemies had labeled him, and he was not totally irrational in his actions. In some respects, he was a political genius, and his decisions—at least up to the early war years—were perfectly rational in pursuance of his irrational aims. He was a gambler, willing to take unacceptable risks, and he was usually in a hurry. His strengths were his radicalism, his brutality, his megalomania, and his unwillingness to accept compromises. This extremism, the absence of common sense, and the inability to stop while he was ahead were destined to lead to his downfall. The absence of a sense of reality and his belief that willpower could achieve anything helped him greatly in his early career. But later they led him into a war for the domination of Europe—and perhaps beyond—well beyond Germany's capacity. On issues that were not central to his beliefs, Hitler would prevaricate or even change position from one day to the next. But he did not swerve from his fundamental beliefs. If his great design utterly failed in the end, it was not (he said) because he had been mistaken or overreached himself but because the German people had been unworthy of a great leader like him.

Hitler was underrated by most early observers of the Munich and Berlin political scene, and he suffered the same fate several decades after his demise when a new school of historians argued that all things considered, Hitler had been a "weak dictator." Frequently he could not make up his mind, and he presided over a bureaucratic chaos, leaving initiatives to his underlings, whom he tended to play one against another. Put more moderately, some historians maintained that the role of the bureaucracy and the old elites was far greater than had been assumed earlier on, that there was a certain automatism in the German situation, with one thing leading to another, until Hitler was no longer the master of the situation but the prisoner of the processes he had set into motion.

Neither argument is borne out by historical facts. Whether a human being is strong or weak (or tall or small, or clever or stupid) is a relative statement because it depends on the yardstick used. Compared with Orwell's *1984*, Nazi Germany was indeed in a state of anarchy. But compared with other systems in history, it was an effective dictatorship. Hitler was not omnipotent; he had little interest in particular areas and did indeed leave the initiative to others, especially after the outbreak of war. Sometimes he acted as a reluctant arbiter, and other times he did not want to be bothered at all. All things considered, it is still astonishing how much he interfered. A random look at the instructions emanating from his chancery shows that he gave orders that Wilhelm Furtwängler, the famous conductor, should not participate in the Salzburg Festival in 1938; that residents of Munich should be permitted to drink "strong beer," thereby opposing a planned reduction of beer's alcohol content; that a public statue at the Rhine should be illuminated by night; that the iron bars on the windows of a museum in Munich should not be painted black but bronze gold; that his aides should wear rubber soles; that the painter Gerhardinger should not be mentioned in the media; that prominent foreign visitors should not be fed canned mushrooms because of the danger of poisoning (this in May 1942!); that foreigners should not be given fishing permits; and that the monthly maximum for renting a garage should be 7 marks all over Germany. He wanted to know how many violins the Vienna Symphony orchestra had (1942) and how much artificial honey was produced in Germany. He ordered that Schiller's *Wilhelm Tell* no longer be performed (June 1941) and that male personnel no longer serve in restaurants. He decided, among many other things, that the physicist Heinrich Hertz, a half Jew, should not become an "unperson" and that in the future the term *kilohertz* should be used.

It may well be that Hitler's instructions concerning fishing permits for foreigners were occasionally disregarded on the local level and that in some places a fee higher than 7 marks was taken for garage rentals. And it is, of course, also true that on many subjects he issued no instructions at all. However, there is overwhelming evidence that on the issues close to his heart—for instance, the destruction of his political enemies at home, the murder of the Jews, rearmament, foreign policy, and the conduct of the war—power was concentrated in his hands, and no one could possibly deviate for any length of time from the guidelines that he set.

There are striking similarities between Hitler and Mussolini. Both grew up in families with a notable lack of warmth. Neither one studied or became a master of a craft, and both went through a period of drifting. At one stage in his life, Mussolini (like Zhirinovsky) considered emigrating to a foreign country. Neither Hitler nor Mussolini drank or smoked, and they both suffered from stomach disorders. They made no small talk and had no close friends. Until they reached age thirty, Hitler and Mussolini frequently changed their opinions, but from early on, they tended toward fierce talk and a belief in violence as their main political weapons. Both tended to invoke the deity and were anticlerical. Both were first-rate speakers, but Hitler was a much weaker writer than Mussolini.

Mussolini had been a revolutionary socialist of some prominence before he became a Fascist. He moved gradually toward an extreme nationalistic stance, but the early Fascist programs that promised liberty to all still betrayed their socialist influence: Land was to be given to the peasants; factories were to be nationalized; the senate was to be abolished; women were to receive the vote; and the regions were to obtain greater autonomy. The anticlerical mood also persisted in the early party program. Once in power, Fascism lost much of its radical impulse, but during the last year of Mussolini's rule in upper Italy (the Republic of Salo) there was a pronounced return to his radical beginnings.

The cult of Mussolini was, if possible, even more all-pervasive than the Hitler cult, but less so than Stalin's or Mao's. His title (Duce) had to be written in capital letters. At one time, he held eight ministries in a government of thirteen.

Hitler was hailed by the German media as the greatest authority on architecture and the stage and later as the greatest military leader and diplomat as well. The German greeting ("Heil Hitler") became the official form of address, replacing "Good Morning" and "Sincerely Yours." Mussolini was predestined, elected by God and history. He was the greatest man who ever lived, the highest incarnation of the Italian race. He was alone and sad, a colossus, a titan, a cyclope, a giant—he could and should not be measured by ordinary standards. He was infinite, like the sky or the ocean, and for this reason it was impossible to describe or define him. Mussolini was the greatest journalist who had ever lived, but an even greater speaker. His speeches were not only great but beautiful, and the youth of Italy was called to learn by heart at least parts of his speeches. He was the greatest poet, musician (he played the violin), and artist. Like Hercules and the centaurs, he had a limitless capacity for work. Like Stalin, he was omnipresent and omnipotent and virtually never slept. His historical mission transcended Italy: Mussolini was the engine of the century, the voice of history pointing the road to all of Europe. The masses loved him because he identified wholly with the people. He was infallible, greater than Caesar, Augustus, and Napoleon, and throughout the years more and more attributes of God were bestowed on him. Predappio, his birthplace, became a place of pilgrimage. Pregnant women would look at Mussolini's picture hoping that their sons would be like him. The blind could see again after the Duce embraced them, and those who kissed his hands would die in peace. Italy, being the country of the theater (and the opera), had a strong theatrical element of bluffing, of operatic effect in his appearance. Mussolini deliberately fostered the impression that he was an excellent horseman, boxer, fencer, and even aviator, and he made no secret of his frequent and intense love affairs. Hitler did not care about sports, except to the extent that they enhanced Germany's prestige in the world, as did hosting the

Olympic Games. His interest in women was strictly limited, and his affair with Eva Braun was kept a secret from the wider public.

Both Hitler and Mussolini suffered from a progressive loss of a sense of reality. In Mussolini's case, this was caused mainly by the flattery of those around him. He was vainer than Hitler, who did not like fancy uniforms and, unlike Mussolini, was not afraid of ageing. Hitler made no secret of his fiftieth birthday, whereas Mussolini would not allow his to be mentioned in the Italian press. In Hitler's case, his loss of a sense of reality was caused more by fanaticism, an innate inability to listen to information undesirable to him, and the virtual isolation into which he had put himself. Neither the Nazi nor the supreme Fascist leader seem to have been interested in amassing money; political power gave them all they wanted. Hitler's tastes were frugal, and Mussolini also was no sybarite. Goering remarked in his Nuremberg prison: "At least I lived decently for twelve years." This would not have been Hitler's or Mussolini's reaction.

How popular were Hitler and Mussolini in fact? This is not easy to determine with any assurance. Public-opinion polls were not permitted in fascist regimes, least of all those concerning the popularity of the leader. Hitler reached the apogee of his popularity after Germany's victory over France in 1940. Even those who had felt uneasy about certain aspects of his domestic policy and were fearful about embarking on a war came to believe at that time that their misgivings had been misplaced, that the instincts of their leader had been right: These had been, after all, the greatest military victories in German history. The results had justified Hitler's daring and political genius. He was a leader who could overcome all obstacles, who had made Germany powerful and would make it prosperous in the near future.

Despite the propagandistic buildup, Mussolini did not enjoy quite the same measure of adulation. His successes at home had been less spectacular, and his ventures abroad had run into difficulties. The majority of the upper class and the intelligentsia had never fully accepted him; the peasants were indifferent; and the workers were less than enthusiastic. The heyday of the Duce at home and abroad was in the late 1920s and early 1930s. The number of those claiming that the Duce was always right did not grow in the 1930s, and with the military setbacks, support for him ebbed away. Four hundred hagiographies on Mussolini were published in his lifetime, some in verse, many of which were to be read by children. But whether they decisively influenced the reception of the Mussolini image is doubtful. Nonetheless, until the very end, both Hitler and Mussolini were more popular than the political parties they led.

A full understanding of the Hitler and Mussolini phenomenon was difficult for contemporaries to explain and, after their deaths, had not been much easier for historians. Attempts to describe Hitler as a gangster (as in one of Brecht's plays) and Mussolini as a second-rate actor have not been helpful. Had they not chosen politics as their profession, they would, in all probability, have lived out their days unnoticed as more or less law-abiding citizens. But instead they situated themselves in the center of the historical stage where they could pursue their criminal aims unfettered by moral restraints, thus causing the violent death of millions and eventually bringing about the ruin of their countries.

Attempts to describe them as slightly deviant politicians in the German and Italian tradition are not convincing. They did not steal, rape, or murder with their own hands. Rather, they were arsonists on a grand scale, setting fire not to a single house but to the whole of Europe. The fact that there had been many wars of aggression before and that mass crimes had been committed under other regimes does not absolve them.

Were they extraordinary people? In some respects, they were, but their talents were magnified by skillful propaganda. Given the right conditions, modern propaganda can sell almost anyone to the public; the mass hysteria in North Korea after the death of Kim Il Sung in 1994 is a recent example. In the late 1930s, during the war, and in its immediate aftermath, the wholly unloveable Stalin commanded as much support, respect, and even love as did Hitler or Mussolini. Yet Stalin was a plodding speaker, and his looks (like Hitler's) were unprepossessing. There was nothing charismatic—let alone demonic—in his appeal, except perhaps the magnitude of his crimes. If even Stalin could generate the feeling that without him his people would be lost like a flock without a shepherd, the phenomenon of the fascist leaders becomes somewhat easier to understand. Some countries in periods of crisis have a greater proclivity than others do to opt for a savior. This instinct is as old as humankind, but it could become fully effective only in the age of mass politics and mass communications.

In analyzing Hitler's record, both academic historians and German patriots have had difficultly recognizing the enormity of his crimes. Hardly anyone expresses full support for Nazi policies. Some argue that it is not the task of the historian to act as judge. Yet there is no such reluctance in regard to an individual person who kills one or two or three others. Someone responsible for the murder of hundreds of thousands or millions was obviously acting on a higher stage, a historical figure motivated by a *raison d'état*, who must be measured by other yardsticks. Marxist and related schools of thought have traditionally deemphasized the role of the individual: If there was crime in the Third Reich, then German society, or at least the ruling class, was to blame, not the leader. Yet others contend that Hitler's full record must be taken into account and that there is no denying that Hitler had been a modernizer of sorts and that Mussolini had given orders to dry the Pontinian marshes and to make the trains run on time.

German patriots wonder how they can explain that a supercriminal could exercise great persuasive power in both his personal conversation and his speeches? The answer is that Hitler did not discuss his worst crimes in his speeches. It is unlikely that he would have been elected if he had announced in 1932/1933 that he wanted to launch a world war that would produce millions of victims and untold suffering. On the other hand, a substantial number of the German people were willing to abdicate their democratic rights and their freedom to an adventurer whose aims were, at the very least, suspect. Thus attempts to explain the Hitler phenomenon must take into account not just the individual but also those who supported him, the specific situation in which all this occurred, and the novel means of propaganda and control that had not existed before. These considerations also apply to Mussolini, albeit to a lesser degree.

Is the leader principle an integral part of all fascist systems? We could imagine a fascist party or a regime headed by a committee, one of whose members acts as a primus inter pares, such as in Brezhnev's Russia or in China after Mao. But there is no precedent: In all fascist movements so far, the personality of the leader had played a crucial role. Not all leaders have had equally forceful and charismatic personalities, and some of them were interchangeable if need be. But leadership as an institution and as a symbol has been an essential part of fascism and one of its specific characteristics, in contrast to earlier forms of dictatorship, such as military rule.

The State and the Party

After Hitler's and Mussolini's takeovers, all other political parties were liquidated, and their movements obtained a monopoly of power. But the role of Hitler's and Mussolini's parties in the new state was not remotely as important as had been widely expected. It was not the party that ruled but the Führer and the Duce, their aides, and the bureaucracy. Eventually 8 million Germans belonged to the Nazi Party, but because the number was so great, membership was not very meaningful. Those who belonged gained certain career advantages, but generally the party served as a transmission belt conveying orders from the top to the bottom.

In Italy, the party was even less important: It counted 1 million members in 1932 and 2.6 million in 1939, after a law had been passed making it mandatory for civil servants to belong. But by 1932 almost all the old Fascist guard, the *squadristi,* had been purged from positions of real power, and Mussolini ruled the country as the head of state, not as the Duce of Fascism, which was his second title. True, the masses were "mobilized," not in order to participate actively in politics, not to fight in the streets, but to march in occasional mass demonstrations and parades, to listen from time to time to lectures, and to attend similar functions. There was a curious discrepancy between the self-image of Nazism and Fascism in power as a militant movement of fanatic followers imbued with a fighting spirit and an unwillingness to compromise, and the real state of affairs. By 1942 the Fascist Party counted 4.7 million members, and 25 million Italians belonged to some kind of Fascist organization. But these were meaningless statistics.

Mussolini and Hitler came to power not following an armed struggle but as a result of political cabals and intrigues: The "national revolution" was largely a myth. There was no "march on Rome." Mussolini went to the Italian capital in a wagon-lit, and Hitler was invited by Hindenburg to form a government following the intervention of Franz von Papen, his son Oscar, and other men in high places. Because Hitler was the leader of the strongest party in the land, a case could be made for inviting him. Mussolini's first government was a coalition in which all parties except the Socialists and Communists took part; Hitler also entered a coalition with the Conservatives.

Beyond this point, the similarities between the two systems no longer apply: Within four weeks the Nazis took over the police and passed emergency laws that gave them full power. Communist leaders were immediately arrested, and the Social Democratic Party ceased to exist in April 1933, although it was not officially banned until June. During June and July, all other parties disappeared. Alfred Hugenberg, the head of the Conservatives, also left the cabinet in June, and even though a few non-Nazi "technicians" continued to belong to the government in an individual capacity, they held no real power. The Nazi takeover was "legal" in the sense that parliament had passed laws making the dictatorship constitutional; the other parties did not fight the dictatorship but instead collapsed; and parliament surrendered whatever authority it had possessed.

The elimination of the opposition in Italy was a much more protracted process. There still was a relatively free press in the country for years after the "march on Rome" in October 1922. Thus after the murder of the Socialist leader Giacomo Matteotti by Fascist thugs, the Italian papers could still write: "We have a prime minister charged with common crimes." It was only after this murder that the opposition was effectively suppressed. The Italian Socialists were banned in October 1925, and the other parties were abolished one year later following an attempt on Mussolini's life. They already had been harassed for a long time, and so the official ban merely gave official sanction to a state of affairs that had existed for some time. Nonetheless, whereas the Nazis smashed their enemies, Mussolini outmaneuvered and gradually liquidated them. His approach was more similar to the salami tactics practiced by the Communists in Eastern Europe between 1945 and 1948 than to Hitler's.

Both Hitler and Mussolini felt threatened during the early years of their rule by "extremist" elements in their movements. For Hitler, the "national revolution" was completed with the dissolution of the other political parties. For Mussolini, it was over even earlier. But for Ernst Röhm and other leaders of the SA, the "second revolution," the great social transformation, was yet to come. The storm troopers intended to integrate the SA into the army in one great popular militia that would have made them the dominating force in the Third Reich. Hitler faced this challenge to his power—the only serious one between 1933 and 1944—by having the SA leaders (as well as others not connected with this affair) killed on June 30, 1934. A few weeks later, on August 2, 1934, following Hindenburg's death, Hitler became president of Germany in addition to being chancellor and Führer; his power was now absolute.

Although the SA continued to exist, it ceased to be a force of political importance in the Nazi system. The rise of the SS, on the other hand, an elite unit commanded by Heinrich Himmler, who was also minister of police, began as the SA's influence began to decline. The leadership of the SS and most of its members were middle class, in contrast to the "plebeian" character of the SA. Besides establishing its own intelligence service, the SS ran the police as well as a variety of business enterprises. During the war it had its own military units, consisting of both Germans and non-Germans. Eventually the SS became a state within a state, and it was responsible also for the concentration camps and the murder of millions of Jews. Despite its power, the SS never dreamed of opposing Hitler's decisions. It was his praetorian guard, and even as Himmler added to his ministerial responsibilities—during the war he also became minister of the interior—he considered himself, up to the last weeks of the war, Hitler's most faithful follower.

No organization in Italy was comparable to the SS. The purge within the Fascist Party proceeded quietly, and no blood was shed. In the early years of Fascism, the local Fascist bosses played a decisive role in political life, with little coordination between their activities and those of the central party leadership. They also tended to quarrel with one another. Even after the march on Rome, these local bosses continued to argue over who should be responsible for the organization and education of the younger generation, the role of the corporations, the control of cultural life, and many other issues. Mussolini was firmly convinced that the party was not a suitable instrument for political control, and he believed that most party leaders were corrupt. Beginning in the late 1920s, power passed from the party to the state organs, usually in the person of the local prefect and the police. Once a year, party members would see the local secretary and change their membership cards, and they would have to participate in mass demonstrations. Generally, however, membership was not particularly demanding, and in several regions of Italy, particularly in the south, the Fascists were not in complete control. Elsewhere, the party still had some power of patronage, but many Fascists who became members of the state apparatus identified with the state rather than the party.

The role of the party in Nazi Germany was more crucial, inasmuch as the role of the party leaders was more important on the central and local level. The men around Hitler, with only a very few exceptions, were old party stalwarts. Hitler hated bureaucrats, and he used experts only for special assignments. The Nazi Party, as Hitler once said, reached into every house, every workshop, every factory, and every town and village. There were hardly any Germans who were not active in one or other of the satellite organizations established by the party, such as the Labor Service, the Women's League, the Motor and Flying Corps, the Hitler Youth, and the Leagues of Jurists, Teachers, Physicians, Students, and many others. The German party was far better organized than the PNF (the Italian Fascist Party), and in this respect it resembled the Communist Party of the Soviet Union. The main difference between the two parties' organizational structure was that the Communist Party was based principally on the place of work, whereas members of the Nazi Party were organized in cells and blocks according to their place of residence. The role of the Nazi Party was to mobilize the masses, to ensure that the "will of the Führer reached all members of the community" and, on the other hand, to act as a "never failing seismograph," as Robert Ley once put it, "to register the smallest movement, excitement, discontent or consent."

In fact the will of the Führer did not reach every German, and the supreme leadership did not make much use of its "seismograph." There was, rather, a considerable amount of confusion and conflict in Nazi Germany beneath the facade of order, resolution, and unanimity. Sometimes Hitler was not resolute in his decisions, and party leaders on every level quarreled. Sometimes there were open conflicts between the bureaucracy and the party, and orders from the top were ignored or even sabotaged. But such confusion and rebellion seldom concerned issues of fundamental importance. If the Führer had made an important decision, it could be disobeyed only at great risk. Hitler's grip on the army was far stronger than Mussolini's. There was to be no Badoglio in Germany; indeed, it took the Nazis only a short time to deprive the army command from any autonomy.

If there were nevertheless certain limits to Hitler's power—or to Stalin's—this only proves what should have been obvious from the very beginning, that a single person cannot possibly be in total control of a big country, that he (or she) always must depend on the assistants he chooses. And if he delegates power, there is bound to be friction and tension even among people who subscribe with the same fervor to the same ideology. Thus the ambitions of Goebbels clashed with those of Goering, and even the supreme party leaders were afraid of Himmler and Bormann. Some who played an important role in the early days of the movement fell by the wayside because they were incompetent or became an embarrassment for other reasons (Streicher, Rosenberg, Hess).

A similar process took place in Italy, where the party had been, from early on, a coalition between two groups—the Conservative Nationalists and the Radical Populists—that continued to compete for access to the Duce. Radical leaders such as Scorza and Farinacci were always Fascist Party firsters, even though for many years they no longer had any influence.

The longer the Nazi and Fascist dictatorships held power, the more they became the dictatorships of one man. The few elections held were in the form of a plebiscite in which the only choice was between yes and no. In November 1933, 95 percent of German voters opted for Germany's exodus from the League of Nations, and in August 1934, 90 percent voted for merging the posts of president and chancellor. In 1938, following the Anschluss, 99 percent voted for the Nazis; the participation in this election was 99.6 percent. In Italy the process was more gradual: In 1924 the fascist list (Listrone nazionale) obtained 374 out of 535 seats. These were the last more or less normal elections; later on there were only plebiscites.

The German Reichstag and the Italian parliament were convened only rarely. There were three meetings of the Reichstag in 1934, two in 1935, one in 1936, and eleven altogether between 1936 and the end of the war, usually to listen to the announcement made by the Führer on the Anschluss and on various declarations of war. The number of cabinet meetings also decreased sharply (seventy in 1933, eleven in 1935, one in 1936, and none thereafter). In Hitler's view, these meetings were a waste of time. The various ministries existed in order to carry out the will of the Führer. But when there were no meetings or direct consultations, the will of the Führer became a matter of interpretation and speculation, and the result was frequently a bureaucratic nightmare of confusion, uncertainty, and overlapping. Then in 1940, all new laws not connected with the defense of Germany were postponed for the time being.

This loss of delegated power led to a variety of consequences. A strong minister would expand his authority, which would create new problems of administration. Thus, Goering functioned as chief of the "four-year plan" and, at least in theory, became overlord of the economy. But he was also supreme commander of the air force, dabbled in foreign affairs, and had his own private intelligence service that monitored wireless and tele-phonic communications. When Goering's influence waned, Albert Speer was made responsible for war production, and Goebbels, originally the minister of propaganda, was also given broader political and administra-tive authority.

The Italian parliament played no significant role from the late 1920s onward, and in 1939 it was dissolved altogether. The "Grand Fascist Coun-cil," consisting of twenty members, Mussolini used on some occasions, such as to announce in 1938 his anti-Jewish measures, but not on others, such as Italy's entrance into the war. Only after Italy's defeat in the war did the council members suddenly assert their authority and depose Mussolini at a famous meeting in 1943. This was the council's first meeting in four years.

There was no Supreme Nazi Council in Germany, only the annual party conventions in Nuremberg. These conventions were occasions for parades and long speeches made by Hitler; they were not intended for political discussion. In the early days of the Nazi Party, the regional leaders (*Gauleiter*) occasionally met, but after 1934 they were systematically iso-lated from one another, and it was even forbidden for more than two of them to meet.

In theory an omniscient and omnipotent Führer reigned absolute, but since the Führer and the Duce could not possibly be omnipresent, the state was to some extent "polycratic." The situation was further complicated by the emergence of a bureaucracy, which, however much resented by the party leadership, was essential to running the country. And although many bureaucrats had joined the state party, the bureaucracy had a life of its own, and so those who joined it identified primarily with their new assign-ments. Italy never quite became totalitarian, as the church retained its power and the monarchy was not liquidated.

While fascism prevailed, the extent of Hitler's and Mussolini's power was overrated, simply because conflict and dissent—even in a society of this kind—were not acknowledged. More recent is the tendency to exag-gerate the extent of political disorder in such dictatorships. If the fascist regimes were far from perfect in terms of their own aims, they still func-tioned fairly smoothly. They had broad popular support and probably would have continued in power far longer if they had not been defeated militarily.

Fascism and the Church

The attitude of fascism toward organized religion ranged from close co-operation to rejection and persecution. Some groups, such as the Belgian Rexists and the Romanian Iron Guard, drew much of their inspiration from the church, as did the parties ruling "independent" Slovakia and Croatia during World War II. Relations between the two major fascist regimes and the church were less smooth, and to make a complex situation even more confused, there were considerable differences in outlook within the ranks of the Nazi and Fascist Parties, ranging from tolerance to near-total rejection.

In his early years Mussolini was a confirmed atheist, exemplified by his anti-Catholic pamphlets "Life of Hus" and "The Cardinal's Mistress." He also stated on many occasions that Catholicism not only was untenable from an intellectual point of view but also was immoral. The first program of the Fasci (1919) that he drew up provided for the confiscation of ecclesiastic property. Thereafter, however, Mussolini gradually moved toward an accommodation with the church when he finally recognized its enormous influence in Italian life.

Mussolini's policy of reconciliation culminated in the Lateran treaties of 1929, in which Italy solved the "Roman question," which had long plagued it, by recognizing the extraterritorial status of the Vatican. The Catholic Church, on the other hand, committed itself to collaborate with the Fascist regime, which in turn recognized Catholicism as the "dominant faith." On the whole, this arrangement worked well, even though conflicts surfaced from time to time. The Catholics complained that their interests in education were not given sufficient consideration and that the Catholic Action (an organization of lay Catholics), though "outside and above politics," was still subject to occasional harassment. The Fascists' accusations that the organization was meddling in politics were not unjustified, however, for *politics*, as defined by Fascism, referred not only to strictly political activities but also to any kind of social and cultural association.

All such activities were to be controlled by the state, not by the church authorities. Eventually, an uneasy compromise was reached: The Catholic Action was reorganized on a regional rather than nationwide basis, and it promised to refrain from all activities except those for purely religious ends. This was a setback for the church, even though for Mussolini it did not go far enough. From a Fascist point of view, the compromise could still be justified, for it strengthened the support for the regime by the Catholic establishment, which prayed for both the king and the Duce. The pope

himself repeatedly referred to Mussolini as a man sent by divine provi-
dence and offered his full support for Mussolini's foreign political adventures. Even in the conflicts of the 1930s (the papal encyclical *Non abbiamo
bisogno*), the church's complaints were directed not against Fascism as such,
but merely against its attempts to curtail the church's prerogatives.

Some leading Fascists took a more anticlerical line than did Mussolini
himself; for instance, former socialists such as Roberto Farinacci and the
philosopher Giovanni Gentile who was Mussolini's first minister of education and whose works were put on the index by the Vatican. But like the
more extreme antichurch ideologists in Nazi Germany, these men had to
soften their anticlerical line for political reasons. Whatever Mussolini's and
Hitler's personal views, they instinctively understood that it would be
foolish to provoke a *Kulturkampf* prematurely. Although such a conflict
might well have appeared inescapable in the long run, both had more
urgent preoccupations.

Hitler had, on the whole, fewer antichurch resentments than did the
Duce. Although Hitler was not a practicing Catholic, he frequently expressed a preference for some form of "positive Christianity." God is
mentioned only twice in *Mein Kampf*, but Hitler also never proposes a
confrontation with the church. Indeed, one of his first major foreign
political initiatives was the conclusion of a concordat with the Catholic
Church in July 1933.

Nonetheless, the Nazi Party's subsequent relations with the church were
less smooth than they were in Italy. The reasons were both doctrinal and
practical: The ideas of a German racial God-willed supremacy and all that
followed from it were not compatible with the church's desire to bring its
blessing to all people, irrespective of their race. Although the church
would not always live up to its commandments of love and mercy, it
certainly could not entirely deny them. In addition, the Catholic Church
had the complication of its international character, which was anathema in
Nazi eyes. German bishops could be German patriots, but the church as
such could not possibly become German. The Nazis, furthermore, took
their role as a political church, a secular religion, far more seriously than
the Italian Fascists did, and this conflict was bound to lead to a collision.

From the Nazi point of view, Protestantism presented fewer difficulties
because it was German and had given substantial support to Nazism before
1933. After 1933, German Protestantism split into several factions, of
which the pro-Nazi "German Christians" and the Professing (Bekennende)
Church were the most important. Some Protestants resisted both the doctrine of the radical anti-Christians, such as Alfred Rosenberg, who dismissed the Old Testament and advocated a new Nordic religion, and the

so-called Christian Nazis, who merely wanted to replace the revelation of God in Scripture with the revelations of Adolf Hitler. According to Nazi doctrine, the state religion stood above the denominations, independent of all religious dogmas. Seen in this light, the Christian Church had to accept without question the authority of the party and state, as its sole concern was the salvation of souls. The long-term aim of Nazism, however, was not only the destruction of the church but also the abolition of the Christian religion in any meaningful sense of the term.

Thus it was a foregone conclusion that the church in Nazi Germany would come under considerable pressure between 1933 and 1939, even though the church leaders supported Hitler's policy and hardly missed an opportunity to profess loyalty to the new state. Nevertheless, they were frequently accused, in the more radical organs of the Nazi press, of treason and sabotage. The church's hold on education was broken; its social organizations were dissolved; and individual clerics were arrested.

Despite the church's support of Hitler and his policies, such support did have limits. For example, the church might support the Nazis' foreign policy, but it could not tolerate the Nazi's eugenic policies, ranging from compulsory sterilization to euthanasia. Although the church kept silent about the Jews, the fate of Christians of Jewish origin continued to be a worry, though apparently not so much that the church offered any help.

But even if there was not an open confrontation between the church and the Nazi leadership after 1939, it was not because Hitler had changed his views with regard to the church. Rather, he bowed to the political exigencies of the hour: During the war everything had to be subordinated to national solidarity. Goebbels had always been a leader of the Nazi radicals, but he too repeated time and again that no second (domestic) front should be opened while the fighting continued. The time for the final reckoning with the church would come after Germany's final victory. Consequently, the church made far-reaching concessions under Nazi rule, a painful subject in later years for all Christian believers. But there is no doubt that in the long run, even these compromises would have been insufficient, for nothing short of total abdication would have sufficed in the Nazi state of the future.

The Nazi example was not, however, the only pattern for the relationship between fascism and religion. "Independent" Slovakia during World War II is a good example: Andrej Hlinka and Josip Tiso, his successor, were clergymen, and yet the country collaborated closely with Nazi Germany. Slovakia's inspiration was almost exclusively nationalist and religious, and its supreme aim was national autonomy at any price, not the establishment of a new political order. Given the international constellation and Slovakia's proximity to Germany, this aim could be achieved only under Nazi auspices. This is not to say, however, that under different circumstances Slovakia would have become a Western-style liberal democracy.

The cases of Spain and Croatia are again different: The church had a position of considerable strength in Franco's Spain. Although it was reactionary, it was only one of several political factors in a regime that was a conservative, military dictatorship rather than a fascist state. In independent Croatia, a separatist, national-revolutionary movement that had preceded fascism made a serious effort to copy Nazism in building the state. Religion was part of the official Ustasha ideology because it had been an essential part of Croatia's national revival. The church was all the more important because it separated the Roman Catholics from the Orthodox Serbs and the Muslim Bosnians. Even though the Vatican protested from time to time the Ustasha regime's policy of forcible conversion and the massacres of non-Catholics, the local clergy supported them. Ante Pavelic was not dependent on the church, but he and his collaborators still tried to keep on good terms with it all throughout their rule. Still, Croatia's relations with the church were not as close as they were in Slovakia.

Other fascist movements also had a "special relationship" with the church. In Finland, Lapua was very much oriented toward the church. In Belgium, Rex began its political life as a religious youth organization that rebelled against the Catholic establishment and subsequently veered toward a more radical orientation. Its doctrinal base was the Action française, but when the Action was excommunicated by the Vatican, Rex remained faithful to the church. Léon Degrelle, its undisputed leader remained a practicing Catholic, even though the higher clergy gave him little support.

The position of the Iron Guard in Romania was less straightforward. Religious motives played a paramount role in its ideology and practice, and it received considerable support from the lower ranks of the Romanian clergy. At the same time, however, one could argue with some justification that the Iron Guard's mysticism and rituals were only quasi-religious. That is, they had a religious origin but were used for different purposes. The Iron Guard could be regarded as a movement of religious revival, but its substance was always nationalist-populist, religious more in form than in content. Moreover, there was a great distance between its highly idealistic credo and its political practices, which resembled gangsterism rather than religious piety.

In summary, fascists tried whenever possible not to collide with the church. This was of vital importance in countries in which the church's influence was deeply rooted. In some places cooperation with the churches was smooth, but radical fascism was destined to clash sooner or later with the church because of the fundamental differences between its teachings and church doctrine, because fascism was itself a secular religion with a sense of messianic mission and so could not tolerate the activities of a rival organization because it had to dominate all aspects of human life. Had fascism lasted longer and come to power in more countries, this conflict would have been even more apparent.

It was the old question of what should be rendered unto God and what unto Caesar. This had always been a difficult issue, but whereas in the past, coexistence had been possible through temporizing and compromising, in the new era of mass totalitarian movements, this had become a problem that could be resolved only with great difficulty and only for the short term. And since in the totalitarian age Caesar wanted rendered unto him also those things that were not his by right of tradition, accommodation might have been impossible for the long term.

Workers and Peasants

What was the attraction of the successful fascist movements for millions of peasants and workers in some countries and its failure to make inroads elsewhere? In the 1930s, class divisions were more pronounced than they are in the 1990s, and in the 1930s, there were more manual workers in industry than there are sixty years later, and the number of farmers or peasants was many times higher than now.

The Nazi Party came to power under the pretext of saving the peasants. The record of the Italian Fascists, on the other hand, was more dubious. They defended the landowners but engaged in punitive expeditions against unruly landless farmworkers. Agriculture played a far more important role in the Italian economy than in Germany. In 1936 almost half of those gainfully employed were engaged in agriculture (60 percent in the south), which was the most important branch of the Italian economy and represented 44 percent of all exports. It is doubtful, therefore, whether Fascism ever had a comprehensive agricultural policy.

At first, Nazi agricultural policy was largely ideologically, even sentimentally, motivated. The peasants were to have a better deal, and they were also to acquire a new dignity. To the Nazis, the peasants represented everything that was healthy in German tradition; they were the life source of the nation; and their strength was essential to the racial hygiene of the Nordic race. Yet in later years, there was not much difference between Nazism and Italian Fascism.

During its early phase, Italian Fascists promised the division of the big farms, as well as better markets and higher prices. Although the *latifondi* were not split up, higher prices certainly prevailed, but mostly at the expense of the consumer. Both Nazi Germany and Fascist Italy tried hard to increase domestic food production—Italy with its "battle of the grain" and Germany with its battle of production (*Erzeugnisschlacht*). Both countries strove for self-sufficiency, mainly in preparation for war; and both countries had an enormously complicated system of controls and price fixing. Peasants were told what and how much to produce and where to deliver it. Thus, to a considerable extent, Italian agrarian policy was a planned economy. The public sector in agriculture was growing, and there was nothing specifically "fascist" in the principle of fixed food prices. The only specific Nazi contribution to agriculture was the introduction of secure tenure (*Erbhofgesetz*). The grandiose long-term settlement and resettlement plans in both Germany and Eastern Europe scheduled for after the war, were never, of course, realized.

In Nazi agricultural policy the romantic enthusiasm of Walter Darré, an advocate of peasant folklore and an inspiration for the right-wing Green Party gave way to the more pragmatic approach of Herbert Backe. As J. E. Farquharson wrote, "For Hitler the agrarian community was important for practical reasons; it impeded Marxism and yielded food and military material. As these considerations began to take precedence over 'Blood and Soil' from 1937 onwards, Darré began to lose what influence he had ever possessed." Hitler needed airplanes, tanks, and guns, and whatever his sentiments for the racial health of German stock might have been, agriculture could not produce war matériel. Thus the moment that war was envisaged, much greater emphasis had to be put on industry, despite the Nazis' original misgivings about industrialization and the big cities' being the death of the nation. Only a strong, heavy industry could create the base for world power. Seen in this light, the role of agriculture necessarily had to be secondary. It had to provide enough food so that the country would not need to depend on foreign imports.

Nazism and Fascism did succeed in boosting agricultural output, and average incomes also went up, though, of course, much less than the official propaganda proclaimed. Agricultural progress under the Nazis was very slow, however, when compared with the advances made in German and Italian agriculture in the 1950s. Despite all of Mussolini's bragging, the miserable lot of the Italian peasant did not change fundamentally, especially in central and southern Italy. The attitude of Italian peasants toward Fascism was largely passive, and the Germans were probably more positive, although there is no evidence of overwhelming enthusiasm.

In most European countries, fascism was not strongly supported by the peasants, and fascists did not show much interest in mobilizing the peasantry. In a few countries, such as Austria, Romania, and Croatia, fascism had a small following in the countryside, though it took second place to the Christian–Social or the traditional peasant parties. Only one movement got its support mainly from the countryside, the Finnish Lapua Party, whose heyday was between 1929 and 1933. But Finland was clearly an exception, and for many years, much of the support for Finnish Communism also came from poor agricultural (and forest) regions in the north. Lapua searched for a Finnish Hitler and bitterly opposed parliamentary democracy. It was not a conservative party. It played with armed revolt, and it stood for a Greater Finland. Lapua was still an untypical case, however, and so a study of this movement may be more rewarding for an understanding of the strains and stresses of modern Finland than for the mainsprings of fascism.

Some of the other North European fascist parties, such as the Norwegian Vidkun Quisling's National Assembly and the Danish party, also had some rural support—in eastern Norway, with its indebted farmers, and in northern Schleswig. But the numbers were small by any standards; it was predominantly a protest vote. In brief, in the 1930s there was much discontent in European agriculture, but it did not play a significant role in the rise of Nazism or Fascism.

The fascist attitude toward the industrial working class has been subject to widely divergent interpretations. It has been argued on one hand that all fascist movements essentially opposed the working class, that this counter-revolutionary function was indeed their only raison d'être, that they destroyed the trade unions, that they established (or perpetuated) a system of exploitation, that the position of the working class under fascism did not improve, and that the workers were kept quiet by a mixture of mendacious propaganda and brutal terror. Some of this is true: Independent unions were dissolved; wages were frozen; and much of Nazi propaganda was fraudulent, including the very name of the party.

One of the basic tenets of fascism was its opposition to the class struggle. Sooner or later, "left-wing" fascist elements in Germany and Italy were suppressed. Yet despite all this there was little open defiance and not much indirect resistance among the workers. This is difficult to explain if one assumes that none of the Nazis' promises was fulfilled, that fascist policy was nothing but demagogic slogans empty of content. Italian Fascists had a strong tradition of militant syndicalism, and although they rejected the concept of international proletarian solidarity as pure fiction, they also opposed the old-style industrial bossism and engaged in strikes. This led to a conflict between the Fascist workers' corporations, which insisted on their autonomy, and the party, which wanted to turn them into mere administrative organs of the government. The conflict was resolved, in theory at least, by establishing the corporate state, with its law on collective labor relations that banned strikes and lockouts. In Germany the establishment of the Labor Front with its labor code was based on the Führer principle and put an end to independent action by the working class.

Nazism had the good fortune to come to power after Germany's mass unemployment had peaked. During the next four years, through a program of public works, rearmament, and resuscitation of industry, all the unemployed workers were reabsorbed into the economy, more quickly than in other capitalist countries. The regime heralded this accomplishment as a tremendous success, and even though the rise of real wages was only modest—more pronounced in some industries than in others—the new feeling of security did have a substantial political impact: Hitler had succeeded in what the democratic leaders, including those of the Left, had failed.

The achievements of Italian Fascism in regard to the well-being of the workers were more modest. So much more so, in fact, that the official index of wages stopped being published in the late 1920s, as real wages after six years of fascism were lower in Italy than anywhere else in Western Europe. In 1936 Mussolini announced that the days of prosperity were gone forever and that in the future, humanity (meaning the Italian people) would have a lower standard of living. To compensate for the elusive prosperity, Fascist Italy invested heavily in fringe benefits for the masses (*dopo lavoro*), as indeed, did Nazi Germany.

Every German worker was promised a car, but the Volkswagen was not ready by the time the Third Reich collapsed. On the other hand, the number of paid holidays doubled between 1933 and the outbreak of the war. Kraft durch Freude (strength through joy) meant trips abroad on shiny new ships for workers who had never been on a foreign holiday, as well as excursions to German resorts and various cultural activities. Employers did not welcome the cost of these fringe benefits, and they were constantly in conflict with the Nazi Party and its agencies, such as the Labor Front, acting as a mediator. Neither the employers nor the workers were happy with the new arrangements, as shown in the results of the early elections in the factories, in which Nazi candidates sometimes fared badly. Industrial workers were never strongly represented in the Nazi Party, with a relative decrease after 1933. Nonetheless, there was little active discontent in the working class. The output of certain key industries (such as coal mining) doubled between 1933 and 1939, and the enormous industrial war effort—despite air raids and other dislocations right up to the end of the war—shows that from the Nazi point of view the workers were doing their duty to the fatherland.

Fascist Italy's economic performance was less impressive than Nazi Germany's. Industrial output doubled in the 1920s, but the base from which it had started was very low, and in the 1930s it made only modest progress. In 1937, for the first time, industrial output was higher than agricultural output, but real wages in industry between 1929 and 1939 hardly rose at all, and during the war there was, of course, no further advance. In 1935 the forty-hour workweek was introduced, not out of solicitude for the health of the working classes, but in order to cope with unemployment. Italian Fascism also introduced a system of modest family allowances and sickness insurance. But although the main function of the Fascist trade unions was to preserve "labor peace," this meant only preserving their right to negotiate contracts that were not unfavorable to the workers. Thus the Fascists' success among the working class was mixed: The workers constantly complained about Fascist paternalism and its general ineptitude in economic policy. They staged disturbances and even strikes, which during the war assumed major proportions in north Italian centers. At the same time, however, working-class unrest constituted a serious threat to the regime; with all their shortcomings, the Fascist unions served their purpose as far as the regime was concerned.

Some of the minor European fascist movements had considerable working-class support: Workers constituted some 40 to 50 percent of the membership of the Hungarian Arrow Cross, and they were prominently represented in French fascism. The reasons in each case are not difficult to find: Socialism in Hungary was mainly confined to skilled workers. Because the unskilled had no political home, it was among them that the Arrow Cross made its gains. In France it was mainly the personal following of Jacques Doriot among the workers of the Paris *banlieue* that gave French fascism a proletarian base. In its early days, the Spanish Falange also appealed to the Left, and some 50 percent of its early supporters were workers.

Such "working-class fascism," like agrarian fascism, was the exception rather than the rule. Although Nazism and fascism counted many working-class members and supporters, their strength lay in their ability to appeal to all classes. Once in power, however, the fascists destroyed the unions and subordinated the working class's demands and interests to higher national ambitions, mainly in foreign policy. The supreme aim of fascism was to "reintegrate" the working class into the main body of the nation, thereby ending the class war. This goal could not possibly be achieved only through propagandistic slogans, and even though the fascists had no wish to engage in radical social reforms, let alone a social revolution, they had to improve the lot of the industrial workers in order that they would feel that their economic and social position had improved in comparison with the past and was continuing to improve. Although the workers were not to play a leading role in the fascist state of the future, they were still an essential part of society and so had to be kept content. In this, the fascist regimes more or less succeeded. That is, until the last stage of the war, the workers did not actively oppose Nazism and fascism.

Terror

Fascist movements have used terrorism from below when in opposition, and terrorism from above when in power. Violence has always played a central part in fascist philosophy. Without the use of violence, fascism would not have attained power or, having seized it, would not have maintained it. As Mussolini once wrote: "The Socialists ask what is our program? Our program is to smash the skulls of the Socialists." With some rare exceptions, such as in Romania, fascist groups used mass violence, not individual terror, in their struggle for power. Mussolini also occasionally used terrorist assassins. Mass violence meant domination of the street, punitive expeditions, and the disruption and breakup of enemy assemblies. Opponents were beaten up, and some were killed. The fascists introduced as an innovation the forced ingestion of castor oil by their political opponents, who were then humiliated and made a laughingstock. Above all, there were threats of much more force; heads would roll once Fascism and Nazism were in power.

The threat of force was as important as the use of violence. Whereas in a democratic society, political parties have freedom of action within the law, there is no such liberty in a fascist regime: The only activities permitted are those endorsed by the state, in this case, those in the interests of the Nazi and the Fascist order. Nothing against the state, nothing without the state, and nothing outside the state was Mussolini's definition of totalitarianism. But the reality lagged behind the doctrine, in Italy even more than in Germany.

There is no independent judiciary in a fascist regime; instead, the party rules the state, as Hitler announced in 1934. If the Gestapo was dissatisfied with the clemency shown by the courts—and there were such cases in the early years—the victims were sent to a concentration camp anyway. One of the basic differences between the inmates of a camp in the Soviet Union and those in Germany was that the former had been sentenced, whereas the latter were put in "protective custody" for an unlimited period. According to a law passed in 1936, the court of law had no longer any control over the Gestapo, which in fact it had not had since March 1933.

In the early days, the concentration camps were centers of chaos. People moved in and out; some were killed; and others were released after a few weeks. In 1932 there were 37,000 inmates in German prisons, but in 1935 there were 170,000, of which 50,000 were political prisoners. This population did not include that of the concentration camps, which were consolidated after their chaotic inauguration. A special unit, the SS Deathhead Division, with 11,000 members, was in charge of the archipelago KZ, the abbreviation by which the camps were known. The number of inmates fluctuated. During the winter of 1936/1937, the figure shrank to fewer than 10,000. After Kristallnacht, tens of thousands of Jews were rounded up, but most were released within a month or two. Some were able to emigrate during the few months before the outbreak of the war, whereas others perished in the general massacre of Jews.

When the war began, there were about 30,000 inmates in the camps, and during the war their population grew rapidly, with the influx of many foreigners. In January 1945 there were 714,000 inmates in the twenty main camps, which had five hundred branches. The names of the main camps in Germany—Dachau, Sachsenhausen, Buchenwald, Oranienburg, Ravensbrück, Mauthausen—were well known at the time. The primary purpose of these camps was not to kill people, although a high percentage were in fact murdered: 34,000 in Dachau, 56,000 in Buchenwald, and more than 100,000 in Mauthausen. In addition, the extermination camps, or death factories—Auschwitz, Maidanek, Sobibor, Treblinka—were located outside Germany, in which millions of people were exterminated. Finally, one camp, Auschwitz, served as both a labor and an extermination camp.

This enumeration does not take into account the millions of civilians killed by special-action groups (*Einsatzgruppen*), mainly in Eastern Europe, and the millions of prisoners of war and forced laborers who were killed or starved to death. They included 3.3 million. Soviet prisoners of war. Although for many centuries, wars had been fought in Europe, Nazism left behind it a wake of blood, mainly that of civilians, unprecedented in modern history.

Who were the enemies of the state who had to be cowed into submission or physically destroyed? Above all, they were the political activists who had opposed the Nazis' rise to power; particularly severely treated were those who tried to continue their activities after January 1933. In addition there were the members of various undesirable religions—in particular, Jehovah's Witnesses, some Catholics, and a few Protestants. Homosexuals, though not lesbians, and "racially inferior" elements, such as Jews and gypsies, also were targeted. In addition, during the war an attempt was made to destroy segments of the occupied Slavic countries. Draconian punishments were meted out to those in Germany found guilty or suspected of undermining morale: Telling an anti-Nazi joke or listening to a foreign radio station in wartime was sufficient for a death sentence.

Terror was expressed not only in physical violence. The occupied countries were systematically robbed: They had to pay for the upkeep of the German forces stationed there. They had to provide manpower for German industry and agriculture and to supply food, raw materials, and finished products. The occupied Eastern European countries were never promised any payment; but in Western Europe the Nazis' policy was more conciliatory, at least in the abstract. The terms of trade were fixed by the German authorities, who did, however, promise to pay—after the war—or to deliver commodities in exchange. At the end of the war Germany owed France 8.5 billion marks, Holland and Belgium about 6 billion each, and Denmark somewhat less.

There was a basic difference between the use of the police in Nazi Germany and in Fascist Italy: In Germany the political police was administered by the Nazi elite, whereas in Italy it remained under the control of trained bureaucrats. The head of the Italian political police was Arturo Bocchini, a former prefect of Bologna and a bureaucrat of the old school. Unlike his Nazi colleagues of the 1930s, Bocchini saw his main task as prevention rather than persecution. The operations of the Italian political police were more predictable and less personal than those of the Gestapo, and suspects were sometimes given discreet warnings. In Italy the forced residence practiced under Fascism was almost idyllic when compared with the Nazi concentration camps, and the number of those killed or executed in Italy for political reasons is not at all comparable to the number of victims of the Nazi regime. Mussolini, it is true, eventually had second thoughts: "We must have a fascist police," he wrote, "not policemen who are fascists, but fascists who are policemen. This will make many people think again." But he recognized this only in 1943, just a few weeks before his downfall.

In principle there was no difference between the two countries: Italy, like Germany, was in a permanent state of emergency. Like Hitler, Mussolini was bound by neither positive nor natural law; the police could ignore normal legal processes; and the citizens had no rights and no legal redress. If Germany had its Ordinance for the Protection of the People and State (February 1933), Italy had its Legge di publica sicurezza (1926), according to which the function of public security was an activity whose exercise could not be obstructed by absurd preconceptions—meaning individual liberty and due process of law. Hitler said the same, even more emphatically, on various occasions.

It is not possible here to describe in detail the complicated structure of the Nazi terror apparatus, the intrigues among its commanders, and their contests for power. The SD (*Sicherheitsdienst*) was a party intelligence service that, even when it was established, before 1933, specialized in the collection of intelligence, both inside Germany and abroad. The Nazi Party, including the highest functionaries, was not outside its purview. Indeed, one *Gauleiter* complained, "We should not be shadowed by the SD; after all we are not in Russia and we do not need a GPU." But the SD had no executive power, and so it could not arrest, let alone execute, anyone. This was the privilege of the Gestapo, the heir of the old political police. In the Third Reich, the Gestapo was a department of the Main State Security Office.

According to a law passed in 1936, it was the Gestapo's duty to investigate throughout Germany "all forces hostile to the state," but it was not to restrict its activities to those actively hostile. It also was assigned to investigate all "intentions jeopardizing the state," and this eventually became its main task. Many of those working for the Gestapo were old police officials who stayed on to serve under the new masters. Even Heinrich Mueller, the head, had somehow missed to join the party and became a member only after the war started. The Gestapo had fifty-seven regional offices throughout Germany and at the end of the war employed 35,000 to 40,000 full-time officials. In 1939 its number was much smaller, but it greatly expanded during the war, since it eventually had to cover most of Europe. By comparison, the SD had only some 3,000 members. There were other political police units, but they were less numerous than generally believed. The later East German Stasi, for example, had 90,000 full-time employees, even though it covered a country with a quarter of the population of Greater Germany.

The Nazi security forces were more than sufficient to cope with their task, the "total coverage of all people in Germany." In fact, they could have fulfilled their function with an apparatus half their size. Within a few months after the Nazis seized power, all parties ceased to exist, and even the Communists—the only party prepared to carry on illegally—never recovered from the blow. Individual Communists survived, needless to mention, but the moment they made any attempt to renew their activities, they were apprehended. From time to time, even during the war, Communist agents were parachuted into Germany from the Soviet Union, yet with one exception they all were caught within a few days or weeks. (The exception was a Communist of Polish origin who landed in Germany toward the end of the war and survived because he refrained from any activities and was hidden by Polish friends in Upper Silesia.) In only one case (in November 1939) did an assassin even come near to killing Hitler. This was because it was the action of an individual person, against which even the most effective police service is helpless.

Nazi intelligence inside Germany was effective, but Nazi espionage and sabotage in other countries were not very successful. Hitler's blitzkrieg generated the legend of the all-powerful fifth column at work everywhere. But after the war this was revealed as a figment of the imagination. The only conspiracy that might have succeeded (the plot of July 1944) took place less than a year before the war ended, when widespread dislocation had already set in and demoralization was making difficult the work of the Gestapo. Until then, Nazism had never really been challenged from within. The alleged storm troopers' plot in June 1934 was not a conspiracy at all, but a purge of leaders who, Hitler thought, might get in his way at some future date.

The question remains, then: Why was there so little resistance? Germany was a well-organized country, which made police control relatively easy. The Gestapo, furthermore, had many helpers—both ideological informers and "spite informers." But the main deterrent was the Gestapo's reputation as a cruel and efficient tool of the regime. It was believed to be omnipresent, to have agents in every home and office, which, of course, was quite untrue. What made its work so easy was the fact that unlike the police in democratic regimes, the Gestapo could infiltrate all real or supposed conspiracies with total legal impunity, and it did not have to bring the accused to public trial. In addition, it could use torture and other means illegal in democracies. The fear of the Gestapo was such that more often than not, there was no need to apply torture to extract confessions, for those arrested were only too willing to talk.

Those opposed to the regime therefore felt isolated. Precisely because they could not organize for fear of being infiltrated, they had no idea how many like-minded people there were throughout Germany. While the Nazi's winning streak continued, they would have had little support; it was not until 1942 that doubts and even defeatism began to spread.

In the occupied countries, the arm of the Gestapo was not nearly so long. In some Western European countries, the Gestapo had the support of collaborationists, and it also used high rewards to good effect. But elsewhere it failed to penetrate and gain a foothold, either because of national (anti-German) solidarity or because the population was more afraid of the partisans than of the Gestapo. Although the Gestapo acted with great cruelty, it was not spontaneous cruelty (sadism). In most cases, it was bureaucratic cruelty: Orders had been given from above, and the Gestapo obeyed orders.

The number of German opponents (or suspected opponents) of the

Nazi regime who were killed between 1933 and 1945 is, for a variety of reasons, difficult to estimate. If one includes deserters from the army, the number should be measured in the tens of thousands. Was the application of such violence excessive if the Nazis' sole aim was to retain power? The Italian example seems to show that power could be maintained with a minimum of terror. Nor is it true that the Nazi leaders had so many of their opponents killed because they overrated the extent of the opposition. After the war, they admitted that they knew they were always in full control. Thus, the explanation must rest on the belief in needing "preventive violence."

One of the fundamental tenets of Nazism was that the enemy had to be not just defeated but also destroyed. In retrospect, advocates of excessive terrorism could argue that unlike Mussolini, Hitler was not overthrown by a cabal of his closest collaborators. But such comparisons are not wholly convincing because from the very beginning, the situation in Germany was quite unlike the situation in Italy. The Gestapo, like other bureaucracies, had a vested interest in expanding its numbers and budgets. To justify its existence, therefore, it had to magnify the extent of the anti-Nazi threat. On the whole, the security services did not actively participate in politics. They had no ideology, no political will, no attitude of their own. They did not participate in the internal struggle for power but were simply an executive organ.

The Italian political police (the name OVRA was first used around 1930, but the institution was established well before then) was smaller and less well organized, and its exploits have attracted much less attention. Whereas Himmler and Heydrich have become household names, only specialists are familiar with names such as Arturo Bocchini, Carmen Senise, and Renzo Chierici, who were the three heads of Italy's political police from its creation to Mussolini's fall.

The operations of the Italian political police were outrageous by democratic standards: "Socially dangerous individuals" were interned without being tried, and others were kept under special surveillance. It was not uncommon for suspects to be arrested ten or even twenty times in a year, and then to be released after a day or two. Political opponents of the regime were kept on Lipari or Ustica Island. The special tribunals for defending the state meted out sentences totaling tens of thousands of years in prison. But compared with Nazi practice, the OVRA was still a paradigm of moderation and humanism. Only some six thousand "enemies" were sent to the islands or some other forced residence. Bocchini, the OVRA's first chief, systematically blocked any attempt by the Fascist Party to penetrate or control the police. He died in 1940. His successor, Senise, was, as one historian put it, "by temperament a pre-1922 monarchist, by inclination devoid of any fundamental allegiances. Senise plotted with the army and the royal court, and even after he was fired in April 1943, he played a notable role in the conspiracy that led to Mussolini's downfall.

In Italy (and, mutatis mutandis, Germany) there was a great deal of intrigue and infighting among the chief of police, the various ministries, and the other security services. This did not, of course, escape Mussolini's attention. He did not intervene, however, because he did not want too much power concentrated in any single branch of the security services.

Toward the end of Italy's Fascist regime, the political police seemingly lost control, and as a result, there were massive strikes in Milan and Turin, and leading members of opposition parties began to congregate more or less openly. There is every reason to assume that the police was aware of these activities and could have stopped them. In any case, Mussolini's demise was the result not of action by his opponents, but of discontent among the Fascist leadership. When Mussolini, totally dependent on the Nazis, made a revival in late 1943, he completely reorganized the political police under Buffarini-Guidi, and it consequently began to conform much more closely to the German paradigm, which is to say that it behaved with great cruelty.

To summarize, terror played a central role in the rise to power of Nazism and Italian Fascism. In the operation of these two regimes, it was essential, but always in combination with political propaganda. In retrospect it appears that although Fascism could not have continued without the constant use, or threat of use, of terror, propaganda was probably equally important. Though seemingly all-powerful, the Gestapo's power was in fact restricted—partly because there was not one security service but several, scheming against one another, but mainly because the Gestapo was merely an executive organ. Its freedom of maneuver was limited to the manner in which its orders were carried out. It had no monopoly of secret information, and if, in individual cases, the Gestapo was master of life or death, it had no "line" in either domestic or foreign affairs. There was not, nor could there have been, a German Joseph Fouché. The situation in Italy was different, inasmuch as the OVRA had somewhat greater freedom of action than the Gestapo did, simply because Italy was less totalitarian than Nazi Germany.

Propaganda

Terror has been used as a political instrument from time immemorial. The terror of fascism differs from that of other dictatorships not just because it applied terror on such a massive scale, but because it combined the use of terror with widespread, all-pervasive propaganda. Mussolini, Hitler, and Goebbels were not, of course, the first to use propaganda; the essential works on the subject (and on mass psychology) had been written in the century before. Hitler notes in *Mein Kampf* that he learned a great deal from British propaganda in World War I (Viscount Northcliffe) and from the Social Democrats who, in contrast to the bourgeois parties, used agitation on a massive scale in their political activities. But Nazism and fascism as well as Soviet and Chinese Communism used propaganda on an infinitely greater scale than ever before, and this was made possible by the technical development in the twentieth century of the means of mass communications.

Hitler correctly analyzed the failure of official German propaganda before 1918: The authorities had underrated its importance and had also failed to realize that effective propaganda was meant for the consumption of the masses, not the intellectuals. Propaganda, as Hitler envisioned it, consisted of making a few points exclusively for mass consumption and then endlessly repeating them. The masses, as Hitler and Goebbels, his most gifted assistant, saw it, were slow and lazy; their memories were weak; and they reacted only to the thousandfold repetition of the simplest ideas. Furthermore, they were "feminine" in their activities and thought and were motivated by emotion rather than by reason. There was no room for nuance or interpretation: Propaganda had to be positive or negative, based on love or hatred. There could be only right or wrong; and so the ability to see two sides of a question was the very antithesis of propaganda.

As Hitler wrote in *Mein Kampf*:

> Inasmuch as one's own propaganda recognized a shadow of right upon the opponent's side, the ground is prepared for questioning one's own right. The masses are not in a position to distinguish where the opponent's right ends and one's own begins. In such a case they become uncertain and mistrustful. . . . He who would win the masses must know the key that opens the door to their hearts. It is not objectivity, which is a weakness, but will and power. . . . The people sees in unfailing ruthless attack upon an opponent the proof of one's own right. Seen in this light hesitation leads to uncertainty, weakness, and ultimately failure.

If we add to this the recognition that propaganda had to be loud in form and extreme in content, we will have listed all the essentials of Nazi (and fascist) propaganda.

In their struggle for power, the Nazis tried to create as much noise as possible in order to attract attention. Once in power they established a monopoly of propaganda eliminating all potential rivals. The emphasis in fascist propaganda was always much more on the spoken than on the written word, on the assumption that only a minority was reading the political and editorial columns of newspapers. The *Völkische Beobachter*, the central organ of the Nazi party, had some 120,000 subscribers in 1932; that is, only every tenth party member was reading it, and its influence outside the party's ranks was negligible. Goebbels and Mussolini devoted much time and effort to the supervision and guidance of the press once their parties were in power, and they also wrote articles for publication. These articles were essentially guidelines stating the main themes of the party line to be repeated orally by thousands of local speakers and agitators.

Common to Nazi and fascist propaganda were extremist slogans; the building up of the Führer mythos ("the leader is always right"); an aggressive, bellicose approach; and an implacable hostility toward all enemies. Both Goebbels and the Italian Fascists discovered the importance of the radio as a vehicle of propaganda: For the first time in history it was possible to reach many millions of people at one time rather than a few thousand at most. The use of the radio was more widespread in Nazi Germany, as the number of wireless sets in Italy passed the 1 million mark only in 1938. Furthermore, Mussolini preferred the immediate contact with the masses from his balcony in Rome to the impersonal microphone.

Both Goebbels and Mussolini attached great importance to the cinema as a means of propaganda. Mussolini built Cinecitta, thus paving the way for the great resurgence of the Italian cinema after 1945; and Goebbels gave greater freedom to German moviemakers and actors than to any other mass medium. The main difference between Germany and Italy was that Germany generally used the propaganda weapon more systematically and radically than Italy did.

Germany's Ministry of Propaganda was in charge of all the major and minor media, providing daily guidance down to small details. Indeed, by 1937 its budget exceeded that of the Foreign Ministry, which shows how much importance was attached to these activities. In Italy such guidance was sporadic and, in the main, negative (that is, censorship). In 1933 there was a wholesale purge of journalists and radio broadcasters in Germany, whereas after 1923 most Italian journalists were not dismissed but continued in their old jobs. Thus, *Gleichschaltung* (purge) was far more extensive in Germany than in Italy; the only difference in Germany was that there were slightly fewer and more radical periodicals, such as the *Stürmer* or the SS organ *Das Schwarze Korps*.

The techniques of propaganda under Nazism and Fascism have been widely studied. Propaganda was always an instrument, but it was not an autonomous factor in the shaping of policy. In isolation it could achieve nothing; its success depended on physical power. It was *Machtpropaganda*, and it could be said, somewhat crudely, that while the going was good— such as in Germany up to the battle of Stalingrad—even a less accomplished and pervasive propaganda would have succeeded. After the tide of war had turned, however, propaganda did not make much difference to its outcome except helping prolong it: The main function of propaganda was to provide legitimacy to power and to project its achievements and the victors. As such, it helped make Nazism and Fascism popular for years. Nazi and Fascist propaganda outside Germany and Italy never had a strong impact, mainly because it had no monopoly. To the extent that the fascist regimes found admirers, it was for reasons other than the official propaganda.

Nazi and Fascist propaganda were successful before the seizure of power when they had no monopoly and when the use of terror was limited. This can be explained by the propaganda's specific virulence and mendacity and by the fact that it appealed to popular sentiments and traditions (such as nationalism). This is borne out by the fact that foreign propaganda hostile to Nazism had little if any impact inside Germany up to the later war years. In Italy, listening to foreign broadcasts was hardly ever punished, and even Radio Moscow's broadcasting schedules were given in the Italian press during much of the Fascist era.

Propaganda has also been used by other modern regimes, either on a massive scale or in a more subtle way. But comparison between the use of propaganda under fascism and that in democratic regimes is useless because a democratic state lacks, by definition, a monopoly on the dissemination of information. The Communist regimes also attributed crucial importance to propaganda, but their approach differed in certain aspects, such as the division of labor under Communism and between agitation (presenting a few ideas to the masses) and the systematic indoctrination of Marxism–Leninism. Soviet propaganda—appealing, on the whole, less to emotion—depended somewhat less on the use of symbols and rites than the Nazi propaganda did. But the difference was not overwhelming, and they shared considerable similarities in style and content.

Fascist propaganda should be viewed not only as the exploitation of the means of mass communication but also, in a wider framework, as the propagation of political myths, of indoctrination through schools and after-work activities. Once the discrepancy between slogans and reality during the last years of the war became obvious, Hitler and Mussolini fell silent, and although the propaganda apparatus continued to operate at peak capacity, its usefulness rapidly decreased. Experience also shows that the effectiveness and attraction of propaganda erode over time. Even though its very strength is repetition, such repetition causes it to lose some of its impact and credibility. When the mass audiences lose interest, they may still go through the motions of "spontaneous ovations," but their true belief and enthusiasm have dimmed. Fascism did not stay in power long enough to suffer the full consequences of routinization in regard to its propaganda, but there clearly were diminishing returns toward the end.

Fascist Culture

Fascism thought of itself as a movement of cultural revolution, a contention that was not altogether wrong. The Nazis wanted a "healthy" cultural life, the restoration of erstwhile German values, and a purge of all that was alien, decadent, and Jewish—hence the struggle against "cultural Bolshevism" (*Kulturbolschewismus*). But in fact, most of the cultural trends that the Nazis disliked so much (such as modernism in literature, art, and music; sociology; and psychoanalysis) were by no means "Bolshevist," as they were equally disliked in the Soviet Union. Be that as it may, the Nazis burned books, removed "decadent art" from the museums and sold it abroad, and no longer played modern music. Jews, of course, were no longer permitted to participate in Germany's cultural life.

Although it is clear what other cultures the Nazis disliked, the essence and the aims of their own culture are not easy to define. Cultural *Gleichschaltung* meant that art had to be popular, to be part of the overall assignment of social integration. The artist was to create not for other artists but for the people, who were the supreme judges. There was no room for avant-garde trends and constantly changing fashions whose aesthetic value was uncertain. Instead, art had to be heroic or tragic, to preach devotion to the soil, the family, and, above all, the native land. It stood not for bloodless (and rootless) objectivism but, rather, the "healthy instincts" of the people, such as patriotism.

Likewise, the emphasis in education had to be on character and ideals—there was a surfeit of knowledge, as Hitler saw it. All this he had stated in considerable detail in *Mein Kampf*, and what followed in later years were essentially variations on the same theme. Culture must be German, but how did this "German-ness" manifest itself? Sometimes Hitler invoked Richard Wagner ("To be German is to do a thing for its own sake"), and on another occasion he stated that to be German meant to be "clear, logical and true." To the extent that there was a Nazi cultural ideal, it was symbolized by the pictures or sculptures of healthy young men and women. Writers and composers were expected to follow the example of the great nineteenth-century classics.

It was not that the great nineteenth-century figures were bad masters to copy, and it is also true that the modern trends were not always worth following. But it did not make much sense in 1935 to write poems in the style of Goethe and to compose symphonies following the example of Beethoven. Rather, a culture was needed that expressed the spirit of the

Third Reich, and here the aesthetics of Nazism were of no help. Furthermore, the great masters were humanists; Goethe's patriotism always was suspect; and Beethoven (basing himself on Schiller) was embracing all of humankind.

The Nazis' great idol was Richard Wagner. Until the outbreak of war Hitler seldom missed attending the Bayreuth Festival and always paid his respects to Wagner's descendants. But even the *Ring* was not really an example to be emulated. Although Siegfried was an ideal hero, at the same time he was surrounded by intrigues, fratricide, general villainy, and, of course, a tragic ending! *Parsifal* was too Christian; *The Flying Dutchman* was too much of a horror story; *Tristan and Isolde* was too decadent; and so in the end only *Die Meistersinger* remained.

"German physics" was introduced at the suggestion of an overzealous Nazi physicist, but it was never taken very seriously. There was also a "German sociology," but it was a mere stratagem, intended to protect a discipline already suspect to the new masters. Individual Nazis published books on history, philosophy, and economics, but they were few and it is impossible to point to any specific Nazi school in these fields, just as there was no Nazi opera or symphony. The Weimar period had been one of cultural experimentation, and thus of great interest to the rest of the world. But German culture under the Nazis ceased to be of universal interest, which, from the Nazi point of view, was fine, for they loathed the Weimar spirit.

This cultural malaise was most acutely felt in literature and the visual arts. It was less marked in science because there was less censorship and also in the cinema, which enjoyed a greater measure of freedom than did the other artistic genres. If there was a decline in the natural sciences—Germany lost its preeminent position in physics, mathematics, and medicine—it was not so much the result of ideological interference by the Nazi leaders, but the consequence of the emigration, mostly forced, of the leading Jewish and non-Jewish scientists. When David Hilbert, head of the famous Göttingen school of mathematics, was asked by the Nazi minister of education whether his institute had suffered as the result of the purges, he replied: "It has not suffered—it has ceased to exist." The purge of Jews and other so-called undesirable elements aside, Nazism had less impact than commonly believed.

The cultural interests of the Nazi leaders were rather limited; on Hitler's and Goebbels's scale of priorities, culture did not figure very highly. The "old fighters" did not feel comfortable in concert halls, museums, or libraries, though they did go there on important occasions. Their idea of enjoyment was closer to the climate of a beer hall, a strictly male society, with loud talk and laughter, explicit jokes, and popular music performed by military bands. Hitler was interested in architecture and watched many films, and Goebbels also watched movies and made speeches to educated audiences. Goering played the patron of the arts and, through his wife, consorted with people from the theater world. But it is doubtful whether Goering spent much time looking at the many pictures and other objets d'art stolen on his behalf from all over Europe. Unlike Stalin and Zhdanov, Hitler and Goebbels did not instruct German scientists and artists how to perform. It was not excessive modesty that restrained them, however, but the feeling that it was not their business and that they could spend their time better on the truly important things, such as politics.

The party guidelines were neither clear nor consistent. Sometimes a particular writer or artist was warmly praised and promoted by one party institution, only to be attacked by another. And if cultural affairs had a low priority in Nazi politics before the outbreak of World War II, they received even less attention after 1939. During the war there was a certain cultural freedom simply because the troops and the population at home had to be entertained. It was simply part of the war effort, irrespective of whether such works of art served any higher German ideals or even whether they were works of art in the first place.

Political indoctrination in culture was, on the whole, limited to prohibitions; there was no Nazi style in literature comparable to "Socialist realism." Writers and artists thus had to "adjust" themselves to the new spirit if they wanted to publish, exhibit, or perform, and so any direct criticism of Nazi doctrine and practice was ruled out. It was not necessary to write about the party and its Führer or to quote him. There were works that did this, but the educated ignored them, and they had no mass appeal, either.

Indoctrination at the elementary- and secondary-school level and in the universities was limited basically to lessons on racial doctrine and a few lectures on the Nazi worldview. The number of students in Germany fell from 128,000 in 1933 to 58,000 in 1939, but this might have been the result of the introduction of compulsory army service rather than a specific decision to reduce their number.

The cultural policy of Italian Fascism was more tolerant than Nazi Germany's. Fascism made less of a fetish of its antirationalist character, and it derived much of its spiritual inspiration from the Action française, rather than from the murky racial myths of Germany. Some of its main leaders (including Mussolini) were better read and educated than the Nazis, and they were not opposed to modern art. To wit, some of the prewar futurists were among the precursors of Fascism, and so, of course, was D'Annunzio. Pictures symbolizing the spirit of Fascist Italy were in fact considered degenerate in Nazi Germany and could not be shown there. The trend toward monumentalism, so apparent in Nazi Germany and Stalinist Russia came only later in Italy and never reached the same excesses.

Cultural exchanges between Germany and Italy were therefore limited. For the Italians, the Latin spirit was the great idol. Ancient Rome had been the center of the civilized world when the German tribes were still scratching out a living in the dark forests, and there could be no comparison between the German Middle Ages and the Italian Renaissance. For the French fascists, German culture was of no great interest, and the British fascists were preoccupied with their own traditions, as were the Hungarians and the Romanians. Whatever their political affinities, the various fascisms had little in common culturally, except a disdain of the avant-garde.

Italian Fascism was more tolerant of intellectuals known to have reservations about the regime. Indeed, they were protected against some of the more zealous Fascists by Giuseppe Botta, the education minister, and occasionally by Mussolini himself. With the exception of the Jewish academics who left the country when the racial laws were passed in 1938, there were hardly any cultural emigrants at all: Philosophers like Croce and historians and publicists like de Sanctis and Salvatorelli could criticize Fascism while ostensibly writing about philosophy or Hellenistic society or the Risorgimento. The leading Italian philosophical journal was edited by a well-known professor who refused in 1931 to take the loyalty oath to Mussolini. Such "liberal" tolerance was naturally quite incompatible with the true totalitarian spirit. Everyone, including the censor, understood what these critics were doing, but the authorities—rightly, perhaps, from their point of view—did not take them too seriously.

If the overall attitude of the cultural authorities was one of pragmatism, the intellectuals—though not without some grumbling—cooperated. It is impossible to think of any leading writers, musicians (except Toscanini), painters, moviemakers, or scientists who, in protest against the regime, stopped working. This includes the prominent anti-Fascists of the post 1945 period. Moravia, Vittorini, Pratolini, Pavese, and Guttuso all began their careers under Mussolini. The same is true with regard to the Italian film industry, from de Sica, Rosselini, Visconti and Soldati to Anna Magnani.

Whereas in Germany there was a new beginning in 1945, in Italy there was no dramatic break but, on the contrary, a great deal of continuity. In fact, the intellectual climate of Fascist Italy was, after the initial period of enthusiasm and high expectations, mainly one of apathy and indifference. There was, on an abstract level, a Fascist style extolling heroism and similar such qualities. But in practice it was hardly ever in evidence.

Little need be said about the cultural policies of the other European fascist parties. Some had no particular cultural interests, only an extreme and primitive belief in chauvinism. Others regarded fascism primarily as a movement of cultural (and moral) regeneration, such as Pierre Drieu La Rochelle, Robert Brasillach, and José Antonio. These men's ideas are not without interest. Quite often they tried, as Drieu La Rochelle once wrote, to combine contrary ideas: "the nation and Europe, Socialism and aristocracy, freedom of thought and authority, mysticism and anticlericalism." But a discussion of these views and attitudes belongs to a study of modern European intellectual history; they did not constitute a party program, let alone a consistent policy. Indeed, most French or Spanish fascists and fascist sympathizers were not even aware of these ruminations on a rarified, metapolitical level.

In the case of the French fascist intellectuals, there was a curious sado-masochistic ingredient. On one hand, they admired the virile dynamism of Nazi Germany in juxtaposition to the decadent France. Yet on the other hand, the German claims to cultural superiority and their contempt of traditional France offended them, and the depths of the German soul remained forever impenetrable and frightening to them.

If fascism did attract some intellectuals in Europe, who were they? Among the leading writers, composers, and artists and among philosophers, historians, and scientists, there were very few committed Fascists or Nazis before 1922 or 1933, respectively, but there were also no Communists or Socialists: Intellectuals seldom committed themselves without reservation to any political party. But there nonetheless had been latent sympathies all along for elitist movements such as fascism that were by no means limited to Italy and Germany. T. S. Eliot, William Butler Yeats, and D. H. Lawrence were sympathetic to certain aspects of fascism. The sources of attraction were manifold: Some Western intellectuals were attracted by the revolt against "arid intellectualism"; others by the promise of an aristocratic civilization; and still others by a nostalgia for a pagan world. Some saw in fascism an answer to the new machine age and mediocrity, for many believed that culture had been sacrificed to the rule of the masses. Sometimes this was a free-floating fear of anarchy. As Dean Inge wrote in 1933, tyranny was the neurosis of lawlessness, fascism the shield against the ruin of civilization by the slums of the great towns and a few misguided intellectuals.

Fascism attracted romantics resisting the spirit of materialism, and it also inspired the anti-romantic thinkers of the Action française who advocated a return to the classic rationalist French tradition and to harmony, reason, and precision. Fascism appealed to conservatives critical of modern society with its lack of tradition, hierarchy, and religious values. It also brought in young antibourgeois rebels who believed that fascism was a necessary stage in the destruction of capitalism.

Common to all these people was the belief that liberal democracy was bankrupt and that fascism, whatever its shortcomings, was a movement of uncompromising men of firm beliefs and action. These intellectuals were willing to accept restrictions on their liberty because this seemed a small price to be paid for a cultural renaissance that would lead to a national revival, perhaps even to the birth of a new civilization.

Some intellectuals genuinely believed that the artist-hero would be the ruler in this new society created by fascism. But even those who had no such illusions shared the desire for a strong authority that was widespread in the 1920s and 1930s all over Europe. Fascism, as H. G. Wells wrote, was a "bad good thing"; it had purpose and insisted on discipline and public service. George Bernard Shaw predicted that Mussolini would go further in the direction of socialism than the British Labour Party would.

All this strikes one in retrospect as a grotesque misreading of the essence of Italian Fascism—let alone that of National Socialism. But intellectuals have no more specific competence or wisdom in politics than other mortals do, and many of those who sympathized with fascism at the time were basically apolitical men or women who shared a belief that some form of dictatorship was the wave of the future. Although some of them preferred a dictatorship of the left, Communism at that time seemed less congenial than fascism, and the Communists, with their cult of the manual worker, made only sporadic efforts to woo the intelligentsia.

Intellectuals did not fare well under fascist regimes: They were worse off in Germany than in Italy. Generally, however, they accepted their lot, and an overwhelming majority cooperated at least to some extent with the system. There were active antifascists in the working class and among the aristocrats, in the church, and even in the army. But it is difficult to think of intellectuals inside Germany and Italy who perished in the camps or were executed for their beliefs. Those who emigrated were mostly of Jewish origin, and those who were "antifascists at heart" or went into an "inner immigration" still had to conform to some extent. The list of contributors to Goebbels's weekly *Das Reich*, which began to appear during the war, or to the cultural pages of the *Corriere della sera* reads like a list of the members of the "inner immigration." The less said about the French intelligentsia under the German occupation, the better. There were, as always, some exceptions, some shining examples of true humanism, of steadfastness, and even of sacrifice. But they were few and far between in France, as elsewhere.

Achievements

There has never been a regime in history that has not had at least some achievements to its credit, and fascism was no exception. Had it compiled only failures and crimes, it would have had to rest entirely on massive terror in order to stay in power, and this was clearly not the case. Fascism did, in fact, satisfy certain needs and longings of wide sections of society and, at least in some respects, gained its support, respect, and even enthusiasm. The majority of fascist movements, to be sure, never came to power, and so their main function was to challenge the governments that were in power. Even the promised Nazi millennium lasted only twelve years, of which half were spent at war, and the record of Italian Fascism also extended over little more than twenty years.

Italy was affected as much by the Great Depression as other countries were. Even as the national income rose between 1929 and 1939, the per capita income stagnated. Mussolini, however, offered several spectacular campaigns, such as the "battle for wheat" and the draining of the Pontinian marshes. His protectionist policy made possible the postwar development of an Italian car and movie industry. But even so, Italians were not really better off in 1940 than they had been ten or twenty years earlier. Although Mussolini stood for autarky and corporationism, he seemed to have no firm convictions or great interest in economics. In sum, he wanted to make Italy a great power, a paradigm for all humankind, and to him, economic policy was of interest only in this context.

Fascists did take an active interest in the organization of leisure for the workers. Dopo lavoro (after work) was not as extensive as its German equivalent KdF (Kraft durch Freude), but it did help strengthen Fascist influence through social clubs, cheap theater and concert tickets, organized tours, and other such activities. Because Italy was less industrialized at the time than the other major European countries were, it suffered less from the misery of urban unemployment, and the situation in the villages was less likely to meet the public eye. Novels such Carlo Levi's *Christ Stopped at Eboli* and Ignazio Silone's *Fontamara* and *Bread and Wine*—fairly realistic accounts of the situation in the countryside—were published or became known to the wider public only after the war.

The general impression abroad was that under Mussolini the trains were arriving and departing on time and that the Mafia had been all but stamped out. Above all, Italy, "betrayed by its allies" in the postwar peace treaties, had again become an important and respected international power. Thus in 1932 Mussolini could declare that in ten years Europe would be either Fascist or "Fascisized." In theory, Italy was in a permanent state of war even before the first aggressions (Ethiopia in 1935, Spain in 1937) and the irredentist propaganda pronouncing the Mediterranean as *mare nostro* and staking claims not only in North Africa but also Corsica and Nice. All this appealed to substantial sections of the population, including the intellectuals who had long claimed that Italy was a "proletarian nation" that had been discriminated against when the spoils of war were distributed.

Fascism, in brief, was quite popular at home. In a plebiscite in the later 1920s, 99 percent of those who took part—and the results were apparently not falsified—voted for Fascism and Mussolini. There is reason to believe, however, that in the late 1930s and especially after Italy's entry into the war, the popularity of the regime substantially declined.

The economic and social problems facing the Nazis when they came to power were much more acute than those confronting the Italian Fascists: 6 million unemployed and a drop of almost 50 percent in industrial production since 1929. Hitler promised to get the German economy going again. Because he fulfilled his promise, this explains, at least to some extent, his popularity and that of his party. And it is not true that this success was only the result of rearmament: Rearmament on a massive scale began only in 1936, by which time unemployment had been reduced to 2.7 million, that is, by 60 percent (compared with 20 percent in the United States and Britain). In that period, German industrial output rose by almost one-third.

The Nazis had no economic geniuses in their ranks; instead, most of the key positions in the field were given to experts who were not members of their party. But the Nazis opted instinctively for the right solution, a primitive Keynesian strategy: pump priming, deficit spending, major public works. Some of the decisions made by the Nazis early on (and some of the results) had in fact been initiated by earlier governments, just as the *Autobahn* had been envisaged—and the first section built—before 1933. Even though the Nazis appeared as the defendants of small retail trade against the big department stores, the advance of these chain stores had in fact been halted by the Brüning government. However, the Nazis tackled the problems in a more energetic way; for example, public investment rose more than threefold in the 1930s. Public spending made up 35 percent of the national income in 1938 (compared with 23 percent in Britain and 10 percent in the United States). The share of the state in the economy was much larger than that in other countries, and decisions concerning wages and prices were largely made by the bureaucracy. As a result, the recovery in Germany was quicker than elsewhere. The new masters tried to lessen the dependence of Germany's economy on world trade and so cut imports to one-third of what they had been and based business deals on barter. Such measures were helpful for a short time but then caused increasing shortages and imbalances after 1936. Indeed, the whole system might have collapsed if it had not been for the German victories in the early years of the war.

The Nazis' attempts to create jobs at almost any price included the obligatory labor service. Again, the basic idea had been suggested not by the Nazis but by the youth movement in the 1920s. Once rearmament began on a massive scale, unemployment disappeared altogether, and labor became a scarce commodity. The shortage was remedied partly by the return of women workers to the factories; they had been squeezed out during the early years of Nazi rule. Foreign workers were increasingly employed, first on a voluntary and later on a forced basis.

German workers and employees were not well paid during the early years of Nazi rule. The hourly wage of industrial workers declined between 1932 and 1938 while the prices of essential food items, such as for meat and butter, went up. There were acute shortages, but the depressing lines of unemployed disappeared from Germany's streets, and a feeling of optimism gained ground that the crisis had been overcome. The unions had been destroyed, but there were virtually no strikes. In Nazi Germany, in contrast to Fascist Italy, strikes were not banned by law. German agriculture also benefited from the reduction of agricultural imports. The rich did well, though excessive profits and ostentatious spending were discouraged. The big landowners, the *Junker*, escaped expropriation, but their incomes, too, were controlled.

The Nazi regime acquired the reputation of being truly concerned about the fate of the common people. During the winter months, money and clothing were collected for the poor (*Winterhilfe*), and the activities of Kraft durch Freude, founded in November 1933, soon had a wide coverage. Seats in theater and concert halls were made available for a nominal entrance fee of 50 pfennigs, and for 7 marks one could take an eight-day excursion on the Mosel River. In total, 9 million Germans availed themselves of the opportunity to join these cheap excursions, and more people traveled abroad than ever before. This was an age of festivals. The Olympic Games of 1936 and the annual party conventions in Nuremberg were the most widely publicized, but there were also harvest festivals and various parades celebrating some historical event or current political event.

The German boxer Max Schmeling became, for a short while, the world heavy-weight champion, and Rudolf Harbig broke the world record for the half-mile. The Volksempfänger, a cheap but effective radioset, was mass produced, and later the Volkswagen was designed, a car that everyone could afford. Movies and broadcasts radiated optimism and popular satisfaction.

True, the shady sides of life in Germany were not widely featured: Major sections of the population benefited little from the upsurge (for instance, the civil service's wages were frozen), and certain geographical regions such as Silesia, Saxony, and Hesse lagged behind the rest, just as southern Italy did not come close to catching up with the north. But the Weimar social legislation was not revised, and in some respects, the social services in the Third Reich were superior to those provided in earlier years. Robert Ley, head of the German Labor Front, proclaimed on every possible occasion that the new regime stood for social justice and that all had an equal chance in the Third Reich. There were not many cases of workers and peasants moving into key positions in the economy or politics. But the leadership favored such upward mobility and claimed that it was only a question of time until inherited wealth and privilege would disappear.

Was fascism "modern," and did it aim at a society in line with new social and technical developments? Some latter-day writers have stressed these aspects, but is this emphasis justified? The issue is of limited interest today, for our main concern is with the attractiveness of fascism for contemporaries, not how it appeared to subsequent generations. Italian Fascism and Nazism were in some respects a modernizing force, albeit often indirectly and against their original intention. Both Hitler and Mussolini were fascinated with modern technologies and used them as often as possible. For example, Hitler was the first politician to use the airplane on a daily basis to appear in many cities during the election campaigns.

But Nazi ideology was backward looking, and so was Fascist doctrine, with the Roman Empire and the German Middle Ages as the ideal forms of existence. Nazism painted a grim picture of the horrible effects of urbanization and industrialization in comparison with the calm, idyllic life in a medieval village, a small town, or the Nuremberg of *Die Meistersinger*. Even though Himmler was one of the most powerful men in the Third Reich, the commander of its elite forces, his view of life was shaped by all kinds of abstruse and ridiculous ideas on every possible subject. Likewise, Nazi doctrine was essentially irrational, stressing blood, sentiment, and instinct, rather than reason.

Many years after the event, observers have detected strong elements of modernist planning and rationalization (of industry and agriculture), but few contemporaries were aware of this kind of modernism. If fascism was compelled to deviate in its practice from its reactionary concepts, it was for strictly pragmatic reasons. However often the Nazis condemned the ugliness of life in the big cities, the majority of Germans continued to live there; and however critical they were of industrial society, for a nation of 70 million, a broader economic basis was needed than agriculture could provide. If Hitler and Mussolini wanted to equip their armed forces with bombers and tanks rather than swords and halberds, they needed a powerful heavy industry.

More and more elements of the original antimodernist thinking had to be discarded. Some Nazi leaders, including Goebbels and Goering, did not need much persuasion, since they had always doubted the validity of the medieval idols. If fascism was modernist, it was so in a reactionary way. It wanted to use the achievements of modern science and technology to accomplish its irrational aims. In the final analysis, Nazism still rejected modern (Western) civilization. Such a combination was by no means impossible—barbarism is not a monopoly of underdeveloped countries and the prescientific age. Stalin was named "Genghis Khan with nuclear bombs," and Muslim fundamentalists do not reject the use of modern high explosives simply because they were first manufactured in the decadent West.

Some of the modernizing measures of fascism have lasted, such as the abolition of confessional schools in Germany. Social changes came about because of the great upheaval of World War II: The misfortune of some is the good luck of others, and mass slaughter makes for upward mobility. But it is still wrong to argue that fascism attracted millions of followers because of the revolutionary changes in society. The great majority of people in the 1930s wanted order and stability, and Hitler was only too aware of their desires. Soon after he seized power, he announced that the national revolution was over and that there would not be another for a thousand years.

The most striking achievements of fascism were in foreign policy, the generation of the feeling that Germany and Italy had become the leading powers in Europe. Although most people were preoccupied with the concerns and hardship of daily life, the depth of the national resentment was also an important political factor. This resentment was directed above all against the victors in World War I who were preventing Germany and Italy from taking their rightful place among the nations. Thus there was broad support for Mussolini's demands for a revision of borders and for annexations. And the Germans had a feeling of pride when the Saar was reunited with Germany in 1935, when German troops entered the Rhineland in 1936—in violation of the Versailles treaty—and when the German army entered Austria in 1938.

Whenever Hitler invaded a country, he announced that this was his "last territorial claim." Most Austrians and most Germans living in Czechoslovakia did want, at that time, to be reunited with the Reich. But finally with the conquest of rump Czechoslovakia at the very latest (March 1939) it became clear that Hitler's ambitions went well beyond national unification. How far, in fact, did his ambitions go? Did he merely want to conquer Europe, or did he envision ultimate world rule? Probably he did not know himself. The comments of his paladins do not offer much guidance. As usual, they followed the Führer, whose vision was infinitely wider, as befitting a man of destiny.

What if Hitler had stopped in 1938, once he had created a powerful, great Germany? In that case there would have been no world war and his state might have survived. Some people have even suggested that Hitler might have entered history as a great and wise leader. David Lloyd George, a former British prime minister, declared in 1934 that Hitler was the "best thing that had happened to Germany since Bismarck, nay since Frederic II." It was a statement typical of the impressions gained by foreigners at the time, but it was based on a profound misjudgment. Bismarck was a statesman who knew rationally and instinctively where to stop. Hitler, in contrast, was a man possessed who could not stop, even if he had realized the necessity of doing so, which he never did. He was a gambler without a sense of reality, and the more he succeeded during the early years, the more he became convinced that he would always prevail over his enemies. Given Germany's limited resources, how could he confront the whole world? Daring turned more and more into recklessness. When the campaign in Russia came to a halt in December 1941, Hitler reacted by declaring war on the United States, a wholly irrational decision, which was contrary to Germany's interests and ensured defeat. This was not a mere miscalculation, such as Mussolini's invasion of Greece; it was a suicidal act. And it was by no means the only one.

Thus, the Nazi victories in foreign policy that made Hitler so popular in the 1930s created a momentum that led Germany into a world war and defeat. But to what extent was this momentum specifically Nazi and Hitlerian? No other brand of fascism would have been able or willing to provoke a world war. On his own, Mussolini might have carried out some colonial expeditions in Africa, but he would not have dared intervene anywhere else, except perhaps in the framework of a civil war.

But even fascism in the smaller countries was militaristic, ultranationalist, and aggressive to the best of its limited ability. It is tempting to speculate what, for instance, relations between a fascist Britain and France, or Nazi Germany and a fascist France, would have been. Their interests would have collided, and they would not have coexisted in peace.

There was an antifascist slogan in the 1930s to the effect that "Hitler means war." It was a primitive slogan, but essentially correct. The ambitions of Nazism precluded a peaceful international order, let alone relations between equals. There was room only for masters and servants. And since, according to fascist philosophy, war was not a disaster but, on the contrary, a necessary event in the annals of nations, with all kinds of curative properties, it was not something to be avoided but, to be welcomed. Some of Hitler's latter-day apologists have claimed that he did not really want war, only its spoils. But on innumerable occasions, Hitler stated the opposite, and he even expressed regret that the Munich treaty of October 1938 had cheated him of a war he wanted.

Wars have been fought since time began. Some were planned, and others broke out accidentally. But never in recent history had war been planned so relentlessly between more or less civilized nations. The Nazi leaders were quite oblivious to the fact that a war in twentieth-century Europe was bound to lead to a huge disaster for vanquished and victors alike. They never seriously considered the cost of war, as this would have been akin to a "slave mentality." Nor did they consider until much later that they who take the sword are destined to perish by the sword.

Did it matter in the end that Mussolini made the trains run on time and that Hitler built an impressive network of Autobahnen if the cities connected by these links were destroyed? It is easy to understand that the early achievements of fascism impressed many. This helps explain the rise of fascism, and it made many forget until too late that such a high price would have to be paid, sooner rather than later.

The Joys of Daily Life

The majority of people in Nazi Germany, as in Stalin's Russia, did not live in acute, paralyzing fear but tried to enjoy themselves. They fell in love; went to concerts, museums, and exhibitions; went on hiking tours in the mountains; swam in the sea; got drunk; celebrated holidays and anniversaries; and watched soccer matches and other sports—active participation in sports was greater than ever before. They went dancing and played cards; enjoyed opera performances, ballet, and musicals; bought cars or at least a new radio; and were interested in new fashions. More people went to the movies than ever before: The number of tickets sold in 1942 was four times that in 1933. Some of the hit songs of the 1930s have lasted and are sung or hummed even today. Movie stars such as Lyubov Orlova in Russia and Hans Albers, Heinrich George, or Zarah Leander in Germany are fondly remembered even now.

What does this all mean? It means that not everyone lived in a state of terror, that not a few people benefited from the regime, and that many more supported it to some extent or at least put up with it and tried to make the best of it. Although daily life was politicized, there were limits that the rulers did not want or thought it unwise to cross. Robert Ley, leader of the German Labor Front, declared in 1937 that only sleep was a private affair in the Third Reich, but no other Nazi ever made such a foolish statement, nor did Ley ever repeat it. The less interest a person had in public affairs and the more he or she ignored politics, the freer that person could feel in his or her private world. The authorities in Nazi Germany and Fascist Italy (and equally in the Soviet Union) used propaganda to an unprecedented extent, but people were still not told what games to play, what movies to watch, what ice cream to eat, or where to spend their holidays. The authorities probably suspected that this would be counterproductive.

Thousands of instructions were issued in totalitarian regimes. Although the Nazis had solemnly promised to get women out of the factories, in 1939, 2 million more women were in the workforce than in 1933. Many instructions were ignored or were merely paid lip service if they did not concern political issues vital to the regime. When Hitler came to power in 1933, only 5 percent of secondary-school teachers belonged to the Nazi Party. Five years later, virtually everyone had to belong to at least one Nazi-sponsored professional organization. But to what extent did this affect life in the schools? It had a certain impact on biology (race theory), history (recent), and German literature (twentieth century). There was a stronger emphasis on physical training. But since contemporary literature and history were hardly covered in school, the curriculum was not radically different from what it had been before. Professional organizations—of lawyers, physicians, war veterans, beekeepers, bowlers, and hunters—came under Nazi control. But on their social evenings they generally did what they had done before 1933 and would do again after 1945.

Instructions were given to pay greater attention to beauty at the workplace and to initiate competition between factories and other workplaces ("socialist competition" in the Soviet Union). More often than not, such orders were simply disregarded. According to the Nazi ideal of female beauty and behavior, German women were to be natural, not "artifical" and fashion conscious. They were not to smoke or to use perfume, except perhaps eau de cologne. But no one but a few fanatics or eccentrics paid attention. Women still wore fur coats or at least dreamed of owning one. They still smoked, and their sex life, as far as can be ascertained, was not fundamentally different from what it had been before 1933.

Studies of entertainment on various levels of sophistication show that little changed in Germany or Italy. True, there was an ideological literature. It was widely bought and given as a present, but it is not at all certain whether it was widely read. Many people leafed through *Mein Kampf*, but few read it from cover to cover. Mussolini's *Italian Encyclopedia* was one of the best works of reference of the time, and if one disregarded Mussolini's own article on fascism, remarkably objective.

What books did Germans and Italians read? Books on World War I were quite popular, but writers considered unreliable by the Nazis because they did not conform with their weltanschauung—such as Hermann Hesse,

Ernst Wiechert, and Hans Fallada—or wholly apolitical writers, were even more widely read. Even those artists who had been sharply critical of the Nazis could find jobs under the new masters, provided they were not Jews or Communists. One example is Erich Kästner, who wrote films under an assumed name. Works by Franz Kafka, Hermann Broch, Elias Canetti, and Robert Musil could be bought in Germany almost up to the outbreak of war. Virtually the whole contemporary American, British, and French literature was read in Germany, many pieces in translation. These works included those by André Maurois, Paul Claudel, Paul Valéry, Virginia Woolf, Evelyn Waugh, T. S. Eliot, D. H. Lawrence, William Faulkner, F. Scott Fitzgerald, William Saroyan, and Graham Greene, and even John Steinbeck, Ernest Hemingway, and the early James Joyce. Those whose books were not translated were at least reviewed in Germany, even in wartime, such as Jean-Paul Sartre, Albert Camus, Jean Anouilh, and Jean Cocteau. There were widely publicized exhibitions denouncing "decadent art," but pictures of this kind were still shown and bought, albeit a bit more surreptitiously. Atonal music was not to be performed in public, but virtually everything else could. "Jewish" psychoanalysis was banned, but something quite similar was practiced under a different name. It was said that 95 percent of post-1945 German authors had been published in the Third Reich; in the case of Italy, the figure was closer to 99 percent and included most of the outstanding writers of the left, such as Alberto Moravia and Roberto Rosselini, the famous film director. It included Salvadore Quasimodo and Caesare Pavese and virtually everyone who had been someone.

What applied to the avant-garde applied even more to mass culture. Up to the outbreak of the war, German radio magazines published the programs of foreign stations. Western best-sellers such as *Gone with the Wind* and *Anthony Adverse* and Pearl Buck's books were read as widely in Germany as in America. Thomas Wolfe had probably a wider and more enthusiastic readership in Germany than in his native country.

The list of hit songs of 1937 shows that young Germans were dreaming of Hawaii, the South Sea Islands, the *Pinien* (pine trees) *von Argentinien*, Cuba, and San Francisco. One of the most popular songs announced that Paris was the most beautiful city of the world, not Berlin, Hamburg, or Munich; others were called "Yes Sir—No Sir" (Zarah Leander), and "Merci, mon ami." The great hero of 1938 was Maupassant's Bel-Ami, the darling of the ladies. There were no hit songs in praise of the Black Forest, the Lüneburg Heath, or the Rhine Valley, even though these regions had much to recommend them. There were no love songs referring to Gretchen at the spinning wheel. With very few exceptions, the German films were unpolitical. Foreign films shown included almost all of Hollywood, from *It Happened One Night* and *Broadway Melody* to *Gone with the Wind* and *San Francisco*.

The incongruence of Nazi cultural policy was perhaps most apparent in dance music. In principle, jazz was banned because of its racially inferior (African American) origin. But it took the Nazis a long time to find out that Benny Goodman was not an Aryan, and they were willing to ignore the fact that Django Reinhard was a gypsy. Leading British and some American jazz orchestras came to visit Berlin and Hamburg right up to the war. They were not officially performing jazz but "swing," and this, in most cases, passed censorship. Dance bands continued to perform during the war, because differentiating between good "German" and bad "foreign" music was virtually impossible.

And what does this all mean? It means that Germans (and Italians) could engage in their hobbies under Nazism and Fascism, provided that they did not show an unhealthy interest in politics and did not collide in daily life with the party and its representatives. In such cases, the tolerance vanished, and the deviant behavior led to quick reprisals and unfortunate consequences. This was particularly true if a person criticized the party and its leaders, publicly disagreed with official policy toward the church or the Führer's architectural projects, or uttered misgivings about the invasion of foreign countries or the way foreigners were treated. If a young man (or woman) refused to join a party-affiliated organization, he could still work in a factory or serve as a soldier but probably would not be able to study at a university. If he did not greet (or return a greeting) with Heil Hitler, he would be suspect. If he complained about some shortcomings (such as the shortage of vegetables or meat) or the conspicuous consumption of a Nazi dignitary and his family, this would be registered as a case of *Miesmacherei* or even spreading hostile propaganda. This would not necessarily land him in prison or a concentration camp, but it would be registered by the *Blockwart*, the local confidential party representative, and could, sooner or later, lead him into all kinds of unpleasantness.

Belonging to one of the mammoth organizations such as the German Labor Front, with 23 million members, or the peasants' organization (Reichsnährstand), with its 15 million, did not really mean much. But not belonging would invariably be interpreted as an act of defiance and would have consequences. People could express their desire that soon there would be peace, but only on the conditions outlined by Hitler.

The terror and the propaganda did not extend to every sphere. People could enjoy themselves if they agreed with the regime's policy or at least ignored its failures and crimes or, if they had misgivings, kept them to themselves. A private sphere of life existed even in Stalinist Russia, where close friends could sometimes talk openly in the safety of a Moscow kitchen. There was a wider such sphere in Nazi Germany than in the Soviet Union, partly because the Nazis had much less time to impose their system on the German people and partly because they had greater confidence in the popularity of their system and so thought total control was unnecessary. This sphere of individual freedom was wider yet in Italy but was always based on the assumption that everyone knew how far one could go, that on basic things everyone had to conform, and that any action considered dangerous to the regime would be punished without mercy.

The Liquidation of Fascism

It took a world war to destroy the fascist regimes. It took millions of people many years to come to terms with the heritage of fascism. Italian Fascism collapsed without fighting to the bitter end; without the massive help from Germany, Mussolini would not have had a second chance with his Republic of Salo established in 1943.

Nazi Germany surprised the world twice, first by continuing to fight for two years after it was clear that it could not win the war. Was it fanaticism, the fear of enemy revenge, or the dreaded Gestapo that prevented a collapse? All these considerations played a role, although fanaticism was probably the least important factor, except to explain the behavior of some die-hard Nazis. More important in regard to the rank and file was sheer inertia and the loyalty among the troops, the refusal to let down one's fellow soldiers.

The second surprise was the total collapse. Once the Nazis no longer held power, the Germans put up no resistance at all, contrary to what many had assumed. Their fighting spirit vanished overnight; no more than a handful of people could be found to defend the old regime. The depth of the commitment of the masses had been overrated.

When the Allies occupied Germany in 1945, they had only vague ideas about reeducation, purges, punishment. Their foremost problem was clearly not dealing with fascism as a doctrine. In any case, its erstwhile magnetic attraction had disappeared, and not until many years later did political groups reappear in Germany that could be regarded in some respect as successors to the Nazi movement.

There was a basic difference between the aftermath of World War I and that of World War II. In 1919 only a small part of Germany was occupied, whereas after 1945 the whole country was under direct Allied control. For years, there was no central German government, as the Allies had come for an unspecified period. If it had not been for the cold war and especially the Communist invasion of Korea, Germany would have regained full sovereignty only after a much longer period. Italy and Austria were treated differently. The purge of fascists was largely left to the local authorities, who, for a variety of reasons, showed much less zeal than the Allies did.

When the Allies entered Germany, they had a list of some 150,000 Nazis who were suspected of various specific crimes. Eventually, 200,000 Germans were interned in the Western occupation zones, and some 120,000 were kept in camps in the Soviet zone. Initially most of them were Nazis, but later on the number of non-Nazis was greater; they were thought to be enemies, or potential enemies, of the new Communist order. At first the Americans intended to investigate millions of people, and many had to answer detailed questionnaires concerning their personal involvement in Nazi Party and subsidiary organizations. An international military tribunal was established to prepare for the Nuremberg trials, which were to give a final verdict on Nazism, which—as the Allies had stated at the Yalta Conference—was to be destroyed.

The charges at Nuremberg referred not to Nazism per se (even though several Nazi organizations were branded as criminal) but to the preparation for aggressive war, crimes against peace, war crimes, and crimes against humanity. The decision to try twenty-four war criminals was somewhat arbitrary. These people included the main figures of the Third Reich (except Hitler, Goebbels, Himmler, and a few others who had committed suicide) but also the economist Horace Greeley Hjalmar Schacht—an opportunist but not a confirmed Nazi—and Hans Fritzsche, a prominent radio commentator.

In later years the Nuremberg trials were criticized for political and legal reasons. But all things considered, justice was done, albeit rough justice. At the time, the great majority of people in the Allied countries (and 80 percent of all Germans!) thought the verdicts were just. There was no real alternative, since an independent German judiciary did not exist, nor is it certain that a German court would have reached fairer verdicts.

The purge of Nazis' initially envisaged by the Allies was too ambitious and too indiscriminate. It did not differentiate between fellow travelers and those who had committed major crimes. Thus virtually every civil servant and everyone prominent in business, industry, and agriculture was stripped of his or her position, whereas Nazi teachers went on teaching, and commanders of assassination squads were permitted to return to their old police jobs. The intention of the Allies, above all the Americans, was to eliminate Germany's political, military, social, and business elites. But this was impractical and led to passive opposition among the German population. By 1951 German support for the Nuremberg trial (and its twelve successor trials) had fallen to 10 percent. Gradually, the Allies realized that some authority would soon have to be returned to the Germans. Furthermore, the Allies understood that if they wanted the public services, education, police, and other administrative offices to function, they had to employ people with some experience, even if they had once belonged to a Nazi organization. Ideally, they should have shown clemency to those who had joined the party or its subsidiary groups at a late date or under pressure, mainly out of fear of losing their jobs. But many hundreds of thousands were involved, and the Occupation authorities often lacked the information to differentiate between real villains and those who had merely conformed. As a result, many mistakes were made.

Within a year, between 1946 and 1947, the rigorous Allied policy turned to the other extreme: Most of those who had been sentenced to jail in the Nuremberg trials were released, or their sentences were substantially reduced. Scandalous in particular was the rehabilitation of German judges: Those who had meted out political justice under the Nazis were readmitted, almost without exception, to their old profession. When a group of major criminals were put on trial in Landsberg (Bavaria) in 1950 and five of them were sentenced to death, there was a storm of indignation in Germany, even though each of those condemned had ordered the murder of tens of thousands of civilians, crimes unprecedented in the history of Europe since the Middle Ages. But by that time the belief in *Befehlsnotstand* prevailed in Germany—that every criminal, however highly placed, had merely been obeying orders ("I was only a simple field marshal—what could I possibly do?"). According to this logic, only Hitler was to blame, and since he was dead, there was no point in charging his underlings, several times removed. Thus, after 1947 the persecution of Nazi crimes was gradually discontinued and, by 1957, had virtually come to an end. In the French zone, where 669,000 files had been opened, only 13 persons were found guilty of a major crime, and 958 more were considered implicated.

In the Soviet-occupied zone, the purge was, from the beginning, directed only against major Nazis. It is estimated that one of every ten former Nazi party members were affected, and if a teacher or policeman early on had joined the Socialist Unity (Communist) Party, his previous aberrations were forgiven. However, the higher echelons were more completely purged because the Communists wanted to liquidate the old establishment and install their own, younger cadres replacing the former leading officials. Thus, as a by-product of the Communization of political and social life, the Nazis were cleaned out more thoroughly in East Germany than in the West. The Communists did not fail to stress this point: Their state was truly antifascist, whereas in West Germany the hold of Nazism had not been affected.

In fact, the record of West Germany was mixed. After a lull during the 1950s when the Allies were no longer looking for war criminals and the German authorities were not yet ready to do so, a new wave of trials began. These were mainly of former commanders and executioners in the concentration and death camps. These investigations lasted for years and sometimes decades, and in the meantime some of the main accused died and others fled abroad. But the wheels of justice turned relentlessly, even forty years after the event.

The trials served a useful purpose, inasmuch as they made it difficult to forget the enormity of the Nazi crimes. On the other hand, there was a growing psychological resistance to being made constantly aware of a past that many Germans wanted to forget. Many commiserated with the old men put on trial in the Majdanek trial and other such cases: Surely it made no sense to start proceedings several decades after the event, when memories had faded and witnesses could no longer be trusted. The German attitude toward those who had actively resisted Hitlerism was complex: Many argued that resistance, especially during the war, was tantamount to treason. Even those bitterly opposed to Hitler faced a conflict of conscience, as they feared not only for their and their families' lives but also for their country, and sympathy was due therefore to those who had not resisted.

All in all, the purge of Nazism was neither complete nor consistent. But given the circumstances, the complexity of many issues, the unprepared-ness of the victors, and the reluctance of many Germans to sit in judgment on their own kin, the purge went as well as could be reasonably expected.

Coming to terms with their Nazi past was a protracted and painful process for the Germans. The obvious psychological inclination was to play down the enormity of the crimes: True, excesses had been committed, but this had happened during the war, and the victors also had not been innocent of war crimes. Furthermore, during the first years after the war, all Germans were preoccupied with such problems as getting food for their families or finding shelter, and they had no time or energy left to confront the past. Only when conditions had become more normal, in the late 1950s, were they more willing to do so. But parents were still unwilling to talk openly to their children about what they had done (and seen and heard) under the Nazis, and it took two more decades until some of the truth was digested. By that time Germany was prospering, and a new generation had come to the fore. There was no denying that horrible crimes had been committed in the not-too-distant past. But there could be no collective guilt, and why make young people who wanted to enjoy themselves answer for deeds they had not committed? On the extreme Right, the Nazi war crimes were belittled or altogether denied ("the Auschwitz lie"), and on the Left the facts were not doubted, but the guilt was attributed to capitalism rather than fascism. Whatever the arguments, the conclusion was that too heavy a preoccupation with the Nazi past was undesirable.

It is also true, however, that in the postwar decades, democratic institutions were growing roots in Germany, and so a Nazi revival seemed most unlikely. If there was reluctance to confront the past, this also had to do with the belief that a new generation of Germans should look forward to a democratic Germany in a free (and possibly united) Europe.

Austria

There had been 500,000 registered Nazis in Austria, including some 80,000 who had been party members before 1938 when the party had been illegal. There had been some 60,000 party officials. Of these, 18,000 were arrested by the Allies in 1945. But the status of Austria was different from Germany's, inasmuch as it was considered the Nazi's first victim and therefore a "liberated country." Thus the Austrian purge was much less complete than the German. There was no Nuremberg trial, and the number of those arrested was one-quarter of those detained in Holland. Forty-three death sentences were handed down, out of which 30 were carried out (compared with 750 in France), all of them in connection with specific war crimes. No one was executed or given a long prison sentence for having been a Nazi, however highly placed. Following two amnesties (in 1948 and 1957), those who had been given lengthy prison sentences were released.

Although the Nazis had indeed invaded Austria in 1938, the idea that it was "Hitler's first victim" was still a sham. Enthusiasm for Nazism was at least as widespread in Austria as it was in Germany while the going was good. On the other hand, all Austrian political parties favored clemency, precisely because so many of their fellow Austrians had been Nazis, and they did not want to antagonize the electorate but, rather, to reintegrate the former Nazis as quickly as possible. Thus the chance that highly placed Nazis and even war criminals would escape punishment was much better in Austria than in Germany. According to semiofficial Austrian doctrine, Nazism was something alien that had been imported into Austria. It is impossible to say with certainty whether most Austrians who had lived through the Nazi era ever believed this, but it certainly served the purpose to repress unpleasant memories. This failure to face up to the past also paved the way for a revival of fascist ideas in the 1970s and 1980s.

Italy

If the purge in Austria had a farcical character, the same was true with regard to Italy; historians called it *epurazione mancate,* the purge that did not take place. To be sure, the Italians had taken the first steps to liberate themselves from Fascism on their own and without help from the Allies when Mussolini was overthrown by the Supreme Fascist Council in 1943. The government of free Italy passed a law in July 1944 providing for severe punishment for leading Fascists. Eventually some 10,000 people were brought to court, and 500 to 1,000 death sentences were handed down, out of which 40 to 50 were carried out, considerably fewer than in France. Thousands were given long prison sentences, but after the amnesty of 1946, all but a very few were released. Mussolini and some other leading Fascists, such as Achille Starace and Roberto Farinacci, were lynched, and 10,000 to 15,000 others were killed as the result of partisan, mob, and individual violence at the end of the war and soon after. The victims were primarily militant Fascists or informers, but also several, as in France, were killed as a settlement of personal accounts.

As in Austria, all the major Italian parties, including—after some initial wavering—the Communists, favored a general amnesty as early as 1944. There had been so many Fascists that it seemed impractical to punish even a relatively few: The commandment of the hour, as the parties saw it, was to look forward. Hence there was great continuity, on a personal level, between the Fascist and post-Fascist era and no real confrontation with Fascism after 1945. The leading Fascists did not play a significant role in postwar Italian politics except on a provincial level in the framework of right-wing and center parties. Most of them were careful to dissociate themselves from Mussolini's doctrine. Although most intellectuals turned sharply to the left after the war, they too had no particular desire to engage in individual or collective mea culpas. The Fascist era was neither praised nor strongly condemned; more often than not it was excluded from memory.

Other European Countries

Purges in other European countries were primarily directed against collaborators with the Germans rather than against fascists. Many fascist leaders had not survived (Jacques Doriot was killed in an air raid, and Philippe Henriot was assassinated) or escaped and hid themselves (Marcel Déat and Léon Degrelle), and some were given long prison sentences (Oswald Mosley); a few were executed (Vidkun Quisling and Anton Mussert). In France some ten thousand informers, Vichy militiamen, and other collaborationists were killed at the time of liberation without the benefit of a trial.

Although the great majority were probably guilty, hundreds may have been executed by mistake or as the result of the settlement of private scores, sometimes political and sometimes personal.

More than 120,000 French men and women were convicted of collaborationist crimes, of whom some 30,000 received prison sentences. More than 750 were executed. By the early 1950s the *épuration* was more or less over, and by 1960, following several amnesties, only 9 persons were still in prison. However, a few particularly grave cases lingered on, partly because of bureaucratic complications and partly because the culprits had been hiding. It took almost fifty years until Paul Touvier was brought to justice in 1993. As in other countries, the *épuration* proceeded with varying severity in various parts of France, and the results were sometimes accidental. Accordingly, the influential profascist writer Robert Brasillach was executed; had he remained in hiding for a few more months, he almost certainly would have gotten off with a short prison term. Among those dealt with remarkably lightly were the producers and stars of the film industry—and those in entertainment in general—who had closely collaborated with the Germans and, in many cases, had helped entertain the German troops.

The purge in Norway was particularly severe. Action was brought against every member of the local fascist movement, some 55,000 people and also against 40,000 suspected collaborators. The Norwegians' attitude was rigorous: They did not differentiate between fellow travelers and militants, even though many escaped with only a fine. About 15,000 went to prison, 72 for life, and 25 received death sentences. No attempt was made to reintegrate collaborationists into Norwegian society, and as a result most of them remained defiant: Twenty-five years after the event, 90 percent expressed no regret. But there had been few of them in the first place, and they played no role whatsoever in Norway's postwar history.

Equally drastic were the arrests in the Netherlands, where after the liberation more than 120,000 Nazis and collaborators were detained. Even in June 1946, 70,000 were still in prison. Eventually, 154 death sentences were handed down, out of which 40 were carried out. Some 14,000 went to prison, and 40,000 were temporarily deprived of their civil rights. Most of those given the harshest sentences had been spies and informers or had actively participated in the murder of Dutch citizens. Following the amnesties, the number of political prisoners fell to 3,000 in 1950 and to 4 in 1964. However, despite all this leniency, it would have been unthinkable for a fascist to play a role of any significance in Dutch postwar politics.

The purges in Eastern Europe followed a different pattern. Some countries, such as Poland and the present-day Czech Republic, had not had a fascist party, and collaboration had not been widespread except on the lowest level. In Hungary, Croatia, and present-day Slovakia, the fascist parties had been in power. But the leading Croat fascists had escaped abroad, and the Eastern European Communists, initially small in number, followed a liberal line, especially with regard to the fascist rank and file and the young. In Romania and Hungary, thousands of former Nazis were permitted to join the Communist parties, provided that they had not held prominent positions. Some leading Hungarian and Slovak fascists were executed, but no more than in the rest of Europe. Between 1946 and 1948, as the Communists prepared for the elimination of all other parties, the antifascist purges began to fade or were used for different purposes, for example, to get rid of political foes who had not been fascists but who were now painted with the fascist brush.

Even though antifascism became one of the main planks and slogans in Eastern Europe, there was hardly any real confrontation with the theory and practice of fascism. Few books were published on this subject except in East Germany, and television did not deal with the topic, either. Indeed, it became a forbidden subject because of the features shared by the new and the old system—the one-party dictatorship and the pervasive use of propaganda and terror.

In retrospect, the purges of Nazis and fascists were not handled well. Many who should have been punished for their crimes escaped justice for one reason or other, and some were punished who did not deserve it. There was no concerted effort to explain to the people why fascism had been bad and why it had had such horrible consequences. But there was no precedent for reeducating millions of people, and in any case, such reeducation might have been counterproductive. It had to be left to individual persons to ask the troubling questions. When the Communist regimes disintegrated forty-five years later, it was discovered that the people in those countries knew very little about Nazism and fascism, and so perhaps it is not very surprising that fascist ideas and fascist parties could reenter the scene, unrecognized, through the back door.

The Lessons of Fascism

Our experience with fascism in power is limited. Would our judgment have been radically different if the fascist movements had prevailed in more countries and stayed in power for a longer time? We shall never know. Fascist parties failed where they competed not with liberal or left-wing forces, as in Germany and Italy, but with governments of the authoritarian Right. This is true, above all, with regard to Spain and Romania, but also with regard to Austria, Hungary, and Yugoslavia. Spanish fascism (the Falange) was initially divided between leaders gravitating to the church and the upper classes (José Antonio Primo de Rivera), despite their revolutionary phraseology. Other Spanish fascists originally came from the Left or from the trade unions and tended to take a more radical (syndicalist) position. With the execution of José Antonio by the Republicans, they lost their most gifted leader.

During the civil war the Spanish fascists were forced to subordinate their activities to the nationalist cause. At the helm were military leaders such as General Francisco Franco, who were conservatives in all essential respects. When the civil war ended, Franco was so deeply entrenched that the Falange stood no chance; in this strongly authoritarian (but not fascist) regime, there was no room for a political opposition. The fascists became junior partners in the government, and as such, they had to accept responsibility for the regime's policy without being able to shape it substantially. Thus Spanish fascism lost whatever impetus it had originally possessed, and when Franco's regime disintegrated, they were in no position to be leading contenders for the succession.

The Romanian Iron Guard under Corneliu Codreanu was the most radical of the European fascist movements and came close to advocating a social revolution. They fought not only the liberals and the Jews but also the ("cosmopolitan") monarchy and the ruling classes. In the elections of 1937 the Iron Guard emerged as the third strongest party. Even the assassination of Codreanu by government agents did not stop their advance. But when World War II broke out, the country was taken over by a military dictator (Ion Antonescu). Although the Iron Guard challenged him, their revolt in 1941 was put down with much bloodshed. The Croatian fascists were luckier: They, too, had failed to overthrow the Yugoslav monarchy, but in 1941 when their country was invaded by the Germans and Italians, the Ustasha, assisted by local church dignitaries, installed themselves as the new rulers.

The situation in Austria was even more complicated, inasmuch as the German Nazis had numerous supporters there, but the right-wing parafascist Heimwehr, which took its inspiration from Mussolini and supported the Christian–Conservative government of the day, bitterly opposed the *Anschluss* (merger with Germany). The Heimwehr was defeated only when the German tanks rolled into Austria in February 1938. True, Nazism had originated in Austria, and Hitler did not even become a German citizen until 1932. But the influence of the Catholic clergy in Austria was strong, and they preferred Austrian independence to a merger with a predominantly Protestant Germany and so favored Mussolini over Hitler.

Fascism in Hungary was surprisingly strong. In the elections of 1939 the

Arrow Cross won almost one-third of the votes. But like the other countries discussed, Hungary was an authoritarian state. Admiral Miklós
Horthy, the dictator, had no wish to share power with the extremists. The
Arrow Cross had its moment of glory in 1944 when Horthy, acknowledg-
ing that the war was lost, initiated peace talks with the Russians and the
Allies. The Germans forced him to resign, occupied Hungary for the few
remaining months, and the Arrow Cross became the new rulers.

Fascism in Western Europe, in contrast to that in the East, grew out of
established political parties. Oswald Mosley had been the great hope of
the British Labour Party (before that he had been a Conservative); Jacques
Doriot had been a member of the French Communist Politburo; Marcel
Déat had been a leading Socialist; Vidkun Quisling had been a conservative; and the Belgian Rexists had originally been the youth movement of
Belgian Catholicism.

Together with their Flemish allies, the Rexists won 19 percent of the
vote in the elections of 1936, showing that they were the strongest of all
the West European fascist parties at the time. Neither the Belgian nor the
Dutch fascists regarded racialism as part of their plank. Like fascism in
Spain and in Britain, Léon Degrelle, the leader of the Belgian fascists, saw
his movement primarily as a revolt of the young against the bankrupt older
generation. The Belgian fascists suffered a decline after 1936, as did the
Nazis in Holland, whose membership shrank by one-third. Both parties
became more radical in the later 1930s and attracted new supporters under
the German occupation.

French fascism was split from the beginning into several groups, but
under the German occupation their main role was assisting the occupants
to run the country. Although this gave them many positions of influence,
collaborationism made it impossible for them to become a truly national
movement. Even patriots of the Right—however much they hated the
British and disliked the Jews—could not identify with collaborators.

No mention has been made of Latin American fascism or of regimes
such as Juan Perón's in Argentina or Getúlio Vargas's "New State" of Brazil
(1938–1945). Even though these movements contained elements of European fascism, they were, in most important respects, quite different: Political conditions in Latin America greatly differed from those in Europe.
World War I with its dire consequences had not reached there; there was
no "Bolshevik danger." In addition, there was a strong counterweight to
fascism in Latin America's deeply entrenched political Catholicism. In
neither Brazil nor Argentina was a formidable state party established.
There was no elaborate doctrine; propaganda was not all-pervasive; and
there were no concentration camps, no strong militarism, and no territorial
aggrandizement. Rather, these regimes were antiliberal and antidemo-

cratic, but not fascist in any meaningful sense. Vargas drew his inspiration from the Portuguese corporate state. Like Antonio Salazar he rejected the Nazis' "pagan Caesarism." Peronism was native populism, more radical in orientation and better at mobilizing the masses, but still not fascist in character.

An examination, however cursory, of these minor or unsuccessful brands of fascism shows that there was a trend toward dictatorship, or at least authoritarian rule, in many countries following the Great Depression and the weakness of the liberal state. A strong hand was wanted, but because of its emphasis on the class struggle, Communism was too divisive and so stood little chance against "integrist" movements that promised to unite all people in one mighty effort. But such a trend still did not lead to full-fledged fascism, sometimes because the local fascists faced conditions less auspicious than in Italy in 1922 and in Germany in 1933, because they were internally divided or lacked leaders of stature, or because they had formidable competition on their own side of the political spectrum.

All this explains why there was not, and could not be, a "fascist International" comparable to the Comintern. Some halfhearted initiatives toward institutionalizing international fascism were undertaken in 1934 and in 1937. If Hitler and Mussolini remarked on various occasions that Nazism and Fascism were "not for export," they may not have meant it. But they were still speaking the truth, for regimes with an extreme, aggressive, nationalist outlook could not have a universal appeal. Although some fascists dreamed of a united fascist Europe, these were fantasies, not realpolitik.

There was also no united antifascist international front. Those who opposed fascism came from across the spectrum. Early on, the Communists and the socialists clashed with the fascists. But the Communists based their assessment of fascism on an profoundly mistaken approach, the idea that the fascists were the "running dogs of monopoly capitalism." The Communists also could not compete with the Nazis and fascists in regard to their nationalist appeal, and their narrow "class approach" led them into denouncing even the Social Democrats as the "left wing of fascism."

When the Communists realized that their approach had been suicidal, they made a radical turn and reappeared as the main sponsors of antifascist popular fronts. But by that time the Soviet Union had been thoroughly Stalinized, and many genuine antifascists were asking themselves whether there even were fundamental differences between Hitler and Stalin. Furthermore, the Communists used the popular front for purposes that had nothing to do with genuine antifascism, such as justifying the Moscow trials and the Stalinist terror. In 1939 the Soviet–German pact brought an end to all Communist anti-Nazi activities, and after the German attack in

1941 the emphasis of Communist propaganda was on patriotism rather than antifascism.

In brief, while the Communists tried to harness the antifascist potential for a number of years, they gave antifascism a bad name by misusing it for partisan purposes, often against enemies from the Left, and this practice continued well after 1945. Individual Communists were among the most militant fighters against Nazism and fascism, but the Communist parties did more harm than good in this struggle. The socialists and the liberals in those countries in which fascism triumphed lacked the political will to offer effective resistance: They had become so accustomed to operating in parliamentary regimes that they were defenseless against an enemy playing by different rules. It took them a long time to understand what fascism really was, and by then it was too late. Moreover, they were unprepared to operate illegally once fascism had been established.

It would be a mistake, however, to regard the victory of Nazism and fascism a foregone conclusion that, like fate in a Greek tragedy, was predestined. More militant and less lethargic democratic leaders would have detained some (or all) fascist leaders and taken strong measures against their followers whenever they violated the law. If they had acted in time, they could have prevented the emergence of the storm troopers as masters of the streets. We can never be sure that such measures would have been sufficient, but they were never tried. What if the Nazis and the Italian Fascists had obtained a parliamentary majority? This was not very likely even at the height of the crisis, as fascist movements came to power only with the support of coalition partners. The success of fascism largely depended on the presence of the leader or, at most, a small group of leaders. With the removal of these leaders their parties would not have been the same since fascism respected violence, they would have been discouraged once they faced determined resistance. Because movements of this kind need constant impetus and success, their influence might have ebbed. But the attempt to resist fascism by force was never made, and given the outlook and psychology of the ruling circles in Germany and Italy at the time, such an attempt was most unlikely.

There were staunch antifascists among conservatives, in the church and indeed among simple, unpolitical people who instinctively understood what more sophisticated people failed to grasp—that fascism was evil and bound to lead to a catastrophe. But the majority—the establishment, the conservatives, the middle class, and the church—was willing to accept Nazism and fascism once they had been victorious. Although this majority did so often without enthusiasm—because fascism seemed too unpredictable and its methods too crude—while the going was good, the assets and achievements of fascism seemed to outweigh in their eyes its negative features. Once the Nazis and fascists were in power, it was too late for organized resistance. The successes of the new masters gained them the sympathies of many who had previously been uncommitted. The fascist state monopolized the media, thereby making it impossible for the opponents to make their views known, and the terror machinery made any organized resistance impossible in the first place. The time to resist fascism was before it gained power.

Why were the warnings not sounded more loudly? One reason was that the essence and the consequences of fascism were not widely understood at the time, except by some, mostly independent observers, fewer politicians and their parties.

It is fascinating to examine in retrospect how fascism was interpreted by contemporaries. Some understood its essential character and its dynamics far better than others did. An interesting case is that of Luigi Salvatorelli, a liberal church historian who, in a series of articles (*Nazional fascismo*) published just before and after Mussolini came to power, astutely analyzed the character of fascism: its origins in the "intervention crisis" of 1915, its nationalist character as a key to its understanding, and its predominantly lower-middle-class backing in the early period. Salvatorelli's essays, written for a daily newspaper, were still being published seventy years after they had first appeared. The same is true with regard to the writings of Angelo Tasca, a leading ex-Communist, which first appeared in 1938 and provided a realistic assessment because it was not dictated by any party line. Tasca's works are still worth reading, but it should be remembered that he was writing fifteen years after the "march on Rome."

In Germany many liberals and democrats, despite their aversion to Nazism, underrated Hitler and his movement. As they viewed him, he was a philistine, a provincial demagogue, a loudmouth appealing to the dregs of society. They also misjudged the explosive character of Nazism until it was too late. Some of the most astute comments came not from politicians or professional political observers but from litterateurs of uncertain standing in their own circles. One was Willi Schlamm, at that time a Leftist who, writing early in 1933, recognized the likely deep impact and endurance of Nazism at a time when such pessimistic assessments were very rare.

One of the most passionate denunciations came from a writer of the extreme Right, whose diaries were published only after the war. As seen from the Left, Fritz Reck Malleczewen opposed Hitler for all the wrong reasons: Hitler was scum personified, a nihilist, a diabolical revolutionary who wanted to overthrow all established order. Precisely because of his strong belief in moral values—an attitude that was not fashionable at the time—Reck Malleczewen came to regard Hitlerism as a total disaster for the German people. He perished in a concentration camp, one of the few men of the Right to suffer this fate.

Some observers in Germany, Italy, and the rest of Europe never harbored any illusions concerning fascism. Nonetheless, most did not recognize it for what it really was, partly perhaps because of their political blindness, but usually because they failed to recognize that fascism was, in basic respects, a new phenomenon. Comparisons with earlier regimes were often downright misleading. Even the Italian experience of the 1920s was not of much help in understanding Nazism ten years later. The differences between the two countries were considerable, and the leaders' ideological motivation and ambitions were quite divergent.

Fascism was not just another extreme right-wing party or military dictatorship. In some respects, fascism was revolutionary; traditional nationalism turned into racial imperialism, and old-fashioned dictatorship was replaced by a totalitarian state, or at least by a regime trying to approximate this ideal.

The appearance of a new political movement usually creates confusion among those who do not belong to it. This was the case in regard to the emergence of Bolshevism and Communism toward the end of World War I. Their opponents confused them with anarchism, taking at face value Lenin's fantasies concerning the "withering away of the state." Many truly believed at the time that under Communism, borders between states would cease to exist and that private property and the ties of family would be abolished. But Communism was not a stranger to socialist leaders such as Karl Kautsky and Rosa Luxemburg. Lenin and Trotsky had been their comrades in the Socialist International, and the extremist interpretation of Marxism was not a novelty to them. Fascism and Nazism, on the other hand, had no known track record, and their ideas had been far less systematically developed. Hitler, Goering, Goebbels, and their comrades had lived before 1933 in a world to which outsiders had no access.

The misinterpretations of fascism did not cease with its downfall. Orthodox Marxists still found it difficult to abandon cherished beliefs concerning fascism as the "agent of monopoly capitalism," and German and Italian nationalists had similar difficulties accepting the enormity of the fascists' crimes. As a result they tried to "historicize" fascism in order to belittle its unique character into what seemed to them the proper perspective, beyond moral judgment and condemnation. Political scientists in search of models for generic fascism opted for new aspects and revisionist approaches.

Such attempts to find a definition or at least a common denominator for fascism were always hampered by the fact—to which reference has been made repeatedly—that there was not one fascism but many, differing one from another. In the circumstances, all that could reasonably be expected was a "fascist minimum" such as the common belief in nationalism, hierarchical structures, and the "leader principle." All fascisms were antiliberal and anti-Marxist, but they were also anticonservative, inasmuch as they did not want to submit to the old establishment but to replace it with a new elite. Fascism rested on the existence of a state party and, to varying degrees, on a monopoly over propaganda and the threat and use of violence against opponents. Such a "fascist minimum" is far from perfect, but it is sufficient for most purposes. Attempts to go beyond it have failed in the past and are unlikely to succeed in future.

2

NEOFASCISM

Neofascist Ideology

In what way does neofascism differ from historical fascism? Is it merely a new, weaker version of Italian and German fascism in the 1930s? An unequivocal answer is impossible, as there were many varieties of fascism then and just as many now. Some are in the tradition of the extreme Right; others are national revolutionary or even national Bolshevist; and still others fashion themselves faithfully after historical fascism. The dividing lines, furthermore, are seldom clear. All these versions share certain important features, such as a rabid nationalism, a belief in the power of the state and the purity of the people, a hatred of the liberal-parliamentary order, and an opposition to Communism, on the one hand, and to capitalism on the other. There have been strange combinations, such as the "fascist Maoism" spearheaded by the Belgian Jean-François Thiriart, whose Jeune Europe had followers in several countries, and the Italian Serafino di Luia of the Lotta di Popolo group.

The new fascism can gather strength only if it adjusts to the changed conditions. The cult of the Führer and the Duce has gone out of fashion, and similar leaders have not appeared on the scene. The impact of the media (propaganda) is as strong as ever as the government of Silvio Berlusconi in Italy in 1993/1994 demonstrated. A new *telekratie* has emerged that can work miracles for at least a little while. Although the appeal of nationalism is still strong, in Europe it is a defensive rather than an aggressive force; war seems to be ruled out. And the extreme Right does not have a monopoly on nationalism; in a country like Greece, the Left and the Right are equally nationalistic.

Having realized that military aggression and conquest are no longer feasible, neofascism has opted for the defense of Europe. This is by no means a revolutionary turn, for when he began losing the war, Hitler too still appeared as the defender of Europe and, after him, Mosley. But it is an approach born more out of frustration than of genuine conviction.

The defense of Europe has a certain logic for movements in search of a mission: The economic and demographic (and ultimately also the political) pressures on Europe are increasing even as the immediate danger from the east has passed. But an effective defense of Europe must be based on much closer integration than most neofascists envisage, and it collides with their innate nationalism and xenophobia.

Neofascists praise Europe's great past and future. They are not concerned with the present, the real Europe, the European Union (which many of them oppose). They are against Maastricht and a Eurocurrency. They are preoccupied with a "certain idea of Europe" that does not yet exist but, they claim, will eventually be created under their leadership. Some neofascists, mainly those in Eastern Europe, are not anxious, for a variety of reasons, to associate too closely with the neofascists in Western Europe.

The new fascism opposes Communism, but Communism has ceased to be a threat. As America reduces its presence in Europe, the American threat is also declining, except perhaps on a spiritual–cultural level. The extreme Right in Europe, in the Middle East, and in Asia has always been anti-American. It has usually favored some form of neutralism (often called "the third way"), even while the cold war was raging. Some grudgingly accepted NATO, and others joined the antinuclear demonstrations. The idea of Europe's being an "occupied continent" was never far from the surface.

Socialism, Soviet style, is dead, and consequently anticapitalism is sure to come to the fore among the extreme Right, even though they lack an alternative socioeconomic program. They have opposed all along liberal capitalism, free trade, and multinational corporations, and "Wall Street," but they have never made clear what alternative they would offer. In the 1930s the fascists usually advocated autarky, but this is no longer feasible nor do the neofascists promise to abolish the stock exchange or to increase state ownership. They do not clarify their position with regard to the welfare state and taxation. They promise to protect the "national middle class" against foreign capitalists (*compradors*). But this is an old Leninist concept, not applicable to late-twentieth-century conditions. Some (but not all) fascists favor greater state intervention in the economy than customary in the United States. But this idea they share with many other parties, especially those on the Left.

Neofascists promise to take tougher action against drug users and pornographers and to restore family values. These "value conservatives" (*Wertkonservative*) also invoke the need to do more for the environment; indeed, ecological concerns have become a central issue in their propaganda in the 1990s. But they were not the first in the field, and so any attempts to interpret Nazis, with their "blood-and-soil" credo, as premature and misjudged Greens are not persuasive. In their publications, the neofascists frequently refer to the death of the forests, the excessive ozone content of the air, and the dangers of pollution. They express disapproval of contemporary feminism, but this is not one of their foremost concerns. Even though they ridicule the homosexual subculture, some of their leading figures, such as the German Michael Kühnen (who died of AIDS), are homosexual.

There is no neofascist party line with regard to religion. Some neofascists are practicing Christians who favor close cooperation with the church, such as in Russia, without becoming too dependent on it. The more sectarian elements favor a new paganism, but their pagan gods are by no means identical. Whereas some on the extreme Right, out of either genuine conviction or opportunism, proclaim their attachment to traditional Christianity, others opt for sects in the theosophical tradition of Helena Blavatsky and Alice Bailey. These various esoteric creeds reappeared in the 1960s as part of the hippies' conscience-raising cults. Though not nationalist, or even political in a narrow sense, the teachings of the esoterics are deeply antirational and tend to blur the differences between good and evil. Morality is replaced by bioethics, and good is what is good for the planet. This is not unprecedented, however; occult ideas preached by charlatans played a role in the birth of Nazism, less so in the case of Italian Fascism. Such ideas often appear together with a new (green) utopianism (or "ecofascism") envisaging the depopulation of continents. There is an ideological affinity between sections of New Age and neofascist ideas: If good is what is good for me, all kinds of extreme measures against others can be justified. Seen in this light, neofascism could be interpreted as part of a movement trying to fill the spiritual void created by the decline of religion.

There is now a dearth of truly new political ideas. It is nearly impossible to advocate a fascist dictatorship, and as a result, the neofascists have their work cut out for them. But ideological vagueness also has certain advantages. The neofascists' main hope is to appear as the unsullied alternative to the breakdown of the old liberal-democratic system (as in Italy) or to the chaotic conditions following the collapse of Communism in the former Soviet Union and Eastern Europe. In these circumstances it is best if the neofascists do not define their aims too closely, for this would antagonize some of the people they want to attract.

It may be enough for the neofascists to appear as the party of order, of national regeneration, and of the defense of their country (and Europe) against rapacious or parasitic aliens. It is more important to acquire respectability than to have a detailed and consistent doctrinal platform. Seventy years ago the Nazis and the Italian Fascists had very short programs, and hardly anyone paid attention to them. But their absence did not significantly impede their political progress. Neofascism, to be sure, does need an ideology and gurus, but its function must be viewed in proper perspective: It is not a matter of paramount importance. The basic tenets of neofascism are few and simple, sufficient for current political action. The ideological superstructure is something that can be left to the intellectuals. Neofascist militants worth their salt will know instinctively what they stand for, even if they do not have an advanced degree in political philosophy.

Fascism has traditionally been based on myths, intuition, instinct (such as the will to power and the voice of the blood), and the irrational, rather than on a closely argued system based on a detailed analysis of historical political and economic trends. This has not changed. The ideologues of fascism have always been marginal figures such as Alfred Rosenberg, author of the famous *Myth of the Twentieth Century*. But it is doubtful whether a single German was converted to Nazism as the result of reading Rosenberg's magnum opus, and the same is true with regard to Italian Fascism. The ideologists had to be marginal figures because they were merely interpreters: The Führer and the Duce were the prophets, the repository of all wisdom. However, in contrast to Lenin and Stalin, Hitler and Mussolini had few ideological ambitions. Their ambition was to make history rather than to interpret it; they wanted to be men of action rather than thinkers. The basic tenets of fascism were (and are) self-evident: nationalism; social Darwinism; racialism; the need for leadership, a new aristocracy, and obedience; and the negation of the ideals of the Enlightenment and the French Revolution.

No skinhead, no "fascho," and no "hooligan" ever read a page of Giulio Evola or Alain de Benoist, and the same is true with regard to most of the voters for Jean-Marie Le Pen's party, the German or British far Right, the Austrians, and other European groups of the extreme Right. Rather, these groups acquired an ideology as an afterthought, since they would have felt incomplete without a theory.

Those thinkers who did exert some influence on the political leadership of the extreme Right and on the literate elements among the militants are largely unknown outside this camp. Among them are Giulio Evola (1898–1974), who first appeared on the Italian scene as an outspoken anticlerical (anti-Catholic) writer belonging to the extreme wing of historical fascism. In this respect, one can find some similarity between him and Rosenberg, except perhaps that Rosenberg, hanged at Nuremberg, was quite famous in his lifetime but totally forgotten after his death. Evola, on the other hand, became influential after the defeat of Fascism; he had not belonged to the top leadership under Mussolini. The Duce thought of him as a somewhat exalted intellectual—no praise in the Fascist vocabulary—of a certain usefulness, because Fascism had few true believers who could also write articles and books. Evola was a rabid anti-Semite and an even more fanatic enemy of the Freemasons. He was severely wounded and crippled in an air raid toward the end of the war. But since he had not been a war criminal in the strict legal sense of the term, he escaped with a short prison sentence and continued to publish. Among those he influenced was Pino Rauti, Gianfranco Fini's predecessor as leader of Italy's neofascists. Giorgio Almirante hailed him as "our Marcuse, only better." Some of Evola's works also appeared in French and German; a conference at the Sorbonne was devoted to him; and after 1988 a few thinkers of the Russian extreme Right embraced him as their new spiritual guide.

What were Evola's ideas? We have mentioned his paganism. He claimed that Christianity had caused the downfall of the Roman Empire, a thesis he shared with de Benoist, but this had been argued since Gibbon, at the very latest. For his anti-Catholic writings Evola was taken to task by Giovanni Montini, the future Pope Paul VI, for "surrendering the search for truth in favor of intellectual excitation, that is to say those strange forms of cerebralism and neurasthenia, of intensive cultivation of incomprehensibility, of pseudo-mystic preciosity, of cabalistic fascination magically evaporated by the refined drugs of Oriental erudition."[1] This characterization of the twenty-six-year-old Evola is as accurate as any later comment. The future pope should also have included Dadaism, for Evola had begun his career as a Dadaist poet and painter, and there were elements of pure nonsense also in his later work. (A few of his paintings of this period can still be found in a Rome museum.) He considered himself both a traditionalist and a revolutionary second to none, an antihistorical metaphysician, an antiegalitarian, an antihumanist, an advocate of intuition over reason, and a believer in hierarchy and "spiritual virility." He opposed modern civilization and freedom: The modern free man was merely the slave emancipated and the pariah glorified.

These and similar ideas were in no way novel, however, as they can be found in European intellectual history of the late nineteenth and early twentieth century, with a bit of Nietzsche and a little Sorel, and the concept of the "political soldier" borrowed from Jünger, as well as traces of Bergson and Weininger and the right-wing German *Kulturpessimisten*, and a bit of Mosca and Pareto. Some of the young Italian rebels of 1905 would have found in Evola a kindred if not quite an original spirit.

How can we explain the enduring interest in Evola in some circles after 1945? His style was extravagant, and people not familiar with Evola's sources could reach the mistaken conclusion that his pyrotechnics and deliberate obscurity were manifestations of originality, wisdom, and depth. In addition, Evola used a modified Spenglerian cyclical theory of history and made frequent references to Eastern, mainly Indian, philosophy. Such practices were intended to create an impression of great erudition.

Even though Evola professed to engage in pure philosophical thought ("metapolitics"), he did not refrain from commenting on recent history and current affairs. His judgment was usually disastrous. In the 1960s he opted for terrorism rather than making neofascism respectable. His great heroes were not Hitler and Mussolini but Codreanu, the mystic Romanian terrorist, who was the most radical of the fascists in the interwar period. Although Evola opposed Communism and the Soviet Union, he was equally anti-Western in outlook. America stood for democracy, and anyway, there was no basic difference between Communism and democracy, generally referred to as a "syphilis of the spirit." Evola had considerable influence on the extraparliamentary Italian Right, such as Ordine nuovo. When he was brought to trial, his disciples claimed that their revolutionism was not violent, except in self-defense. In truth, the Italian extreme Right was not strong enough to engage in systematic terrorist struggle. They would have been smashed by the state and so wisely refrained from such a confrontation. When Evola died in 1972, Italian neofascism was weak, with little hope for a revival. When it got a fresh impetus in the 1990s it was not because of Evola's wisdom.

What Goethe said about Klopstock is certainly true with regard to Evola. Everyone (on the far Right) lauded Evola, but few read him. Evola's roots were in a period that had ended with the Duce. His writings were not relevant to the contemporary world, except perhaps the general laments about decline and decadence, about materialism and mass democracy, about drugs and perversion. But these complaints are not a monopoly of the extreme Right. Evola was a learned charlatan, an eclecticist, not an innovator.

The attempt to provide a more modern doctrine was made by the French New Right, a group of young intellectuals—the best known of which was Alain de Benoist—whose writings received much publicity in their own country and abroad. Interest in their doctrine peaked in the 1970s and early 1980s, after which time they no longer received much attention, partly because of internal divisions but mainly because, having had their say, they were merely repeating themselves.

The New Right deliberately contrasted itself with the traditional Right. Even though they thought that much in historical fascism had been correct and healthy, they realized that it was no longer relevant to the contemporary world. So for the traditional Right, the New Right had only contempt. Totalitarianism (pace Mussolini and Hitler) they regarded a major danger, a menace equal only to the American way of life, which threatened to engulf Europe. They did not preach territorial expansion and wars of aggression—imbued as they were with French patriotism, there was a heavy emphasis on Europe in their doctrine. Nor did de Benoist and his companions favor vulgar biological racism. As they saw it, every race and national group had the right of self-expression and self-determination ("ethnopluralism"). Instead, their concept of a hierarchy of races was "truly scientific," based on the findings of ethology (Konrad Lorenz) and behaviorist psychology, as well as modern genetics. Intellectually, the New Right was willing to borrow from left-wing thinkers such as Antonio Gramsci. To frighten the French *bien pensant,* de Benoist made it known on the eve of an election for the European parliament that he would vote for the Communists. But because there was no great danger that the Communists would win the elections owing to de Benoist's vote, the threat was not taken very seriously.

After some initial hesitation, the New Right doctrine was considered as lacking novelty as much as seriousness. But for the fact that its leading spokesmen had been graduates of the prestigious *grand écoles,* not much attention would have been paid to them in the first place. True, its thinkers had read widely and borrowed from a great variety of sources: Action française and the German conservative revolutionaries (1920–1932), Nietzsche, Carl Schmitt, Evola, and anti-Americanism. From Evola the New Right took its neopaganism and its conviction that the Judaeo–Christian tradition was largely responsible for all that had gone wrong in Western history during the last two thousand years. Such views not only were bound to offend sections of the German extreme Right, but they also were a bone of contention in France, where Le Pen and other leading figures of the far Right were either practicing Catholics or, at the very least, wanted untroubled relations with the church.

The New Right was a reaction against the socialist egalitarianism that had prevailed in the French academic world since World War II. Yet at the very time that the Nouvelle droite became fashionable, pro-Sovietism virtually disappeared on the French Left. Because de Benoist realized that it was pointless to flog a dead horse (Marxism), the main brunt of his attack was against "Americanism" (also known as the "Coca-Cola culture" and "McDonaldism"), liberalism, and Western-style capitalism. He offered no clear alternatives other than general references to the need for new elites and the baneful effects of arithmetical democracy. The New Right always prided itself on its preoccupation with a long-term cultural revolution. Among its publications are far more numerous movie reviews than articles on economic issues. Indeed, an examination of the New Right's ideology is like a visit to a supermarket (or a cemetery) of ideas and ideologies that have been selected in an attempt to produce a new synthesis.

The Nouvelle droite, and related groups tried to find an antileft ideological alternative. But unlike historical fascism, they had to proceed from a position of political weakness. In the nuclear age, no single European country can aspire to great-power status; a united Europe is at best a distant dream; and war is ruled out as a means to achieve political aims. In historical fascism, however, power and (military) glory, sacrifice and heroism played a crucial role. Its successors must find different ideas and idols.

Neofascists have accused the New Right of wasting their time in fruitless theoretical discussions, following the example of the New Left. This is true to a certain extent, but the neofascists are facing exactly the same problem, of a political stage much reduced in size, leaving little scope for dreams of glory, of fascism adjusted to conditions in Lilliput. The ideological equipment of the New Right is quite similar to that of Italian Fascism, that is, meaning nonbiological racialism, the danger of the Americanization of European society and culture (decadence), the paramountcy of elites, the hierarchical structure of political institutions, and the rejection of the parliamentary system. The appeal for an "orientation toward the East" is reminiscent of the national Bolshevism of the 1920s.

The New Right and fascism differ inasmuch as the latter accepted the fact that only the mobilization of the masses could effect political change. Conversely, the New Right wanted to return to the earlier nineteenth-century ideas of an elitism that would keep the common people out of politics. Fascism bereft of aggressive chauvinism, of military force and war, is at most fascism on the defensive, promising to save Europe from an invasion of foreigners. The fascism of the welfare state could still be a radical force in the spiritual realm, but political realities narrowly confine its freedom of action in Europe. It is rooted in protest and feelings of resentment rather than in a belief in a coming national renaissance and political messianism. If the extreme Right had a revival in the 1980s and 1990s, it was connected with general dissatisfaction, crime, immigrants, and the malfunctioning of the political system. It had little to do with the "heroic pessimism" of Evola, de Benoit, and their popularizers.

Italy

Italian neofascism was the first on the scene in Europe after World War II, and it was also the first, in 1994, to come to power, temporarily, in a right-wing–populist coalition. The MSI (Movimento sociale italiano) was founded in 1946 in the ruins of an even earlier quasi-fascist group, Uomo qualunque, the "movement of the common people." Its main spokesman and secretary-general at the very beginning and again from 1969 to 1987 was Giorgio Almirante, the editor of *Difesa della razza* (Defense of the Race) under Mussolini and a highly placed official in the Ministry of Propaganda of the Republic of Salo (1943–1945), the second and more radical embodiment of Italian fascism.

The story of Italian neofascism over almost five decades is one of ups and downs. Having won just 1 percent of the votes in 1948, it attracted 2.7 million voters in 1972, with fifty-six members in parliament (8.7 percent), only to decline again during the next twenty years. It then reached a new height in 1994, attracting 13 percent of the votes, making it the third strongest party in Italy and a key component of the Berlusconi government.

Because the postwar Italian constitution prohibits fascism, the MSI could not openly declare its attachment to Mussolini's theories and practice. But it made no secret that it regarded the Republic of Salo (which by 1990, most Italians had nearly forgotten) as its idol. The MSI did not call for the abolition of parliamentary democracy but instead proposed direct elections for the presidency; strong, centralized state power; and a limitation on the influence of the political parties.

From the beginning the MSI has followed a double strategy of proclaiming its attachment to the values and the good government of Mussolini while asserting at the same time that it, the MSI, was "postfascist," that not everything about fascism had been admirable, and that in any case, the political situation was no longer what it had been in 1922 or 1943. While promoting violence in the streets, at the same time, the MSI wanted to gain respectability as a pillar of Italian democracy. And it is true that in retrospect the pragmatists favoring the double-breasted suit over the terrorist bomb served the party better than did those openly advocating violence. If the Italian political system eventually collapsed, it was because of its own failures, not because it had been destabilized by bombs placed in railway stations.

How genuine was the conversion of the MSI from the spirit of the Republic of Salo—very similar in inspiration to Nazi Germany—to the democratic rules of the game? This question cannot easily be answered because historical fascism meant different things to different people. Fascism as the opposition before the "march on Rome" was certainly more radical than Mussolini's regime in the 1930s and 1940s, and the Republic of Salo was a return to the beginnings of fascism, as we have noted on previous occasions. The MSI also was not a monolithic party. It had always had a right wing, a left wing, and a center. Its history is one of many divisions and mergers.

The early MSI under Prince Junio Borghese, its first president (a submarine commander and antipartisan fighter) was certainly radical in its proclamations. But after 1950, moderation prevailed. The anti-American, anti-Western, anti-NATO orientation lingered for another few years, resurfacing in the 1970s and, to some extent, persisting to this very day. On the home front the MSI became domesticated during the 1950s. It helped the Christian Democrats elect the president of the republic, and it did not bring down Christian-Democratic governments based on small majorities. Indeed, it was courted by successive Christian-Democratic governments, and in 1953 an attempt was even made to establish a Catholic–MSI coalition in Rome. All this changed in the 1960s, however, when Christian-Democratic influence waned and the Christian Democrats had to accept an "opening to the Left," that is, to cooperate with the Socialists. In these circumstances the MSI was no longer needed but, on the contrary, became something of an embarrassment.

This was a blow for the conservative forces in the MSI (who had been joined in the meantime by the monarchists) who advocated a parliamentary approach. The MSI "Left," sharply critical of the alleged "betrayal" by their leadership of the old fascist ideals, had favored an extraparliamentary strategy all along. This meant violence and a "strategy of tension." The MSI's left was influenced by the activities of antiparliamentarian leftist groups such as the Red Brigades. The "revolutionary" wing of the MSI was spearheaded by the party's youth and student sections and gave birth to Ordine nuovo and Avanguardia nazionale, headed by Pino Rauti and Stefano delle Chiaie, respectively. Their guru was Giulio Evola. At the same time they admired Che Guevara ("a real fascist"—the highest praise they could bestow) and China's Mao Zedong.

Almirante, originally a supporter of the radical line, was reappointed in 1970 and tried to combine the respectable approach with the enthusiasm of the illegal or semilegal youth groups who emulated the violence of the Red Brigades. Major terrorist attacks took place in Milan and subsequently in Brescia and Bologna, and at the same time amateurish plots were hatched to carry out a coup, Greek or Chilean style, with the help of the army or the secret services. In the 1972 elections the MSI had its greatest success, not as the result of the random bombings or the conspiracies, but because part of the population, frightened by the left-wing–anarchist terror, was anxious to support a counterweight.

But the Red Brigade's campaign was running out of steam, and far from destabilizing society it had strengthened—temporarily at least—solidarity among the democratic forces. The country calmed down, and in the wake of the antiterrorist campaign, the violent men of the Right suffered as much as did those of the Left. Their organizations were smashed, and their leaders and militants had to flee abroad or were arrested. By the late 1970s the MSI had to drop its revolutionary stance and return to the safer ground of "good Catholicism" and conservativism. It took a leading part in the campaign against abortion, against divorce, and for the introduction of capital punishment. Bettino Craxi, the Socialist prime minister in the

1980s, met with MSI leaders. Earlier he had expressed his desire that the extreme Right not be left in the wilderness but be reintegrated into the political spectrum. But despite such gestures, the MSI remained in isolation, its parliamentary faction ignored. It mounted no effective opposition to the government, and its share of votes stagnated or even fell.

When Almirante resigned in 1987, he was succeeded for a while by Rauti, the leader of the revolutionary wing, and eventually by his chosen heir, Fini, a younger leader who, impatient with a strategy that had led the MSI into the wilderness, advocated "a postfascist orientation." He led his party to victory in the elections of 1994. Accordingly, at a convention in Fiuggi in January 1995, the MSI decided to transform itself into a broader political movement and also to change its name to Alleanza nazionale.

The composition of the electorate and of the membership of the former MSI is fairly accurately known. It has been predominantly a party of the south, with its stronghold in Rome and south of Rome. Even when its fortunes had sunk to their lowest, it could count on about 10 percent of the electorate in cities such as Rome and Naples and up to 20 percent in Catania and other Sicilian towns. In the industrial north the MSI has always been considerably weaker, as it has had to confront the Left and, in later years, also the Lombard League. In Rome much of the MSI's support initially came from former beneficiaries of the fascist regime—state and party employees who had lost their jobs. (The survival of the Communist vote in East Berlin after the dissolution of the republic is based on the same phenomenon.)

The MSI is a party of the nonreligious right, and its radical, even revolutionary, slogans frighten the Catholic clergy, which supported, as long as feasible, the Christian Democrats. It is a party of the young and the old, rather than the middle aged, and it has traditionally attracted more men than women. (Women gravitating to the right were more likely to vote for Berlusconi in the 1994 elections.) The party has, however, attracted some intellectuals and other dignitaries. Two of its ministers in the Berlusconi government of 1994 were not party members but fellow travelers.

Generally, however, the legacy that Fini inherited from Almirante was unpromising. The party still made no progress; on the contrary, it scored losses in the Euro-election of 1989. The wind was taken out of its sails by other parties; the Communist danger had disappeared; and if there were a growing sentiment against foreigners, it was not a MSI monopoly. In addition, the Lombard League (and the other leagues) syphoned off support that might have gone to the neofascists. The leagues argued that the prosperous north was being systematically exploited and subverted by the backward and corrupt south.

The MSI could not use this argument, for it stood for Italian unity. It could not possibly turn its back on the south, its traditional base of strength. If the MSI's fortunes dramatically improved after 1992, it was in part due to Fini's leadership, as he realized even more strongly than Almirante did that the party had to get rid of its violent elements or at least silence them. But at the same time Fini could not disavow the hard-core fascists and so had to balance carefully under the slogan "Non rinnegare—non restaurare" (not to renege—not to revive).

Fini declared that Mussolini had been the greatest statesman of the twentieth century, but at the same time he laid a wreath at the Ardeatine caves, where the Nazis had committed a massacre toward the end of the war. He made most of the noises befitting a good European and at the same time made it clear that he considered the Adriatic an Italian sea. Italy, he asserted, had justified its territorial claims against the Croats and Slovenes. Fini also changed the name of the party, so that Mussolini's granddaughter could announce that she was not a fascist but a "Mussolinian." When Fini was asked whether fascism had been a mistake, he replied that it had been a historic phase, a force for social progress with a tradition of honesty and good governing and so should not be demonized.

Astute maneuvering alone would not, however, have catapulted the postfascists into a position of strength. If it had not been for the crisis and ultimate downfall of the old regime, the fascists would not have made a breakthrough. The Christian Democrats—alone or in cooperation with other parties, including the Socialists—had ruled the country without interruption since 1945. There had been no political alternative for the non-Communist Italian electorate as long as the Soviet bloc existed with the Communists as the second strongest party (and becoming stronger). But as soon as Communism in Eastern Europe collapsed, these considerations ceased to be of paramount importance. The dissatisfaction with the old faces and the general boredom were manifested in the growing number of antiestablishment votes and in the indifference to the democratic system. Was this "one-party system" worth defending?

Furthermore, the revelations of corruption—suspected for a long time but seldom proved—shook the country as a new cohort of independent judges probed the activities of leading politicians. This resulted in the arrest of Giulio Andreotti, de Michelis, and other pillars of the old regime, as well as leading state officials and businessmen, and it created a political earthquake. Only two major parties had not been substantially involved in corruption, the former Communists and the MSI. But the Communists—even though they had also changed their name and made common cause with other forces of the Left in 1993/1994—were handicapped by the setbacks of Communism elsewhere. In these circumstances the "postfascists" were destined to be the main beneficiaries. Nonetheless, there is reason to assume that they, too, had cooperated with the Mafia in southern Italy and Sicily, but these were not big deals compared with the sums that had changed hands in the north.

The phenomenal rise of the MSI was foreshadowed in the local election of autumn 1993 and continued in the general elections of March 1994. Fini, with 47 percent, and Alessandra Mussolini narrowly missed being elected the mayors of Rome and Naples. They were coalition candidates, with the vote for the Alleanza proper being 25 percent and 19 percent, respectively, in these two cities. In the general election the Alleanza nationale doubled its share. It became the third strongest party, and it had a good chance of further improving its position. But there is no certainty, for more than ever before there is in Italy a huge mass of floating voters who could be driven by the tide in almost any direction.

France

The extreme Right in France has a tradition dating back more than a century, but to what extent is it neofascist? For the German neo-Nazis and Italian neofascists, there are the nostalgic examples of the 1930s when the Axis powers were strong. For the French, however, there is only Vichy and even the staunchest defenders of Marshal Philippe Pétain do not believe that his regime could serve as an example to be emulated.

The French right-wing extremist potential has gone through several transfigurations since World War II. In the first years after 1945 its main pillar was the successor groups of the monarchist, elitist Action française, the prewar halfway house between traditional conservatism and fascism. Their ranks were swelled by the victims of the postwar purges—beneficiaries of the Vichy regime and minor leaders of the fascist parties of the 1930s, many of whom escaped punishment. But these groups amounted to little, either in parliament or on the street: The memories of the German occupation were too fresh to enable a major fascist revival. The few sympathizers could be seen on Sunday mornings selling their literature in front of churches, but there were not many takers.

A new resurgence came in 1953 when Pierre Poujade's Union de défense des commercants et artisans appeared on the scene. In the elections of 1956, almost out of the blue, they won 12.5 percent of the vote, or 2.5 million. The Poujadists used antiliberal, anti-Semitic, nationalist, and, generally, antiforeign slogans. But the movement was essentially just what the name indicated, a big lobby of farmers and small traders fighting against high taxes. Its base was regional, with most of its support in the more backward south and west of France. The Poujadists lasted a few years and then faded away as economic modernization gathered speed and other issues came to the fore.

This movement was replaced by action groups of French persons of North African origin who wanted to keep Algeria French and were fighting the "traitors" in Paris who were willing to surrender the French positions. But the ultras headed by the (OAS) the underground armed organization, were fighting a losing battle. Following France's defeat in Vietnam, the country was sick and tired of colonial wars. Everyone wanted to keep North Africa, but few wanted to fight for it.

The North African crisis brought Charles de Gaulle to power, and while he was president, the extreme Right faced lean years. With his vision of a great France he could not be outflanked from the Right.

After its defeat under the Gaullist regime, the far Right engaged in some ideological rethinking of its basic positions and tried to shape a new doctrine. This New Right differed in important aspects from its predecessors: It was not monarchist or Catholic, nor did it regard Germany as the archenemy. It did not dream of reconquering North Africa but merely wanted to get the North Africans out of France. Although the ideas of the New Right influenced neofascist ideologues in Italy, Belgium, Spain, and even Germany, their political effect at home was small. While the Nouvelle droite published articles about "biological realism" and a European "third way" between the Soviet Union and America—between Communism and capitalism—the extreme Right in France continued to fracture. In the parliamentary elections between 1967 and 1982 its various factions did not attract more than 1.4 percent of the vote, a dispiriting performance considering that even Tixier-Vignancourt, their candidate for president in 1965, had received 5 percent running against de Gaulle and that 9 percent of the Right had voted against de Gaulle in 1962.

In 1972 in a plebiscite, yet another attempt was made to unite the splinter groups; this was the Front national headed by Jean-Marie Le Pen, a man from Brittany who had spent his apprenticeship first among the Poujadists, whom he represented in parliament, and later in the war in Algeria. It took the new party more than ten years to become a major factor in French politics, but Le Pen, an effective speaker with considerable debating skills and generally a dynamic figure, must have felt that the long-term prospects were not bad and that various trends favored a resurgence of the extreme Right.

The National Front was not a monolithic party but a coalition of half a dozen groups cooperating because they knew that on its own none of them had any chance. Le Pen was the leader of one of these groupuscules, called the "New Order." His leadership was accepted, though often grudgingly, because he was thought to be the most effective vote getter. Le Pen's ascendancy became secure only in the 1980s, after the party had made its electoral breakthrough.

Politically, the National Front's task became easier with de Gaulle's disappearance from the political scene. Neither Georges Pompidou nor Valéry Giscard d'Estaing, however competent they might have been, were figures of equal caliber, nor could they rival de Gaulle's extreme nationalism. At the same time the decline of French Communism began and opened a new reservoir of potential voters for the National Front. Within a few years, Marseille, a stronghold—first of the Socialists and later of the Communists—became a fortress for the National Front.

Social and economic trends favored the rise of the extreme Right. The loss of North Africa had resulted in the exodus of French from these territories, and their sympathies were not with the Left or the Center. More important yet, following the North African war, many Algerians and Moroccans and also some black Africans settled in France. Despite rigorous measures limiting immigration that were taken in the early 1970s, the immigrants multiplied and constituted a substantial segment of the population, first in southern France and Paris and later also in other parts of the country. Although the North Africans were looking for a better life in France, many of them had no wish to adopt French ways; indeed, they were eager to preserve their religion, language, and way of life. Thus tensions developed between them and the local population that were aggravated by the structural unemployment that was characteristic of the economic development in the 1970s and 1980s. Le Pen's slogan was "1 million [later 3 million] unemployed—this means 1 million [3 million] foreigners too many."

Finally, there was a growing dissatisfaction—a common European phenomenon—with the parties in power. After the economic miracle of the 1950s and 1960s, more and more people had come to believe that the rapid rise in prosperity would continue indefinitely. Then, when the economy stagnated and the quality of life did not improve, there was a backlash, from which the party in power invariably suffered. People in France also felt, as they did in other European countries, that the government did not devote enough attention to the growing crime rate. Since the Communists were not an attractive alternative, the extreme Right was in position to profit from this protest vote.

All this does not, however, explain how a party that in 1982 counted for nothing in French politics, that had a membership of only a few hundred, became within a year a major force. There had not been a major upheaval—political, economic, or social. In 1981 the right-wing coalition that had ruled France since de Gaulle came to power was replaced by a

Socialist government, which at first included a few Communist ministers. Some have argued that it was precisely this swing to the left that drove the traditionally anti-Communist voters to the National Front, because the legitimate Right was dispirited and disunited following its defeat. There might be a grain of truth in this explanation, but since Communism was on the decline and since the Communist ministers were squeezed out by François Mitterrand soon thereafter, this could not possibly account for the dramatic swing to the extreme right.

Other factors included the organizational competence shown by Le Pen's lieutenants in building a countrywide political network. Above all was the tremendous amount of publicity that Le Pen suddenly received. Before 1983 the National Front had not been well known outside its few strongholds. But then its first electoral victories at provincial elections, and especially the Euro-elections of 1984 in which it scored 11 percent of the vote, gave it unprecedented exposure. At the time, the media considered the National Front's achievements to be the most important event in French political life. Le Pen and his aides were constantly interviewed in the media and more people flocked to his meetings and watched Le Pen's television appearances, which he handled with skill. In the parliamentary election of 1986 the National Front received 9.9 percent of the total vote, and in the presidential election of 1988, 14.4 percent (4.4 million) voted for the National Front. It did even better with more than 15 percent in the presidential elections of 1985.

The National Front has become a party with a countrywide following, which, given the multipolarity of the French political system, made it on more than one occasion the arbiter between superior forces. It now has support in all regions of France and in all age groups. The National Front has been particularly strong in Greater Paris and the southern departments, including Marseille, Toulon, and Nice, and in the Alpes maritimes, Var, and Bouches-du-Rhône departments. But it also polled more than 14 percent in Alsace and Lorraine. The party did particularly well in Mulhouse, a city that has suffered from the decline of the local smokestack industries, but it did also well in Strasbourg and Colmar, which have no major heavy industries. It succeeded especially in regions with many foreigners, but it also made inroads in places with relatively few foreigners, in which their presence was merely feared. The National Front did better among workers than among intellectuals and the haut-bourgeoisie, but it can count sympathizers in all parts of France.

What attracted so many different people to the National Front? We could point to its catchall, populist slogans and, at the same time, its successful attempt to create an image of a reliable, responsible, and nonextremist party. Although the National Front is anti-Semitic, Le Pen's statements have never been extreme, nor has the party made the Jewish question a major plank in its platform. It has appeased the industrialists and the *grand capital* with its support for private enterprise; it has praised President Ronald Reagan's and Prime Minister Margaret Thatcher's economic policies as popular capitalism and privatization. But at the same time Le Pen has been the friend of the workers and has promised to help small traders and artisans against competition at home and from abroad. The National Front has appeared as the party of law and order and, as such, the best friend of the security forces. Le Pen has attracted the far Right, the "integrists," and practicing Catholics, but he has also found a place in his movement for the anti-Christians of the Nouvelle droite. Although he has attacked the government bureaucracy, always a popular theme, he has assured the bureaucrats that nothing untoward would happen to them and their jobs if Le Pen should come to power. He has been "European" and anti-American, but this too has long been part of the French consensus. And the National Front promises to cut taxation but to maintain current social services, except for foreigners, who should be deported.

The National Front's efforts to create and maintain a moderate image have been, on the whole, successful. But on occasion they have given way to manifestations of what many outsiders believe is its true character. For example, in 1991, Le Pen went to Baghdad to shake Saddam Hussein's hand and express his solidarity. No doubt, Le Pen's political instinct told him that there was no possible benefit from this gesture, yet he must have felt an overwhelming inner urge to identify with a kindred spirit. Hence the belief is widespread that the National Front has another face, which is dictatorial and terrorist. While the party is, for now, far away from gaining power—except perhaps on the local level—it will preserve its outwardly democratic character. But its true attachment to the democratic rules seems to be only skin deep, and this thin veneer could quickly and dramatically evaporate once the party was in a position of power.

The National Front has benefited from the weakening of the country's major power blocs, first the Gaullists and the moderate right and later the Communists and the Socialists. But its advance has been limited: In the European elections of 1994, the National Front won only 10 percent of the vote. Most French people are unlikely to support a movement still considered radical and unpredictable, unless of course, some major political or economic disaster should occur.

Much of the National Front's achievement has been the work of one man, and although no one is irreplaceable, it might take years for an equally effective new leader to emerge. In the process the old fissures in the National Front could reappear and weaken it.

In any case, it is clear that the party is basically a protest movement with little positive content. True, its goals are popular—to reduce the number of immigrants or at least to prevent a further increase, to restore law and order, to combat excessive government intervention and taxation. But the majority also knows that the National Front has no more panaceas than the other parties do. If there is distrust of political leaders and parties, the National Front and Le Pen are not excluded. According to several polls, a majority of National Front voters opted for this party mainly to protest the political system; a significant proportion had no great desire to see their own party in power. Above all, the National Front lacks the enthusiasm, even idealism, that once permeated elements of the Nazi Party and Italian Fascism. Its supporters may engage in isolated acts of violence, but at bottom, they are indignant interest groups rather than fanatics. They are unwilling to sacrifice too much of their time and energy (let alone their property or life) for this political movement. This is not the stuff of which fighters for a neofascist France are made.

Germany

Neo-Nazism in Germany has been less successful than its supporters hoped and its enemies feared. The reasons inhibiting the growth of neo-Nazism are as obvious as those conducive to its spread. At the end of World War II, millions of former members of the National Socialist German Labor Party (to give it its full name) continued to work and live in their native land. Not all had joined the party out of opportunism, and not all believed after the defeat that the Nazi regime had been evil. A third or more of all Germans continued to express their belief that Nazism had had various positive features. Even in 1989 just over half of all Germans rejected Nazism as "mainly negative," and almost 40 percent thought that Hitler had been one of the leading statesmen of the century. According to various investigations, 10 to 15 percent identified with the values and ideals of the extreme Right, and this applied to the young as well as to the elderly. In other respects, such as law and order and the attitude toward foreigners living in Germany, these investigations revealed a substantial reservoir of right-wing extremist feeling.

During fifty years of postwar German history, however, this reservoir has not been converted into political action and into votes for right-wing extremist parties. Only on two occasions did the forces of the far Right succeed in gaining a significant foothold on even a regional level. This refers to the National Democratic Party (NPD) in the 1960s and the Republican Party in the 1980s. But in neither case did their success last, nor could these parties be classified as neo-Nazi. Most of their members would, no doubt, have welcomed Hitler in 1933. But times have changed, and old-style Nazism is no longer a player on the German political scene.

The growth of Nazism in postwar Germany has been limited for many reasons. First was the economic miracle, the prosperity that began ten years after the war. At the same time, even those Germans who looked back with nostalgia to the Third Reich did not altogether reject the new political order and the institutions that had emerged. The fact that Nazism had been defeated and that it had led the country to ruin had had a negative effect on the popular image of Nazism. After World War I, "traitors" had been blamed for "stabbing the country in the back." But after 1945 no one could blame the opposition, for there had been none while Hitler had been in power. The fact that the Nazis fought to the bitter end (unlike the kaiser and his generals in 1918) only hastened Germany's democratization. Finally, Nazi activities were outlawed in the constitution, and although this did not deter the die-hards, it deterred fellow travelers.

The first groups advocating extreme right-wing positions appeared as political parties, which were readmitted by the Allies in 1946/1947. They were the Deutsche Reichspartei, which was followed in 1949 by the Sozialistische Reichspartei, which was represented by five deputies (twenty-two later on) in the first Bundestag (the German parliament) in 1949.

One of the main heroes of this first blossoming of the extreme Right was Major (later General) Otto Remer, the officer who had stopped the officers' revolt in July 1944 and thus saved the Nazi regime. The party's supporters were mainly Nazis and war veterans who had suffered a social decline as the result of the defeat and had not benefited from the postwar prosperity. The others had not been prominent Nazis but disliked the new order even more. At its peak, the Reichspartei counted eighty thousand members, but only two thousand to three thousand young followers. It achieved some success in certain north German regions such as Lower Saxony and Bremen but attracted few capable people in any profession who could have acted as leaders. The extreme Right established various social and cultural institutions and edited periodicals (such as *Nation Europa*) preaching its gospel. But it was preaching to the converted and did not succeed in converting the politically uncommitted.

In 1962 the Reichspartei was banned by the German Supreme Court; it had not hidden its pro-Nazi sentiments well enough. In fact, the party decided to disband even before this judgment was handed down. But it would not have done this if it had not been for the feeling that it had no real chance to compete against the major parties: The time was yet not ripe.

During the next twelve years, new neo-Nazi sects were established, but not one of them has survived. Extremist feelings have been expressed in the desecration of Jewish cemeteries and the publication of nostalgic literature recalling the Nazis' achievements, both political and military. Politically, however, the neo-Nazis themselves have remained insignificant.

Another opportunity was presented in late 1964 when, under the leadership of Adolf von Thadden, most of the factions belonging to the far Right united under the roof of the National Democratic Party (NPD). In contrast to its predecessors, the NPD had stronger working-class support, and it was able to find followers in south Germany (Baden-Wurttemberg, for instance) as well as in the north. But it did not succeed in establishing a foothold in parliament, failing to overcome the 5 percent hurdle fixed in the constitution. Then it was torn by internal strife between a conservative and a radical wing, gravitating toward extraparliamentary action. When the party failed in the general elections (1969), it became more radical and its internal dissention more intense. Von Thadden resigned in 1971, and although the party continues to exist, it is no longer a factor of political importance: Whereas in 1972 it had five hundred representatives in local councils, ten years later only twelve were left.

The NPD carefully stressed its attachment to conservative values and the "national idea." It defined itself as an assembly of freedom-loving German patriots living within a framework of the constitution and legality. In fact, as befitting a law-and-order party it emphasized on every occasion that the *Rechtsstaat* (the laws and their application) should be observed. The NPD had certainly learned from the mistakes committed by the Reichspartei. To be a militant of the extreme Right in Germany requires, by necessity, a good deal of dissimulation. But there were other considerations: Some of the NPD's supporters were not radicals but reactionaries, and they were frightened by the revolutionary talk of the neo-Nazi hotheads who wanted radical change and were calling for violent action.

On the fringes of the legal far Right have been, all along, extraparliamentary groups collecting arms and providing military training for their members. In the late 1970s, with the decline of the NPD, right-wing terrorism became more frequent. In the best-remembered incident, the explosion at the Munich Octoberfest in 1980, thirteen people were killed. But in the final analysis, right-wing terrorism was even less effective than that of the left-wing Baader-Meinhof gang.

The NPD had no wish to risk state action as the result of such violence. The same is true with regard to Gerhard Frey's Munich-based publishing empire, out of which yet another party evolved, the DVU (Deutsche Volksunion). The publications were successful—the weekly *Deutsche Nationale Zeitung* sold 120,000 copies, which was more than the Social Democratic *Vorwärts* did. But readership did not translate into votes: Frey, who was behind the propaganda campaigns of the most extreme right-wing groups, was a successful businessman and lawyer, not a charismatic political leader.

A price had to be paid, however, for sticking to legality. If the NPD and the other parties of the far Right were just strict conservatives, as they claimed, why did they not make common cause with the right wing of the ruling Christian-Democratic (CDU) rather than wasting their votes in an endeavor without real prospects? To this question they had no answer. The honest reply would have been that there in fact were basic differences between them and the conservatives but that these could not be spelled out because it would have resulted in a loss of votes and the possible outlawing of the party under Articles 9 or 21 of the constitution.

The issue of legality had also faced the Nazis before 1933, but under the Weimar Republic it had been less risky to defy the constitution. In any case, the members of the NPD were not motivated by similar fanatism. Neither von Thadden nor Frey would risk a four-year prison sentence, like that given to Michael Kühnen, a former Bundeswehr lieutenant who in the 1980s had been the leader of an outspoken neo-Nazi group. Consequently, Frey's periodicals concentrated on relatively safe subjects—that World War II had been started by the Allies rather than Hitler, that the gas chambers were a giant hoax perpetrated by world Jewry, that Germany belonged to the Germans, and that foreigners should be expelled.

As the popularity of the NPD declined, however, the issue of foreign workers became more acute. In 1981 the demand was first voiced to make them return to their country of origin. But the NPD lacked the dynamism to exploit this mood. A void existed on the far Right of the political spectrum that was filled only in 1983 with the establishment of the Republican Party. The Republican Party was a radical offshoot of the Bavarian CSU. It was headed by Franz Schönhuber, who, as a young man, had served in a SS division, had a career as a television producer in Munich, had joined the Social Democrats, and had subsequently become a member of the ruling Bavarian Party, the Christian Socials. Schönhuber was replaced in 1994 by Rolf Schlierer, a much younger man whose idol was the Austrian Jörg Haider, whose mixture of populism and nationalism had found greater resonance than did the approach of the leaders of the German far Right.

The Republicans did well in Berlin, the Rhineland, Baden Wurttemberg, and some other *Länder* in the regional elections in 1989, and so they entered the local parliaments. They also succeeded in electing several Euromembers of parliament in the same year but again failed to clear the 5 percent hurdle in the elections to the Bundestag. In the regional election in

Hesse in 1993 the Republicans won 8 percent of the total vote and, in Frankfurt, 10 percent. But countrywide they were in decline, despite the growing antiforeigner sentiment that was manifested in acts of violence, sometimes spontaneous and sometimes instigated by the far Right.

It is difficult to point to specific reasons for the changing fortunes of the far Right. Their elected representatives were uninspired people who made no noticeable impact and showed more interest in drawing salaries and expenses (and being reelected) rather than promoting the cause of their party. There were very few doctrinal differences between the Republicans and the NPD, which also continued to exist. In regard to electoral geography, they had few differences as well: The Republicans were strongest in the very regions that had been the stronghold of the NPD fifteen years earlier. But one important difference was that until the 1980s there had been a significant proportion of ex-Nazis in the extreme right-wing parties, but they had gradually died and younger voters had replaced them. There was no clear pattern. Some German analysts claimed that the Republicans were a party of the losers, the victims of the modernization process. Indeed, the Republicans did relatively well in the poorer sections in the big cities. But on the other hand, they did not do well in East Germany, where the protest sentiment was strongest, and they also scored above average in some prosperous districts in the West. Almost without exemption, the NPD and the Republicans did better among men than among women. The whole spectrum of German politics moved somewhat toward the right in the 1980s, as it also did in France, Italy, and Russia. But this did not help the Republicans; on the contrary, it tended to make them redundant.

All things considered, the story of neo-Nazism in postwar Germany has been one of failure. As the old Nazis disappeared, the tradition has been maintained by younger admirers of Hitler's ideas. But they are not many: Most of the sects have fewer than 1,000 members, and even the Republicans have no more than 12,000 to 24,000 (the former figure is based on outside estimates, the latter is their own figure). Although there is a large reservoir of goodwill for law-and-order slogans and anti-immigration sentiment, just as there is in Britain—but not in France, Italy, or Russia—this has not been converted into a mass movement.

The main reasons for the neo-Nazis' failure are, first, the economic and political achievements of the new democratic order. Furthermore, not everyone who desires law and order or resents immigrants is a neo-Nazi. Even those expressing great dissatisfaction with the current state of affairs are not willing to mount the barricades, as many Nazis did in 1932. Germany has been reunited, but not because of the efforts of the NPD or the Republicans. They are proud of the German military tradition, including the wars of aggression. But they have no wish to engage in new wars, not even to increase military spending. There is resentment of foreigners, including Americans, but there is no hatred of British and French among the extreme Right, and if Poles and Czechs are far from popular, few people believe that Germany should go to war to recover the territories it lost in 1945.

One of the main handicaps of the German extreme Right is the constant internal division. Unlike the situation in France and Italy they have never been united in one party, under one flag, following one leader. But this lack of unity is probably not accidental: It reflects their inherent differences of opinion. Would they have been much more successful if they had joined forces? In the 1980s Germany did face serious social and economic problems, and as in other countries, German developed a growing aversion against the big established parties. But few Germans believe that the NPD and Republicans could cope more effectively with a problem such as unemployment than can the CDU or the Social Democrats. Thus, all the extreme Right can hope for is an unprecedented general crisis, not some minor temporary setback or stagnation. An earthquake is needed to put German democratic institutions to a real test.

Fascism and the Extreme Right: Some Case Studies

Since the end of World War II, there have been military dictatorships, some of them cruel and bloody, and also populist movements of the Left or the Right. In these regimes and parties, certain fascist elements can be discerned, and from Chile under Pinochet to Greece under the colonels they have been denounced as "fascist." But such labeling is neither correct nor helpful. One could endlessly debate whether the Pol Pot regime in Cambodia was left wing or right wing, or neither. It might be an oversimplification to argue that if Pinochet, the Greek colonels, and their kind had been true fascists, they would still be in power. But there is a grain of truth in this argument: These regimes were not totalitarian in the modern sense, as there was no state party controlling all spheres of life, no all-embracing doctrine, no propaganda machinery. Rather, they were updated versions of traditional military dictatorships, reprehensible and reactionary but not fascist. For this reason, they either abdicated, as in Chile, or were easily overthrown, as in Greece.

Authoritarian regimes continued to exist after 1945 in Spain and Portugal. But neither Salazar's "New State" nor Franco's national Catholicism was fascist, and if they had been totalitarian, these countries' transition to a democratic order in the 1960s would have taken much longer. The Russian example shows how difficult it is to transform a truly totalitarian regime. Thus, the ease with which this was accomplished on the Iberian Peninsula demonstrates better than any theoretical debate that the differences between authoritarian and totalitarian regimes are indeed great.

After Franco's death and with the transition to democracy, Spain still had a far Right, which had begun with the Falange and its leader, José Antonio Primo de Rivera, who had been killed at the outbreak of the civil war in 1936. This rightist party was the Fuerza nueva, headed by Blas Pinar, a leading figure in the late Franco regime. (His party was later renamed the Frente nacional.) It had some success in the late 1970s but virtually disappeared in the 1980s. Some of its slogans—denouncing the permissive society (and drugs) and promoting law and order—were popular. The Fuerza nueva was religious in inspiration and denounced leading Catholic clergy whom it thought too liberal vis-à-vis the new democratic order. But despite Spain's social and political tensions (a high percentage of unemployment, mainly in the south and among the young,) the Fuerza nueva could not make any significant inroads, partly because the Socialists were too popular and had much more prestige. Later, when the Socialists stumbled, there was an effective conservative alternative under José María Aznar. In such circumstances, there was no room for a party so closely identified with the inefficient and hated Franco regime. In addition, nationalism as an ideology had little appeal in post-Franco Spain. Spain had no territorial disputes, and the parties generally agreed on the Basque problem.

The number of foreigners in Spain was relatively small, and it was not a crucial issue. If the Spanish harbored any popular resentment, it was directed against North Africans—that is, against regimes with which the Spanish far Right felt a certain affinity—and so they were reluctant to exploit the issue. But Spanish fascism was not particularly racist; indeed, it was probably the only European fascism not to attack gypsies but to welcome them in their ranks. The experience of the Franco regime had been too recent and, all things considered, too negative to make fascism an attractive option. Even those who had supported Franco's regime had to admit that in recent decades a political, social, and economic revolution had taken place in Spain and that the Franco regime could not be resuscitated. Spanish fascism erred in claiming that the Franco regime had been part of the old order (which it disavowed) and then not providing a new ideology rather than reviving the old Falange slogans. But even if the neofascists had been more enterprising, it is not clear what kind of modern alternative they could have produced and how they would have fared.

The extreme Right fared better in Belgium and Austria. The reason was not economic crisis or social conflict. In fact, Austria's economy has done better than those of most other European countries in recent years, and in fact, Belgium, the decline of its traditional heavy industries and mining has affected the Walloons much more than the Flemish. But it is precisely among the relatively prosperous Flemish that the far Right has made progress.

The reason that the extreme Right has been successful in Austria is primarily political. Austria has never been properly de-Nazified, and former Nazis have been able to keep their positions. Unlike in Germany, there was no admission of guilt; responsibility for the Nazi era was rejected. Austria, it was claimed, had been an occupied country and, as such, a "victim of Nazism," not an enthusiastic collaborator. According to the postwar "Austrian ideology," the Austrian-born Hitler had really been a German, whereas Beethoven, a German who settled in Austria at the age of thirty, had really been an Austrian. In brief, Nazism had nothing to do with Austria, and the sooner this whole episode was forgotten, the better.

Since 1945 Austrian politics has been dominated by the Social Democrats and the Christian Social Party, usually in a coalition. The third "liberal" party (FPO) was much smaller, winning no more than 6 percent of the vote, even while serving as a shelter for ex-nazis almost from the beginning. (Like the Italian neofascists, the FPO decided to change its name in 1994.) Then in 1980 a series of scandals undermined the two major parties, and the economy stagnated. The two ruling parties could no longer offer their members the same direct and indirect benefits. At the same time Jörg Haider took over the leadership of the FPO. He is a populist demagogue and effective speaker and has made the most of the popular grumbling and general negativism, features well known to students of Austria. Haider justifies Nazism—up to a point. After all, he declared, the Nazis had had an effective employment policy. Haider is anti-Slav, anti-immigrant, and despite joining the World Union of Liberal Parties, he advocates antiliberal policies. In 1994 his party captured 33 percent of the vote in Haider's native Carinthia and even 22 percent in cosmopolitan Vienna, a clear indication that a new force had arrived, reversing the old pattern of Austrian domestic politics. And in the general elections of 1994 he won 22 percent of the vote countrywide.

Is the FPO a fascist party? Not in the traditional sense, even though Haider welcomed old Nazis at his meetings and went out of his way to address SS veterans. Anti-Communism also is not an important issue for the FPO, in view of the small number of Communists in Austria. Although Haider wants to deprive the Slovenes living in Austria of their cultural autonomy and to get immigrants out of the country, his party does not advocate the overthrow of the democratic order or the use of violence. It is not revanchist or militarist: Given Austria's geopolitical position, Haider has no desire to reestablish the old Austro-Hungarian Empire. There is no danger of dictatorship or aggressive war; instead, the FPO is concentrating on domestic affairs. It wants reunion with Germany, but it also realizes that few people in Germany are eager for this.

At the same time, it would be wrong to dismiss the Austrian phenomenon as inconsequential simply because it does not constitute a danger to the outside world. True, the fact that the old political system was discredited because there had been no real change in fifty years contributed to a political earthquake, as it did in Italy. But there is no reason to believe that the FPO voters were more morally sensitive than were other Austrian citizens. Since Haider's progress occurred at a time when unemployment and inflation were low and per capita income was still rising, we can conclude that what the FPO stands for is very much in line with deeply rooted trends in modern Austrian history—nationalism, xenophobic populism, authoritarianism—not quite fascist, more in the tradition of Lueger, the legendary nineteenth-century Viennese mayor, than of Hitler. But it is also true that Nazism was at least as popular in Austria as it was in Germany, and very likely more so.

The extreme Right in Belgium has made little progress among the Walloons despite the economic malaise in the regions close to the French border and the support of Le Pen's National Front. The Right has been more successful among the Flemish majority (which constitutes 57 percent of the total population). How can the electoral success of the Vlaams Blok be explained in cities such as Antwerp (20 percent in the 1989 elections, even more in 1994, and 10 percent of the total Flemish vote in 1991). The Flemish insist on more autonomy for their regions, claiming, for instance, that the Walloons benefit disproportionately from the welfare state. But these demands are common to all Flemish parties, and through constitutional reform the country has moved far in the direction of greater autonomy.

The Flemish bloc is strong in those parts of Antwerp with heavy concentrations of foreigners (and rising crime). The exceptions to this rule in Belgium merely demonstrate that racial tension is not the only factor involved. Karel Dillen has been the undisputed leader of the Blok, and he joined, without hesitation, the "technical faction" in the European parliament. This move was not a surprise in view of his lifelong career on the extreme Right.

It is therefore difficult to define the Blok as a radical party or to predict success for Belgian fascism. The Nazi occupation of Belgium discredited the cause of the extreme Right and the collaborators. Democracy is deeply rooted in the country, and so it is unlikely that national tensions and the presence of foreigners will destroy the political system.

Similar considerations apply to the neighboring Netherlands. Far Right political groups such as the peasants' (agrarian) party had an upsurge in the 1980s, which, notwithstanding its name, drew its main support in the cities. But it never polled more than 3 percent of the total vote, and the party was not neofascist in any meaningful sense. It was replaced by other groups—in the 1970s by the NVU and in 1986 by two parties, both of which used the term *Centrum* in their name. The NVU concentrated its attacks almost exclusively against immigrants but failed to elect a member to parliament. The two Centrum parties were somewhat more successful in pressing home the same message of too many immigrants. They attracted enough votes in 1994 to elect local councillors in the major cities who were ostracized by the democratic parties. As in the case of Belgium, there is much overlapping of the Centrum vote with the poorer, lower-class white regions in the cities in which Moroccans and Turks reside.

The Dutch extreme Right has been even more eager than the Belgians to stress that it is not fascist ("Neither right nor left"), but suspicions concerning their real intentions linger. The party regards itself as the spearhead of a "Greater Netherlands" including not only Belgium and Luxembourg but also parts of northern France. It has collaborated with the German National Democrats, the British National Party, and the far Right in the Balkans. Like the Flemish bloc, it is anti-American and has reservations about European unity. In response, the Dutch government has combined restrictions on immigration with a multicultural policy, and foreigners have been given the right to vote. Such policies may not be sufficient to change the belief of the majority that there are still too many foreigners in the country, but they seem to be enough to contain it.

In both Belgium and the Netherlands, a vote for the extreme Right represents protest, not just against the presence of foreigners, but also against the "system." And since the extreme Left has been eclipsed, at least temporarily, such protest has gone to the Right. The weakness of the system is manifested in a multiplicity of political parties, frequent changes of government, and long periods without government. This weakness, combined with resentment against permissive policies (crimes, drugs, prostitution) has produced a backlash, as the result of which successive governments have retreated from the permissive positions taken in the 1970s. Given such widespread resentment, it is not the very modest achievements of the extreme Right that are surprising but the fact that it has not been more successful.

We have not mentioned neofascism in Britain mainly because it has not been very significant or in any way original. In the 1930s the fascists had the British Union of Fascists, with Oswald Mosley as its leader, but during World War II it was rejected as unpatriotic; Mosley was detained; and the group disbanded.

In the 1950s and 1960s the remnants attempted to reassemble, capitaliz-ing on the antiforeigner feeling, which increased with the mass immigra-tion from Africa and the Caribbean. But the National Front and other groups on the extreme Right were not able to exploit this dissatisfaction except occasionally on a local, municipal level. Like other fascist groups, the British were beset by internal division, and they also had no leader of stature. The National Front did not even come near electing a member of parliament. Although a few fringe members of the Conservative Party showed some sympathy, there was no room for a party to the right of the Tories under Margaret Thatcher, just as there was no room in Germany for a movement to the right of Franz Josef Strauss. Britain's only contribution to neofascism was the skinhead culture which in the end gained more support outside Britain and faded away in its country of origin. Thus it did not come as surprise that a chief propagandist of the extreme Right, David Irving, the most prolific of the revisionists and Holocaust deniers, moved his business to the Continent.

In other European countries, neofascist groups are mere sects, even though there has been great resistance against uncontrolled immigration. Thus the Norwegian Freedom Party gained—to everyone's surprise—13 percent of the vote in the 1989 elections, with its main plank, "halting immigration now." Its support was subsequently halved, and in any case, it is not a fascist party in any meaningful sense. The same applies to the Progress Party in Denmark, founded in 1972, which at one time, was Denmark's second largest party. Beginning with libertarian positions—opposing taxation and state regulation in general—it has moved steadily to the right in search of popular proposals such as a ban on immigration. In Sweden, neo-Nazi activities have been limited to sects and skinhead groups, none of which has more than a few hundred members.

Neofascist activities in postwar Europe show certain patterns that pre-dict success or failure. We have already cited the immigrant issue, which favors the growth of the extreme Right. The other predictive factor is the crisis of the democratic system, as the Italian example has shown.

Equally obvious are the factors inhibiting the growth of neofascism. The fact that Nazism was discredited after 1945 provided some immunization. As Europeans became more prosperous, even the unemployed were far better off than they ever had been before. Nonetheless, every country still contained a reservoir of votes for the extreme Right and an even greater potential for protest. But even if the anger was great, the fanaticism was missing. Whereas fascism in prewar Europe had been an aggressive, belli-cose movement, neofascists realize that a war in Europe is not a possibility, and they even have joined most other parties in the endeavor to keep defense spending down. In fact, most of those on the far Right are opposed to civil war and terrorism—too many people have too much to lose. Neofascism is often a single-issue movement, and so there is always the danger that as the result of government action (such as restricting or stopping immigration) they may lose their raison d' être.

Italian neofascism scored high, even before the elections of 1993/1994, in Alto Adige (south Tyrol), with 25 percent of the vote in Bolzano (Bozen). The reason was obvious: the belief among the local Italians that Rome was spending too much on the Tyrolians. But since the Italians also benefited from the general prosperity, their indignation did not go beyond registering a protest vote; there was no civil war in the lovely resorts surrounded by mountains and forests.

In the postwar period, there have been no outstanding leaders among the neofascists. Although Le Pen and Haider are capable politicians, they are not Hitler and Mussolini. Some neofascists have been dismissed as mere showmen or clowns; Zhirinovsky is a contemporary example. Conversely, in the 1930s, whatever the madness of a Codreanu or a José Antonio, no one ever doubted that they meant what they said and were willing to pay with their lives. Indeed, some of the prewar fascist groups encouraged sacrifice and death, to which the postwar groups would not be as likely to aspire. The ideologues of the 1930s, such as Rosenberg, had been true believers, but it is not clear whether postwar gurus such as Evola and David Irving were true believers or mainly wanted to attract attention.

It might be tempting, therefore, to write off neofascism or to consider it tamed and now part of the system, in the same way that the extreme Left has become domesticated. But even if neofascism is much less of a danger now than it was sixty years ago, it would be premature to dismiss it as inconsequential. Under certain circumstances, a second coming could not be excluded, and there is no evidence that the neofascists have permanently accepted the democratic rules of the game. Even though they have done so out of weakness, whether they would do it in a position of strength is less certain. There is a danger of crying "wolf" too often, and it is true that very often since 1945 the danger of neofascism has been exaggerated and groups have been branded as neofascist that only vaguely resembled the real thing. It is equally dangerous, however, to ignore the fact that the ground is still fertile for antidemocratic movements and regimes.

Right-Wing Extremism: An Alternative Way of Life

Neofascism, like Communism in France and Italy during its heyday, is not primarily an ideology or a political party but an alternative way of life. Its supporters were and are advised to reject mass culture and not to watch movies and only a minimum of television unless the extreme Right has a strong foothold in the media. They are expected to read the patriotic writers of their country and not to waste time on decadent literature and art. The prescribed patriotic taste is not unlike Stalin's socialist realism, but with a nationalist content. This rules out most of twentieth-century culture, all the modernist trends, psychoanalysis, and other subversive influences. Neofascists should not read the establishment's daily newspapers—except perhaps for the sports sections and advertisements—but subscribe instead to the periodical literature put out by their own kind. They celebrate Hitler's birthday, Rudolf Hess's death, and the great military victories of the German armies during World War II. The Russian far Right celebrates Russian victories such as the battle of Kulikovo. Germans collect Nazi memorabilia, Iron Crosses, brass replicas of Thor's hammer, and German weapons of World War II vintage. Russians seek out relics of the last monarchs and the White Armies as well as icons, Cossack uniforms, and St. George's crosses.

The religious-minded neofascists meet to pray to the Nordic gods such as Wotan and Freya (their sects are named Armans, Goden, Gylfilits, and "Wotan's folk"), and they have their own Druid-like priests and priestesses. Some Russians call themselves Vedy, and follow Indian traditions; others pray to Dash Bog and the pre-Christian Slavic gods. To them, the Christian Bible is a document of alien origin, and so its injunctions should be disregarded. Instead, neofascists celebrate solstices and harvest festivals, study old Nordic and Germanic symbols, and visit cemeteries in which soldiers of the two world wars are buried. Wind surfing and motorbike races are concessions to modern life.

Marriages between believers are encouraged, and having as many children as possible is a neofascist's patriotic duty. Some are fierce fighters for abstinence, as they consider the excessive consumption of alcohol one of the main reasons for the people's declining health, particularly in Russia. A few are vegetarians. But the cause of antialcoholism has been an uphill struggle, since the consumption of beer, Schnaps (in Germany), and vodka continues to be as great on the far Right as on other parts of the political spectrum. The skinheads would not give up beer at any cost. A variety of esoteric cults have their fervent followers on the extreme Right, in Russia perhaps more than in any other country. Nationalist astrology is particularly popular, as are patriotic magic and various cults, theosophical and mystical, some home grown and many imported from both the West and the East. Numerology is rampant among Louis Farrakhan's Nation of Islam.

Above all, neofascists believe in a world conspiracy against the Aryan (or Slavic or Gallic or Roman) race that, unless thwarted, will lead to the destruction of all that is positive and valuable. This superplot involves the devil, the Jews, the Rosicrucians, the Freemasons, and generally all international ("global") or "mondialist" organizations aiming at world domination and the destruction of the nation-state. This conspiracy is omnipotent and omnipresent; nothing in the world happens by chance. Everyone (except only the neofascists themselves) is manipulated by the forces of darkness. Much of this paranoia can be traced back to before the revolution in Russia and before Hitler came to power in Germany. Its deeper sources are in the obscurantism of the Middle Ages and even further back. Such fears are less frequently found among Italian neofascists and the French far Right, though the belief in conspiracies is as widespread in Italy and the Mediterranean as in north and east Europe.

Modern technology is used to spread old ideas: videos of Hitler's and Mussolini's speeches and refutations of the "Auschwitz lie," computer games instructing youngsters how to run concentration and extermination camps, and neofascist computer networks.

During the 1970s and 1980s the extreme Right showed an interest in ecological concerns. Some of their leaders even declared that in the future such concerns would be of central importance and hold political promise for the extreme Right. In Russia the "green wave" began with the "village writers'" rediscovery of the Russian countryside. At the same time regional meetings and demonstrations were held to protest the systematic poisoning of the atmosphere, forests, rivers, and lakes (including Lakes Baikal and Aral and the Black Sea); the rerouting of the Siberian rivers; and the emissions of poisonous gases and other noxious substances. The Chernobyl disaster gave additional impetus to this movement. Although these initiatives were not initially sponsored by the extreme Right, as popular causes they helped the extreme Right find new supporters and be accepted among the wider public.

In Germany the extreme Right realized the political potential of environmentalism relatively late. It intensified its initiatives in north Germany, mindful of the fact that National Socialism had obtained much of its early support in these regions. But during the past seventy years, the number of farmers has greatly diminished. Vested agricultural interests still have a certain political clout in France, but much less so in Germany. Farmers receive enormous state subsidies for not producing food at costs that are not competitive. To support the agricultural lobby in these circumstances would not be popular. As a result, the extreme Right has expressed merely "platonic" support for "healthy farmers," for it was in the villages that the nation and national culture originated. Some extreme right-wingers also call for the establishment of new settlements in the countryside, far from the unhealthy life of the big cities. But such suggestions have been made in various quarters for at least a hundred years, and the response has not been overwhelming.

Both national revolutionaries and die-hard National Socialists have infiltrated existing Green parties or established new ones. The national revolutionaries have been more sincere in their enthusiasm for a new harmony with nature. But rather than winning over other Greens to their cause, they have defected to the ecologists and have been lost to the far Right. The neo-Nazis sometimes have chosen a village as their headquarters, but they have not opted for agriculture as a way of life. They are still preoccupied with producing their brochures on the heroic deeds of SS units in World War II, on the *Protocols of the Elders of Zion*, and on nefarious Americans and Poles, and there is no obvious connection between such propaganda and the rural environment. At one time the Russian Pamyat established a farm outside Moscow, but its main purpose was to make money to finance political activities. German and French neofascists sometimes express sympathy with ecological movements, even if these groups have dissociated themselves from fascist ideas. But such declarations are mainly based on electoral calculations: The Green parties are useful because they weaken the established major parties and, as a result, the whole system, which the neofascists want to bring down.

The extreme Right has traditionally taken a strong stand on cultural issues. Its taste was shaped less by the monumental style of Nazi Germany, Fascist Italy, and the Soviet Union and more by the classicist–conservative tradition, especially in Germany, Austria, Eastern Europe, and Russia. The French and Italian New Right is more sophisticated and somewhat more liberal in outlook. Unlike the Germans and the Russians, they are not as extreme in their condemnation of modern art as the Nazis had been with their denunciation of "decadent art."

The ideologues of the extreme Right are moving in territory that offers certain promise: The cultural crisis that they invoke is not a figment of their imagination. Avant-garde artists—in the plastic arts and music even more than in literature—have moved far ahead of public taste and frequently encounter a lack of understanding or rejection. In this situation, gurus of the far Right make themselves the spokespeople of those who demand that paintings (or photographs or music) offensive to the public not be supported by public funds.

The idea that great art should be popular is widespread and can be found on the Left and Center as much as on the Right. German and Russian conservatives lament the loss of beauty in art as in life and the chaos that has replaced it. As the Nordic neofascists see it, the plastic arts should depict peasants or small-town scenes, landscapes, and handsome young men and women, mixed in with portraits and paintings of animals.

Most politicians are not fervent adherents of twelve-tone or electronic music and abstract art, but in contrast to the new-Nazis, they think that the state should stay out of culture. The extreme Right, on the other hand, wants to spearhead the battle against modernity and for patriotism. But they do not have a monopoly: The instructions to French television and radio that at least half the songs broadcast be of French rather than foreign origin were given by the government, not by the National Front.

The extreme Right advocates a *Kulturkampf* from below against decadence and liberal and permissive trends in general. It is antimodern and irrational in ways not altogether dissimilar to the beliefs of the postmodernists. But they agree only on what they reject, and they do not offer an alternative way of life or a culture combining their ideals and values with the present human condition. This struggle against multiculturalism has become one of the neofascists' central and seemingly most promising rallying cries. But it is a strange *Kulturkampf*, since on neither side in this political struggle is there a passionate interest in, or commitment to, culture. There are interesting affinities with New Age and other *fin de siècle* trends such as the assumption that Western liberalism, with its stress on the rights of the individual and free political institutions, is doomed. Hence the opposition to the tradition of the Enlightenment and rationalism in general, the spread of various irrational cults, the reemergence of gurus such as Nietzsche and Heidegger. All this does not, of course, amount to a fully fledged fascist ideology, and its political impact is strictly limited for the time being. But it recalls the mood of an earlier *fin de siècle* in which the spiritual precursors of historical fascism made their first appearance.

The Skinheads

In the 1970s and 1980s, groups of adolescents, more often male than female, in strange attires, and with names such as skinheads, "fashos," hooligans, bovver brigades, psychos, bootboys, and psychobillies, caused amazement and even shock in the streets of Britain, Germany, and other European countries. Their heads were shaved, and they wore T-shirts; donkey jackets (tonic jackets for girls); heavy boots, biker boots, monkey boots, or Doc Martens with iron nails and razor chains; crombies and Harringtons; belts with metal sheets; and rings showing snakes, scorpions, deathheads, and a variety of other strange items. Swastikas and, occasionally, an Iron Cross, had been painted or affixed on their shirts. Some skinheads were heavily tattooed, and they all shouted "Sieg Heil," "Heil

Hitler" (and also "Anarchy" and "Juden raus" [throw out the Jews]). In their songs they advocated killing Turks and other foreigners, as well as homosexuals, hippies, vagrants, and the handicapped. Their feelings with regard to rival street gangs were not noticeably warmer. Unlike the punks the skinheads were not individualists but roamed in packs and cliques.[2]

The beginning of the new youth subculture was on the soccer fields and in the discos of England; the movement had begun spontaneously and was predominantly working class. In most other countries, including West and East Germany, Spain, and Hungary, the connection between soccer crowds and skinheads was equally apparent. In Spain the skinheads originated in the fan clubs of Real Madrid and the two Barcelona football teams.[3] The exception was the United States, where soccer is not widely played. In America the skinheads emerged at the fringes of various organizations of the extreme Right, such as the Ku Klux Klan and the White Aryan Resistance. Whereas European skinheads are mainly working class in origin, American skinheads seem to be more strongly middle class, with a pronounced criminal element. Among their favorite bands were at first the Skrewdrivers; latter-day skinhead bands were named Blood and Honour, Aggravader, Assault, No Remorse, Klansmen, and Bound for Glory.

The names of the skinhead magazines are even more revealing: *Un Jour viendra, Rebelle blanc, Der Angriff, Erwache, Totenkopf, Stahlfront, Das Reich, Zyklon B,* and *Solução final.* It is only fair to add that most of these have a circulation of a few hundred copies only. Their music was fashioned first on the lines of reggae and ska (imports from the Caribbean) but later gravitated to *oi* ("the sound of the street") with songs on the "long nights of Auschwitz" and Zyklon B.

Oi was the invention of a group named Cockney Rejects and replaced the "one, two, three, four" that had earlier introduced a new song. It became the symbol of violence with songs such as "Someone's Gonna Die, Tonight" and "Violence in Our Minds" abounding and neo-Nazis figuring prominently in the new fashion; the second *oi* album was entitled *Strength Through Oi.*

To the uninitiated it was not easy to differentiate among the various gangs, also called packs and brigades. Some tried to project an image of male virility, flaunting their female companions, whereas others deliberately minimized the difference between the sexes. Their magazines (called fanzines) do not offer many clues concerning their ideas, as they communicated through music rather than the written word. The British skinheads began their career in the later 1970s with "paki bashing," and the Germans, with *Türken* and *Neger Klatschen.* The German skinheads became politicized only in the late 1980s; earlier they had been active on the margins of various fan clubs, trying to create mayhem by attacking passersby in the street, smashing shop windows, and generally searching for outlets for their aggression.

In East Germany the skinheads arrived well before the Communist regime collapsed. Subsequently, it was revealed that the Stasi (the state security service) had to send as many as two thousand agents to certain soccer games to keep order. The skinheads (not yet known by that name) no longer had any respect for the police. Even so, the East German police arrested some of the leading figures of the scene, which for a while noticeably cut down on the skinheads' activities.

The political orientation of most of these groups was uncertain: The early skinheads in West Germany could be found among the demonstrators supporting the Baader–Meinhof terrorists. Their main aim was to provoke and shock the older generation, and it did not take them long to realize that the swastika and "Heil Hitler" were more likely to annoy people and attract attention than was support for any left-wing cause or random violence.

During the 1980s some of the right-wing extremist groups in England and in Germany decided to experiment with a strategy of "entryism" (that is, infiltration and mobilization) on the soccer fields and in the discos. This they did with more success in Germany and Eastern Europe than in Britain. It was facilitated by the growing youth unemployment, on one hand, and the feeling of boredom, on the other. "Ghost Town" one of the last songs of the Specials, a British band, vividly described this mood, and the reaction of some young Germans (and later Poles and Russians) was similar: There was nothing to do . . .

Youth subcultures emphasizing autonomy and rebellion against the generation of the parents had existed in Europe for a long time. Nowhere had they been more prevalent than in Germany, the home of the classic Jugendbewegung, which came to an end with Hitler's rise to power. But in crucial respects the skinheads, "fashos," and hooligans were the very antithesis of their predecessors: The members of the earlier youth movement were from the middle class, whereas, the new movement was lower class in origin. The earlier youth group was educated, idealistic, and romantic and favored "life reform," a healthier way of life. It wanted to change the human condition by means of a cultural revolution through self-improvement. The new youth culture had no such ambitions, was inchoate, and its instincts were violent and its ideas incoherent. Its ideal was not harmony and beauty, inward or outward, but shocking others through deliberate ugliness in their makeup, slogans, and songs. The cacophony and brutality were intentional, even though European skinheads did not, as a rule, carry weapons as often as American street gangs do. (There were twenty-eight skinhead murders in the United States between 1987 and 1993, more than in Europe, even though the total number of American skinheads—perhaps 3,500—was smaller than that in Europe).

The skinhead subculture provided a source for the recruitment of neo-Nazis in Germany and Britain, even though the older generation of neo-Nazis rejected their "jungle music" as a decadent manifestation of subhuman elements. The younger generation of neo-Nazis had no such misgivings and tried actively to mobilize the skinheads for their cause, from London to Budapest. In the Mediterranean countries, in contrast, the neofascists regarded the skinheads as a negative element. In France and Italy, skinheads were considered a manifestation of British and American decadence.

This was the view of, among others, Domenico Fisichella, minister of culture in the Berlusconi government. Fini, the leader of the MSI, called the Italian "shaven heads"—"empty heads": "I would send them all to work in the mines." The Polish extreme Right, harping on the evils of mass culture, took a similar line. The Russian neofascists' view of rock music and rock culture was likewise one of uncompromising hostility. They regarded it as one of the devices that the worst enemies of the Russian people (Satan, the West, the Jews) used to corrupt its soul. These feelings prevailed, however, among the older generation; the younger were more tolerant, as they saw kindred spirits in the right-wing rock stars and their followers. The bard Igor Talkov, who was killed in circumstances not clear to this day, was a supporter of Pamyat, and the heavy-metal fans from Lyuberi, a working-class satellite town to the west of Moscow, played at one time (1987–1990) a role similar to that of the skinheads in the West. Nazi symbols, relics, and rites became fashionable among certain groups of Russian youth—the motivation and the social origins of those involved were quite similar to those of the skinheads in the West.

The skinheads and other such groups attracted wide attention after their attacks (sometimes with fatal consequences) against foreigners in Germany and also, to a lesser extent, in other European countries. Skinhead rock stars were singing the praises of Nazism and Adolf Hitler from Budapest to Stockholm. Skinhead magazines, in a variety of languages, announced that National Socialism was the only means to save Germany, Europe, and the white race—and to "destroy the people who do not belong to us." The Skrewdrivers, founded in Blackpool, organized white-power rock concerts, and in Germany annual processions were arranged in honor of Rudolf Hess's death. Some groups carried the swastika, and others, the U.S. Confederate flag. Some were violently anti-Irish, but others identified with the IRA, whom they considered fellow national freedom fighters.

Many punk-style skinheads (*Glatzen* in German) used Nazi symbols and rituals mainly in order to annoy their families, teachers, and authority in general. How deep was their real attachment to fascism? When asked by interviewers about their political ideas, their responses were as loud and emphatic as they were inarticulate. They wanted their national culture and way of life to be kept pure, but in fact they were not well informed—to put it mildly—about their own cultural heritage. They told everyone who wanted to listen that they felt overwhelming *frust* (frustration), that they hated everyone who did not share their feelings, and that violent action was the only way to reduce their own tensions and to put their enemies in their place. They drank and smoked heavily but opposed using drugs, in contrast to their counterparts in America, where rap and drugs often overlap.

Much heart searching has been caused among outside observers by the appearance of the skinheads in their various mutations. Social psychologists and social workers have had difficulty understanding this unexpected and shocking phenomenon. As a result, the belief that virtually everyone was almost infinitely educationable was put to a hard test. True, one could argue that this strange subculture was essentially a way of resisting the impact of capitalism on young peoples' lives. Bourgeois (or petty bourgeois) society was generating frustration, and frustration in turn was leading to aggression. Furthermore, European society was deeply racialist and thus bound to lead to excesses.

The frustration–aggression hypothesis was resurrected, as it had been used to explain the left-wing terrorism of the 1960s and 1970s and crime in general. But its factual basis has always been tenuous: Violence, criminal and political, can exist without significant repression. And in any case, people always must accept a certain amount of frustration and not succumb to all of their inclinations and instincts.

Furthermore, European society has been and is racialist, if by this we are referring to an awareness of the differences among races and peoples. Europeans are not automatically amicably disposed toward others who look different and have different beliefs, lifestyles, and values. All societies are intolerant in this sense, some more and some less; there is a racialism of the majority as well as of ethnic minorities, and the latter is by no means less dangerous or morally superior.

The idea that skinheads and the like could be brought under control as a result of humanist, pacifist, and antiracist indoctrination was overoptimistic. In dictatorships, both ancient and modern, people of this kind would be beaten up and arrested by the police and thus deterred, at least for a while. In democracies, especially those believing in permissiveness, skinheads can find little to entertain and amuse them or keep them busy, but violence is not used against them, except in extreme cases.

Those people studying skinheads are at a loss as to what can be done about these rebels without a real cause. Humans have always been predisposed toward violence, and it is not helpful to argue that such an inclination does not exist or that it can be easily reasoned away.

Groups such as the skinheads and their successors will probably continue to exist in one form or another. How important are they to the spread of neofascism? For reasons that we have discussed, the skinheads are unreliable allies and an undependable source for recruitment. There is little that unites them, and they lack identity as much as continuity. There are few skinheads over thirty, with new street gangs appearing and disappearing as quickly as fashions in music. Although they can be mobilized for certain actions against foreigners, they lack motivation, discipline, and stamina for concerted action. Furthermore, they antagonize many more of their fellow citizens than they attract, and neofascists stand for law and order rather than chaos.

The skinheads' influence is limited to a specific social milieu and a certain age group (fifteen to twenty-one). There is nothing specifically national, let alone patriotic, about their existence. Their ideas, their dress, and their music are a mix of international elements, mainly Afro-Anglo-American. The young people attracted by these gangs are not the material likely to be of much use to the neofascists. Moreover, they are few in number, being a minority within a minority. In 1992, the total number of skinheads in Germany was estimated at six thousand, about half of them in East Germany. About two-thirds of them identified with the extreme Right; the others were apolitical. They are, in brief, a problem for the police and the educators, rather than the politicians.

According to some estimates, a considerably larger segment—15 to 20 percent—of the young generation in Germany sympathizes with extreme right-wing groups. But it is still unlikely that they would become a political force in the forseeable future.

Two questions remain to be answered: Why is it that such small groups of young people have attracted so much attention? Hard-core neo-Nazi skinheads are very few, even though some of their records, cassettes, and discs have sold well. The same question was asked in 1975 with even greater justification in regard to a handful of terrorists. Although they numbered no more than a few dozens, their deliberately outrageous behavior brought them enormous publicity, which, of course, was what they wanted. In the end, there was a book and several articles on terrorism for every active European terrorist, and learned treatises were written about their psychology, social origin, and general motivation. This was a hopeless enterprise, however, because the social sciences can perhaps account for mass movements, but certainly not for the behavior of tiny groups. True, the skinheads of the extreme Right are more numerous than the terrorists were. They do have in common with the terrorists and early fascists the desire to shock the public by means of unconventional behavior. This, in the final analysis, is the reason for the great publicity.

But why did the skinheads adopt views of the extreme Right rather than the Left; why did they not stay out of politics, as they did at first? Around 1970, at the time of the ferment in the schools and universities, such a movement would have gravitated to the extreme Left or to anarchism, to the Chaoten or Spontis. But the zeitgeist of the 1990s is different. The extreme Left has little allure for a movement of resentment and free-floating violence. It is too ideological for people of little education, and it does not single out for attack obvious, popular targets—such as foreigners. Nor can the "no-future" generation (and the one following it) turn to the Greens, who are too intellectual and too tame. Thus it is only natural that in many countries, neo-Nazi symbols and ideas should gain support on the rock scene. The skinheads' political significance should not be overrated: Future historians will probably find them a fascinating footnote in the history of late-twenty-century customs and manners rather than politics.

The Fear of Immigrants

Nationalist aspirations and the grievances of national minorities played an important role in the rise of historical fascism. But Europe became more homogenous as the result of the redrawing of borders and ethnic cleansing (that is, expulsions) after the war.[4] Nazism drew much of its strength from the Germans' hatred of France (Germany's traditional archenemy) and of Poland. Such feelings are no longer so acute but have been replaced by new tensions that could not be envisaged in the 1920s and 1930s.

In the 1970s, political sociologists in Western Europe discovered "new social movements" that they thought would be of considerable political significance in the future, but only a very few paid attention to the emergence of new ethnic minorities which, within a few years, did become an important political problem. Among the issues that led to a revival of fascism in Europe, none was greater than the fear of being overwhelmed by immigrants. Immigration did not play a crucial role in the resurgence of Italian or Russian neofascism. But it was not entirely absent even in those countries, and it was a factor of paramount importance in virtually all other European countries. By immigrants, we are referring mainly to the migration of West Indians and Asians to Britain; of North Africans to France; of Turks, Moroccans, and others to Germany; and of Yugoslavs to Switzerland and Sweden, but also to the migration of "Caucasians" to Moscow and other major cities in European Russia, and to the influx of gypsies.

Until the 1960s, migration in Europe had been predominantly internal, principally from eastern and southeastern to northern and western Europe. In the 1970s Turkey and North Africa emerged as the main countries of emigration, followed by immigrants from sub-Saharan Africa and South Asia. Until the early 1970s the great majority of the immigrants were hired as guest workers. Then, with the rise in unemployment, the Western European governments adopted measures to bring this immigration to a halt. For a variety of reasons, however (such as the reunion of families and a high birthrate), these measures had only a limited effect. For example, although the number of actively employed foreigners in Germany decreased between 1972 and 1992, their total number doubled, from about 3.5 million to 7 million. Developments in France (with about 4 million) and Britain (with perhaps 3 million) were, broadly speaking, similar. In addition to these official figures was an unknown number of illegal foreign residents. As long as there was a seemingly unlimited demand for labor, few Europeans complained about the presence of the immigrants. But as the number of unemployed native-born Europeans rose and when it appeared that most of the guest workers did not wish to return to their native countries, the issue became one of central political importance. By 1989, 79 percent of Germans and 75 percent of Italians expressed the view that there were too many foreigners in their midst; the figures for France and Britain were in the 80 percent to 90 percent range. Even in tolerant Holland, a substantial majority of citizens thought that the country did not benefit from the presence of so many foreigners, only a quarter of whom were believed to work, with the rest supported one way or another by social security.

Resentment of foreigners was by no means limited to the extreme Right. Prime Minister Thatcher made it known in 1978 that Britain was "swamped by foreign cultures," and President Mitterrand declared that in France the "threshold of tolerance" had been reached. In every European country, Socialists as well as Communists voted for measures on both the local and the national level to limit immigration. The principal difference between the neofascists and right-wing extremists and the other parties was that whereas the first two groups wanted to get rid of all foreigners in one way or another, the others, however grudgingly, were willing to accept those already in their midst. But if the immigrants did not want to return to their home country, they were expected to make greater efforts to become acculturated, to conform with local customs and traditions.

Many Europeans resented that they had never been asked whether they wanted so many aliens in their midst. Nor had they been requested to vote for or against a multicultural society—they were faced with a fait accompli.

The social and cultural absorption of the new immigrants has been made difficult by their concentration in certain regions, mainly in the big cities and in certain districts in these cities. This has resulted in a disproportionate pressure on social services (such as housing and schooling) and a decline in the qualities of these services. Before World War II, Poles settling in France, or East European Jews settling in Germany, Britain, or France, tried to assimilate to the culture of their host country. But immigrants from North Africa, the Middle East, and other parts of the world who arrived in Europe in the 1970s and 1980s often did not wish to be integrated but, rather, wanted to preserve their way of life, their customs and values, even if these conflicted with the traditions of the host country. Furthermore, the new arrivals were usually more easily recognized by the color of their skin and sometimes their attire.

By 1980 many European inner cities had assumed a distinctly Balkan-Middle Eastern, North African, and Third World character. Even though such variety appealed to those in search of exotic cuisines, the reaction of the local residents was usually less enthusiastic. They resented not just the sights, smells, and the relative lack of cleanliness, but they complained also of a breakdown of law and order, of vast amounts of public money being spent on foreigners they had not invited in the first place. Such a lack of hospitality may be regrettable but it is not altogether surprising. Citizens of France, Germany, or Britain are not welcome settling in a North African, Middle Eastern, or indeed any other country. In some places, such as Algeria, they would quite likely be killed, and in any case, they would be expected to adapt to their host country's religious customs and native traditions.

Enmity directed against foreigners can be found all over western, northern, and southern Europe, not just in the major cities, but also in the smaller towns in Holland and Britain, in Alsace as well as in East Germany, where their total number was small. Some antiracialist observers argue that there is little or no connection between the rise of neofascism and the presence of immigrants. But an analysis of election results shows that this is generally not true. The case of Vienna is instructive: All Austrian parties have agreed on limiting immigration to a very low level (27,000 annually). Nevertheless, the number of foreigners grew by 75 percent between 1981 and 1991, and it was precisely during this period that Haider's party with its anti-immigrant platform made its greatest progress even in Socialist Vienna: Once a certain limit was reached, antagonism against foreigners became a major political issue.

In most cases there is a direct link between the presence of foreigners—

especially from overseas and to a lesser degree from Eastern Europe and the Balkans—and the strength of parties opposed to their presence.[5] "Asylum seekers"—more often than not a misnomer—caused the emergence of a stop-immigration party even in Norway, and an anti-Somali hysteria even in distant Finland.

If Le Pen's National Front had significant electoral successes in the 1980s and 1990s, it was not because of the virtues of the philosophers of the Nouvelle droite but because of the resentment and fear of wide sections of the population—and Le Pen's invocation of Jeanne d'Arc to help stem the tide of foreign invaders, mainly from North Africa.

The issue of immigration and of the perceived danger of a foreign presence has become a more central and potent factor than the perceived danger of the Communists or the Jews ever was after 1945. The anti-Communism of the extreme Right was always somewhat suspect, since they professed to hate equally liberalism, capitalism, and the parliamentary system. Furthermore, they shared their opposition to Communism with most other parties. And after the war, there were so few Jews left in Europe that they were not an issue.

Uncontrolled immigration is an issue of concern even for those not afraid of a multicultural society, for it means the decline, and possible the breakdown, of the welfare state. Some argue that the rich countries of the West have a moral obligation to share their wealth with the poor of the Third World and to give political asylum to those asking for it. They also reason that for purely selfish reasons, Western societies have a vital interest in continuing to accept immigrants. In their view of these countries' demographic structure (a shrinking labor force and an ageing population), foreign workers are needed to keep the factories operating. Hence the need for antiracialist, antidiscriminatory legislation and, generally, the education of both young and old in the benefits of a multicultural society.

These arguments do contain elements of truth, as few European workers would be willing to do the menial and badly paid work in industry and the services if the guest workers were made to leave. The cultural chauvinism of the extreme Right is equally groundless, for all too often the most radical are young men (and, to a lesser extent, women) whose cultural interests are limited to soccer, skinheads, and right-wing rock. The antiracialists are right to protest against violent attacks against foreigners. Yet at the same time they are combating deeply rooted feelings. The great majority of the asylum seekers did not go to Europe because of acute political persecution but in order to better their living standards. This was a perfectly legitimate aspiration, and there might have been no valid reason to oppose them had Europeans resources been unlimited. But they were not and this inevitably led to the establishment of priorities. Preaching tolerance to the Germans, French, and others was laudable, but since there was not much tolerance on the part of Islamic fundamentalists—to adduce only the most blatant example—such arguments fall flat. Ethnic strife has been a global phenomenon: If Tutsis and Huttus, Hindus and Muslims, Turks and Greeks, Tamils and Singhalese, Arabs and Jews, Bosnians and Serbs, Armenians and Azerbaijanis, and Irish and Irish could not live in peace, it was unrealistic that Europe alone among all continents would be an exception.

The attacks against foreigners in Europe, culminating in the 1990s, were, of course, criminal and the antiforeigner hysteria was irrational. But beyond the outrages committed by the least savory elements of society, there were genuine problems that could not be solved by antiracist slogans, legislation, and indoctrination. It was a misjudgment on the part of well-meaning "antifascists" to assume that the antiforeign sentiment exploited by the extreme Right was merely a passing phenomenon caused by a downturn in the economy and high unemployment and bound to vanish in due course. The high unemployment rate, for all one knew, was structural and thus unlikely to disappear in the forseeable future.

Will immigration play in future the central role it does in European politics at the present time? No party in Europe favors unlimited immigration, and almost all have adopted or favor strict control: The extreme Right has no monopoly in this field. But despite the insistence of Muslim fundamentalists, for example, on political and cultural apartheid and on the preservation of their traditional way of life, at least part of the younger generation of immigrants in Europe will be culturally absorbed into the mainstream of modern, secular European civilization.

But experience shows that such integration—expressing itself in language, manners, and customs—does not necessarily lead to greater ethnic harmony in the short run. On the contrary, the second and third generation of immigrants often faces an identity crisis greater than their fathers or grandfathers did. They no longer have roots in their country of origin, but feel as though they are not treated as equals in the country in which they were born. Hence their greater assertiveness, hence the making of more severe ethnic strife.

These problems are relevant inasmuch as they contribute to the potential growth of neofascist parties. If, in the best case, immigration is limited or halted, and if on the basis of good will and mutual tolerance, something akin to a multicultural society will emerge, fascism will derive no benefit from the birth pangs of this new society.

But this scenario is unlikely, for even if some kind of multiculturalism prevails in the long run, it still will create tensions during the long transition period. In addition, there will be strong demographic pressure on (a relatively) prosperous Europe as a result of the high birthrate in Asia and Africa, particularly North Africa and the Middle East. Islamic radicalism aggravates this pressure inasmuch as the modern (European) sector of societies taken over by Khomeinism is decimated and those affected flee. One and a half million Iranians escaped after the return of Khomeini, and a similar exodus seems likely in Algeria, Egypt, and even Turkey if the fundamentalists should assert themselves there. But there is the potentially much larger exodus of the nonmodern sections—because of unemployment and the ineffectiveness of the Islamists to build a viable economy.

The worst-case scenario would be the creation of a fortress-Europe climate in which neofascist and similar movements could prosper. The possibility of ethnic conflict, rather than economic crisis, is, at the present, the best—perhaps the only—real hope of the extreme Right in Europe.

Anti–Semitism and Denial of the Holocaust

Anti-Semitism was a crucial ingredient of Nazism and of some fascist movements in Central and Eastern Europe. It was of minor importance in Italian and Spanish fascism, because of the small Jewish presence in these countries. Nor was it the paramount factor in French, Belgian, and Dutch fascism, even though hatred of the Jews had deep roots in France. At the time of the Dreyfus affair, such feelings were probably as widespread in France as in Germany. According to anti-Semitic doctrine, the Jews are the forerunners of a global conspiracy also consisting of Freemasons and other subversive elements such as liberals, finance capitalists, and revolutionary socialists. But after World War II, anti-Semitism lost some of its relevance as a factor in politics, even in Eastern Europe and Russia. Even though the Communists had engaged in anti-Semitic actions and propaganda, this was done in a certain ritual way—under the guise of "anti-Zionism." Fascism needed the image of an enemy, but the number of Jews had dwindled as the result of the mass murder. Anti-Semitism has been reported also in the absence of Jews. In political practice, but for the presence of a minimum critical mass, it is virtually impossible to conjure up the image of an all-powerful enemy against whom all true patriots should unite.

Nonetheless, anti-Semitism has continued to exist even after 1945, and activities hostile to the Jewish communities have been reported in many countries. It is also true that for the anti-Semitic sects, the Jewish issue remains paramount. But even if basic attitudes have not changed significantly, the far Right (except the sectarians), for strategic as much as for tactical reasons, have softened its rhetoric. One reason, of course, was the murder of millions of Jews by the Nazis during World War II. The anti-Semites either deny the mass murder or try to "put it into historical perspective," that is, interpret it as a mere footnote to twentieth-century history, as Le Pen once put it. Although they might welcome in their heart the elimination of the Jews, they would not say this openly because it would be politically unwise. Neofascists crave respectability, and justifying mass murder would not improve their image.

If the number of Jews has greatly diminished in most European countries, other foreigners have arrived to take their place: the guest workers from Turkey and North Africa, asylum seekers from various Third World countries, gypsies, and others. Thus the Jews are now only one of several scapegoats and, in most cases, no longer the most important one, as public opinion polls in Germany and elsewhere show. Strong or fairly strong anti-Jewish prejudices are admitted by some 30 percent of the population, but their feelings about these other groups are even more negative.

Typical in this regard were the attitudes of the Russian extreme Right emerging under *glasnost*. Those calling for removing the Jews as the main and most urgent concern were initially very prominent in the public eye. But as time passed, the more farsighted leaders of the extreme Right realized that even though anti-Semitism was an inalienable part of their ideological heritage, to make it the central issue would be to condemn them to a role of marginal significance.

Jews were hardly represented in the ranks of the Russian mafia, about whom everybody complained, or among the speculators on the stock markets; they were not among those who hijacked or shot Russians in the Caucasus or Central Asia or abused them in the Ukraine. A considerable part of Soviet Jewry left the country between 1988 and 1992. To blame those who remained behind for all the misfortunes that had befallen the Russian people lacked persuasion; even the least sophisticated elements in the population knew that one had to look for the real culprits elsewhere. Extreme anti-Semitism also involved the Russian neofascists in all kinds of contradictions: Under Communism, the professional anti-Semites had denounced the "Zionists" as the most active anti-Soviet element. As Communism collapsed, the Russian neofascists, without stopping for reflection, went over to the other extreme: The Jews had been the most ardent Bolsheviks, instrumental in the victory of Communism in 1917 and the maintenance of the regime in the years after. The Bolshevik Party, as they now claimed, had been largely a Jewish party.

After 1991 yet another change took place, when the Russian extreme Right and the neofascists realized that the (neo) Communists were their natural allies. They shared a distaste for capitalism and liberalism. Those on the extreme Right had to make both political and doctrinal concessions to their partners. Communism, according to the new version, had not been all wrong, and the influence of Marx and Lenin could be expurgated only up to a point. Thus the "Red–Brown alliance" that emerged strongly disliked the Jews but could not make anti-Semitism the central plank in its program.

Traditional, hard-core neofascists in Europe and America spent much time and energy on attempting to refute the "Auschwitz lie," that is, the facts about the mass murder of Jews. Their argument was, very briefly, that no written evidence for an order to kill millions of people had ever been found, nor had physical evidence for the existence of gas chambers. The Jews might have been deported to the east because they were considered security risks. Because of the severe climatic conditions, lack of food, and spread of diseases, some of them might indeed have died, perhaps as many as 100,000, perhaps even 300,000. Perhaps they had been dealt with harshly, but then the Western Allies had also committed war crimes, and so it was unjust to single out Hitler.

There were slightly different versions: Russian neofascists, for instance, were less reluctant to concede that mass murder had been committed, as millions of Russians, after all, had also been killed. But they argued that this had been mainly the fault of the Zionists, who had engineered the mass murder so that they could get their own state after the war, as a first stage on the road to world domination, and so they also could blackmail Germany and other countries to give them reparations. Some Germans contended that "harsh measures" might have been taken against the Jews in wartime but that they were justified because the Jewish people had declared war on Germany. That is, they were "enemies of the state" and had to be dealt with accordingly.

A Canadian engineer was found who claimed in a report of 132 pages that it was technically impossible to burn thousands of corpses a day, as was the case at Auschwitz. In 1993, however, it was revealed that the engineer was no engineer, and in the newly accessible archives in Moscow, technical drafts and specifications were found, provided by Topf and Co. in Erfurt, for stoves with a capacity for disposing of 4,700 corpses a day in Auschwitz.

Those denying the Holocaust deliberately confused the concentration camps located in Germany with the extermination camps in the east. The camps in Germany such as Dachau, Buchenwald, Mauthausen, Neuengamme, and Bergen-Belsen were not primarily death camps, even though most of those who entered them never returned: in the case of Mauthausen, 102,000 of 197,000 died; Bergen-Belsen, about 50,000 out of 125,000; and

Neuengamme, 55,000 out of 106,000. The camps in the east had no other function but to dispose of a maximum number of people in a minimum amount of time. Special SS units had been employed for more than a year in the east in 1943/1944 to obliterate traces of the murder. It is also true that no general order signed by Hitler referring to the destruction of European Jewry has ever been found. But this did not come as a great surprise to historians, who know that throughout history the greater the crime, the less is the likelihood that written evidence will ever be found.

Nonetheless, there is more than enough evidence from the various war crime trials after 1945. The German "Auschwitz trials" began in 1960 and ended in 1981, in which admissions were made by those who had directed and operated the death camps, and evidence also was offered by the survivors. Neither Adolf Eichmann nor Rudolf Hess, the commander of Auschwitz, ever denied the essential facts of the mass murder. But this does not impress the Holocaust deniers, who argue that the camp commanders had made these mendacious admissions because they had been tortured and that the eyewitnesses suffered from delusions or were lying. As for the written evidence—for instance, the reports of the *Einsatzgruppen* in Russia, giving the numbers of those killed—these, too, were falsifications. According to the deniers, both the Red Cross and the United Nations have made it known that mass murder had not taken place. The Red Cross and the United Nations have said nothing of the kind, nothing even remotely like such assertions.

But it is futile to argue with the deniers, for as soon as one allegation is disproved, they come up with another. If it were not the Red Cross, perhaps some other international organization had been involved. And if Hitler had announced in a speech to the Reichstag in January 1939 that if world Jewry succeeded in unleashing another war, European Jewry would be destroyed, why, that did not signify anything. Furthermore, if there had been a mass murder of Jews, surely Churchill, Roosevelt, and Stalin would have known about it. And since they were only too eager to engage in anti-German propaganda, they would have revealed it to the world as soon as they heard about it. Seen in this light, this fact—that the news about the Holocaust spread only after the war had ended—proves that it never took place.

Jewish institutions nevertheless continue their confrontation with the deniers, assuming that even though they are only an insignificant minority, their literature could have an impact on many others not very well informed about what had really happened. Psychologists know that people are inclined to believe that the truth is somewhere in the middle between two "extremes," that there is no smoke without fire; hence the danger that the deniers' arguments, however spurious, might fall on open ears.

These exchanges with the deniers should not be confused with the "revisionist debate" after 1986 which involved German as well as American, French, and British historians. These polemics did not concern the facts: that millions of Jewish civilians and others had been exterminated. Rather, the issues at stake in this dispute were whether the Nazis' Jewish policy had been deliberate from the beginning and consistent or had been opportunistic in the sense that it wanted to get rid of the Jews but considered various ways, bloody and less bloody, to accomplish this. One of the bones of contention, for instance, is whether the decisions to engage in mass murder were made in 1940 or early 1941, or only six or nine months later, whether Hitler himself decided this or whether his underlings (or the bureaucracy) confronted him with the fait accompli. Whatever the merits of the revisionist arguments, they do not deny the Holocaust but merely want to downgrade it.

The revisionists deplore the "ritual repetition" of the allegation that the murder of the Jews was a unique crime. They believe, instead, that Germany is the victim of a systematic campaign by foreigners and the left-wing intelligentsia bent on perpetuating the Germans' guilt. They argue that the Holocaust was by no means unique but comparable to civil wars such as that in Bosnia. "Auschwitz," as they see it, is invoked to prevent the free expression of opinion in this matter.[6] It is difficult to ascertain whether the "Auschwitz relativists" truly believe that the mass murder was just another crime like those that have frequently been committed by governments and individuals throughout history or whether they recognize its uniqueness but believe that the only way to relieve the Germans' remorse is to play down the issue's historical importance.

Who are the Holocaust deniers? Most of them are old Nazis or neofascists. The more successful far Right parties do not want to be identified too closely with the deniers, even if they occasionally use their arguments. They know that the Holocaust took place, and they want respectability—and at the same time they want to appear as the protagonists of the most burning issues preoccupying the public. Denying the Holocaust is therefore not an issue of paramount importance for the neofascists except, for obvious reasons, in Germany, where a special urge exists to refurbish the historical record or, at the very least, to show that the mass murder was by no means unique but merely one of many crimes committed during the war. Those on the German far Right firmly believe that the time has come to bury once and for all this skeleton, and such suggestions are by no means unpopular.

Some of the Holocaust deniers are professional naysayers, the kind of people that can be found in every group that disagrees when faced with a fact, however indisputable and irrefutable. Their belief could not be shaken. It is doubtful whether such folly, however wicked, can be cured by law. On the whole, such beliefs are limited to sectarians; their arguments are too outlandish to make them acceptable to normal people. But there is always the danger that in a major crisis the views of fringe groups may be spread beyond their normal habitat. The *Protocols of the Elders of Zion* is still published today on the fringes of the neo-Nazi movement, and the belief in an international Judeo–Masonic–Communist–high-finance conspiracy lingers on. For Muslim fundamentalists, the Jewish issue is basic from a theological point of view, and the Jews are among the main targets of their propaganda and terrorist actions. Sectarianism on the extreme Right continues to believe in old-style anti-Semitism, with Boleslaw Tejkowski's (Polish) National Community as a typical example. The Catholic Church in Poland (he claims) has been "Judaized," Solidarity is referred to as "Judeo-Solidarity," Cardinals Glemp and Macharski are said to be Jews or servants of Jews, as are Lech Walesa, Tadeusz Mazowiecki, and virtually every Polish prime minister or cabinet minister, scientist, and artist. The propaganda of such groups follows the tradition of the prewar extremists in Poland as elsewhere. But these are the views of individuals, and they have been criticized by more enlightened spokesmen of the far Right for clinging slavishly to an outdated, prewar party line. Some anti-Semitism, they realize, may be essential, but focusing on it relentlessly is traveling the road into the political wilderness.

The policy of the more successful neofascist parties has been more circumspect, partly because of tactical considerations and fears of legal consequences. Fini, the leader of the Italian postfascists, has refrained from anti-Semitic remarks, and although Le Pen has never claimed to be a friend of the Jews, astute politician that he is, he realized long ago that there was not much political profit in belaboring the Jewish issue. The Republicans in Germany became openly anti-Semitic only when they were in decline, when it seemed they had nothing to lose. Haider's Austrian "liberal" party has been careful not to single out Jews as the group mainly responsible for Austria's misfortunes. And anti-Semitism has played a relatively inconspicuous role in Zhirinovsky's propaganda. The other radical patriotic–Communist groups have been more outspokenly anti-Semitic, especially the sectarians, who prefer "purity of doctrine" over popular success. Anti-Semitism could again become a central issue in the case of a major political, social, or economic upheaval, but there is little likelihood that it will do so in the forseeable future. Although political anti-Semitism is by no means finished, it has declined in importance, except among those for whom it is an article of religious faith.

International Fascism

Cooperation between fascist movements and states was common in the 1930s, but a fascist International never was established along the lines of the Comintern. Germany and Italy provided money, logistic support, and, on occasion, weapons to weaker fascist organizations, especially those in the Balkans. But neither Hitler nor Mussolini had high hopes with regard to the political prospects of these groups, terrorist or nonterrorist. Fascism was the antithesis of an internationalist movement; there was no reason that, say, a Hungarian and a Romanian fascist should consider the other a comrade in arms.

After World War II, the Nazis and fascists cooperated in helping war criminals escape to Latin America and the Middle East. Even later, they exchanged information and propaganda material and held small international gatherings in Malmo, Sweden, and Dixmuiden, Belgium. In 1962 Oswald Mosley, the veteran British fascist leader, met with his peers of the Italian, German, and Belgian far Right, and they passed a resolution (the Declaration of Venice) calling for a Europe-wide fascist party. But this came to naught, and subsequent exchanges between Spanish and Italian fascist groups and other international meetings in the 1970s and 1980s led nowhere either.

American neo-Nazis thought Germany a more promising ground for their propaganda than their native country and frequently visited Europe. The French and Belgian New Right supplied literature and apparently also some money to Russian neofascist groups. De Benoist, Robert Steukers, and others visited Moscow, and their pronouncements were given much publicity by Aleksandr Prokhanov and Aleksandr Dugin, the chief ideologists of the Russian far Right. It was no accident (old-style Leninists would have said) that a Russian ideological journal named *Elementy* was launched, modeled on the Nouvelle droite organ, *Elements.* (There is also a Flemish *Elemente.*) One of the ideological periodicals of the French extreme Right is named *Identité,* and there is also an Austrian *Identitaet.* Zhirinovsky established contact with Le Pen as well as the German Republicans, Frey's party in Munich, and Austrian extreme right-wingers. But he also tried to enter the World Union of Liberal Parties. Frey, in turn, visited Moscow to address Zhirinovsky's party.

At the meetings of neofascist parties, guests from abroad can be found, representing all kinds of "nationalist parties" with important-sounding names though wholly unknown even to specialists. These honored guests talk emphatically, radically, and, above all, at great length. More often than not it is never clear whether these sectarians represent anyone but themselves, whether they are clinically mad or perhaps agents provocateurs.

There also is an Arab–Middle Eastern connection. A Moscow daily newspaper named *Al Kudz* (Jerusalem), which became one of the papers of the Russian extreme Right, was financed by an Arab "businessman" who was a resident of the Russian capital. Russian and German right-wingers sing the praises of Iraq's Saddam Hussein, probably not without some reciprocal favors, and a neofascist leader has become the chief propagandist of Libya's Mu'ammar Gadhafi in Italy.

Lyndon Larouche's organization, one of the most bizarre sects of the extreme Right and originally Trotskyite in inspiration, has been very active in Germany, has established a branch in Moscow, has cooperated with the Islamists in Sudan and other Arab and North African countries, and has made itself the spokesman of Saddam Hussein and Hamas, the extremist Muslim fundamentalist group. The net results of these and similar activities, however, has been very nearly nil.

More important is the "technical faction" in the European parliament that was created in 1989, consisting of ten deputies of Le Pen's party, six German Republicans, and one Belgian from the Flemish bloc. The technical faction is dominated by the French, because this was the strongest group when it was formed. It adopted the National Front's program as the common platform of all the extreme right-wing groups. At the same time the technical faction was instrumental in setting up the European Confederation of National Youth. This youth group, based mainly on Le Pen's Front and the Italian MSI, meets at "summer universities" in Spain, at marches in honor of Rudolf Hess in Wunsiedel (where he is buried), and at the anniversary of Franco's death at Ulrichsberg, Austria, where Austrian SS veterans and their admirers are addressed by Jörg Haider, the leader of Austria's second largest party.

But the technical faction still has not achieved unity of action. In Brussels, the four Italian neofascists walked out of a meeting because they thought south Tyrol was an integral part of Italy, whereas the German Republicans demanded that it be given the right of self-determination. Even the German Republicans split over the propagation of pro-Nazi ideas; Franz Schönhuber, the leader, proclaimed that the program of the radical faction was "anti-human, neo-Nazi, racialist and extremist." Schönhuber, in turn, was thrown out of his own party in September 1994.

Cooperation among the neofascists is difficult because they do not have a common denominator. The Nietzschean, elitist doctrines of Evola and the French New Right have been rejected by most Russian right-wing extremists as unsuitable and even counterproductive on Russian soil. Moreover, their paganism is highly offensive to the Russian Orthodox Church, with which the right-wing extremists want to be on good terms. Patriots in Moscow claim, not without justice, that the Russians have a tradition of ultranationalism and socialism and that the new-fangled doctrines of Western metaphysicians have no relevance to their country. On the other hand, the Russian cult of anti-Satanism, the adulation of the tsar and (state) church, and the all-pervasive *Konspiratologia* are out of place in Western Europe.

Interest in the ideas of the French Nouvelle droite was pronounced for a while in Britain (traditionally weak in the ideology) and in Germany. During the 1980s British and German journals of the extreme Right regularly published French authors and reported on new trends in Paris. But this enthusiasm lasted for only a few years and then petered out. Only a few intellectuals were interested in these topics; after a while, the subject was exhausted and everyone returned to his or her traditional preoccupations—the "third way" (between West and East), postcapitalist nationalism, the "conservative revolution," and antibourgeois populism.

The history of the Comintern has shown that despite the common international party line, this organization never amounted to very much—and it would have been the same even if it had not been from the beginning a mere instrument of Soviet foreign policy. The Fascintern did not even have such a common ideological denominator except in vague ways, and its prospects are even dimmer.

If there is ever international cooperation among the neofascists, it will be in illegal terrorism. Just as Carlos, Baader-Meinhof, and the leftist terrorists of the 1970s could operate only through an international network of sympathizers (and intelligence services), terrorists of the extreme Right may use their international contacts.

The NSDAP/AO (Auslands Organisation), an American grouplet active mainly in Europe, has published since 1993 a PC journal (with a cover address in Nebraska) that provides instructions for the home production of plastic explosives, napalm-like substances, and detonators. Since these groups do not intend to use their activities for mining, building, or oil prospecting, the purpose of such instructions is obvious. Even though terrorism by the extreme Right will not be more effective than that of its predecessors, past negative experience may not deter it. If external war was an essential component of fascism in a past age, terrorism using weapons of mass destruction could play a central role in the future.

3

POSTFASCISM

Clerical Fascism and the Third World

One species of fascism with a time-honored past had a recent revival and may have a promising future in some parts of the world. This is clerical fascism, which can take various forms, such as the confluence of fascism and radical, fundamentalist religion.

The term *fundamentalism* is as imperfect as most of the terms used in political and general discourse today. But no one so far has produced a concept that fits better and is more widely accepted. If fundamentalism is interpreted as orthodox, going back to the origins, meaning the sacred texts, the legitimacy of present-day fundamentalists is dubious. Often they provide their own, novel interpretations of these texts, which are by no means identical with tradition. Fundamentalism interpreted as antimodernism is more accurate, but since modernity has a variety of meanings, this is not always helpful. Thus, in the final analysis, fundamentalism has come to represent a radical, militant, fanatical movement trying to impose its beliefs on others by means of force, and thus, it is a political movement.

The similarities between fascism and fundamentalism were noted even in the early 1920s, well before Hitler had become a household name. One of the earliest accounts of fundamentalism in the United States was entitled "Faszismus und Fundamentalismus in den USA."[1] The author showed in great detail how political fanatism fueled religious intolerance, how extreme nationalism and populism went hand in hand with radical religion, and how the Ku Klux Klan cooperated with the fundamentalists. Both were based on the same social strata, the poorly educated and discontented looking for primitive and violent solutions.

The term *clerico fascisti* was coined even earlier, in 1922. It refers to a group of Catholic believers in Rome and northern Italy who advocated a synthesis of Catholicism and fascism. The affinities between the Muslim Brotherhood and fascism were observed in the 1930s, as was the fact that the extreme Muslim organizations supported the Axis powers in World War II.

In a remarkable book published in 1937, a German Catholic writer labeled Nazism a new political Islam and Hitler-Mohammed its prophet. Why this "new German" (*neudeutsch*) Islam? According to Hitler from *Mein Kampf* onward, the sword has always been the carrier, prophet, and propagator of a new religion: "Hatred was always the main moving force of all revolutionary change, pervasive fanaticism and even hysteria were impelling the masses rather than any scientific perception."[2]

Nazism contained a pagan element, and Italian Fascism featured an anticlerical trend, but they appeared only at the margins of these movements. Once in power, the fascist states were eager not to jeopardize their relations with the church. On the other hand, the clergy played a crucial role in fascist or profascist regimes and movements. Fascist and parafascist parties in Latin America and the various "integralist" movements rejected the pagan element in Nazism and invoked the need for a Christian spiritual revolution (Father Charles Coughlin in the United States). Sir Oswald Mosley in Britain wrote in retrospect that it had been the weakness of fascism in Britain that it had not been more Christian in inspiration. Neither Engelbert Dollfuss and Kurt von Schuschnigg in Austria nor the Slovak governments of Monsignor Tiso (often labeled at the time as a *clerical fascist*) were inspired by fanatic religiosity; they were authoritarian rather than totalitarian. The Croat state of the Ustasha, on the other hand, provides a good example of the dual impact of religion and fascism resulting in state terrorism unprecedented even by Balkan standards.

It has been argued that there could be no lasting understanding between fascism and religion simply because both were holistic weltanschauungen, staking claims to the whole human being in all respects. "Thou shall have no other gods before me" says the Bible, but it also demands to "render unto Caesar the things that are Caesar's, and unto God the things that are God's," and the Talmud announces unambiguously, "Dina de malkuta dina" (The law of the [worldly] kingdom is the law). But Islam is, according to the fundamentalists, *din va dawla*, both a religion and a political–social system. Islam does not call for Muslims to disobey non-Muslim rulers. But it implies that they should obey only as long as the rule of the infidels lasts.

It also has been contended that a fascist–religious synthesis is impossible because all varieties of fascism are deeply nationalistic, whereas modern secular nationalism is irrelevant, if not anathema, to the world's principal religions. But militant religion and nationalism coexist in Shi'ite Iran, among Jewish fanatics in Israel, among Sikhs in India, and elsewhere in Asia. The Russian Orthodox Church has always been the main pillar of

Russian nationalism, as are the Armenian, Georgian, Ukrainian, and Bulgarian churches of their countries.

Another, more valid argument is that historically some religions have been less fanatical and more tolerant than others. These are therefore unlikely candidates for clerical fascism in any form. Not all religions have tried to establish a theocracy. For example, in the past India was the model country of tolerance, with King Asoka honoring all (other) religions and Akbar preaching religious tolerance.

Similar tolerance was exercised in Europe under Friedrich von Hohenstaufen in the thirteenth century, but this was an exception. The history of Christianity since the early Middle Ages is one of the persecution of heretics, the burning of witches, crusades and pogroms, inquisitions and other forms of intolerance. The power struggle between church and ruler lasted for many centuries and lost its relevance only with the secularization of the state in early modern times or, as in the case of Russia, with the imposition of the will of the tsar (Ivan IV) on the church.

In Islam, Iran offers the best-known example of religious intolerance. This tradition, to be sure, dates back even to pre-Islamic times; as manifested in the persecution of the Turks and Uzbeks and, more recently, in the persecution of various Islamic sects, Bahais, Christians, Jews, and virtually all other religions. The injunction of a holy war (*jihad*) against the non-Islamic world (*dar al harb*) is a collective duty (*fard al kifaya*) of vital importance. The jihad is a permanent revolution in which there may be temporary truces but no real peace. This is the law, but on a practical level, concessions must be made much of the time.

Fundamentalism, is not, of course, an Islamic monopoly, as it can be found in Christianity and Judaism as well as in other religions. In extreme forms it is manifested in political terrorism (such as the antiabortion murders in the United States, in Kahanism in Israel, in Hindu attacks against Muslims in India). Fundamentalists have exerted political pressure on secular governments in America, Europe, and Asia. But only in the Muslim world have radicals acquired positions of power and are likely to have further successes, from Algeria to Afghanistan, Bangladesh, and even beyond. Conversely, in most parts of the West and East secularism has made so much progress that it has made a fundamentalist takeover unlikely.

Hence we shall focus here on the political aspects of Islamic radicalism and the features it shares with fascism. These features include Islamic radicalism's anti-Western, anti-Enlightenment character; its renunciation of the values of a liberal society and of human rights; and its emphasis on the collective rather than the individual; its elite leadership and dictatorial government; its widespread use of propaganda and terror; its all-embracing and aggressive character; and its fanaticism and missionary zeal.

Those who acted as the intellectual pioneers of Italian Fascism and National Socialism preached that the community should be put above the individual personality. They glorified martyrdom for the holy cause; they considered democracy a contemptible heresy; and they believed in the rigid division of the world into friend and foe—*nashe* and *ne-nashe* in the terminology of the Russian far Right of 1990. They put the mystery of leadership on their banners, as well as blind obedience and a near-absolute belief in male supremacy. They declared that there was a fundamental conflict between their creed and that of the decadent West. These were the beliefs of Ludwig Klages and Carl Schmitt, of Hans Freyer and Friedrich Wolters, of the right-wing Protestant theologians of the Weimar Republic, and of others now forgotten.

On another level of intellectual sophistication, these also are the articles of faith of radical Islam. Fundamentalism per se cannot be equated with fascism. In many countries it is primarily backward looking and conservative. In some cases fundamentalism is mainly cultural, and in others it is defensive—the reaction of a minority confronting a lay majority or another majority religion. This is true, for instance, in regard to the ultraorthodox Jews in Israel, the Shi'ites in Iraq, or the Muslims in India. Such fundamentalist minority groups might be extreme in outlook, and they might use violence, even terrorism. But they cannot possibly dream of establishing a theocracy. The most they can strive for is more autonomy.

Elsewhere, as in Indonesia or Malaysia, cultural traditions rule out a fascist regime, or secularization has progressed so far as to make it impossible to turn back. Even though Khomeini's victory in Iran provided fresh impetus to fundamentalists in many Muslim countries, Shi'ite fundamentalism differs in both doctrine and practice from Sunni fundamentalism as taught in Pakistan and Egypt. The Shi'ite rulers are considered sectarians by most Sunni fundamentalists, who reject Iran as a model.

There is thus an unmistakable kinship between Muslim radicalism and fascism. Although not identical they are in essential respects quite similar. Sometimes these affinities are uncanny. When Hitler came to power in 1933 he abolished the trade unions and stopped celebrating May Day. The day of international working-class unity then became National Labor Day and became a paid holiday, which it had not been before. Khomeini did exactly the same. Now the people merely march under different slogans: "Workers, toilers, Islam is for you" and "Our party is that of Allah, our leader is Ruhollah [Khomeini]." In both Germany and Iran, May Day continued to be celebrated in subsequent years, but it became progressively less important.[3] It is unlikely that the ayatollahs knew about the Nazi policy toward the trade unions and the Left and copied them; rather they acted instinctively in the same way.

One student of contemporary Iran compared the Iran of the mullahs not just with European fascism but also with the most extreme of the fascists, the Romanian Iron Guard, which drew its militants in the same way that the Iranian Islamists did, from the wave of young people of peasant origin flooding the universities. Both movements adhered to a practice of suffering, sacrifice, and martyrdom. Priests figured prominently among the Romanian fascists; meetings were preceded by church services; and religious flags were carried in the fascist processions (as in the demonstrations of the Russian Black Hundred). In the words of Cornelieu Codreanu, its leader, the ultimate goal was "resurrection in Christ."[4] The Shi'ites preferred the resurrection of the imam, but the parallels are still astounding.

If radicalization, for whatever reason, should continue in the Islam world, the fascist trend will become stronger. Many Westerners are afraid of the term *fascism*, but fascism outside Europe and North America has not always had such negative connotations: For many Third World militants, Hitler and Mussolini were fighters for national liberation who failed for reasons by no means considered dishonorable.

This theology of the bomb has in common with fascism, above all, its totalitarian character: The fundamentalists are traditionalists in some respects, although they do not want to preserve society and the individual exactly as they are, but to improve them. They want total control and enthusiastic support, not merely passive obedience. Such fundamentalism is profoundly undemocratic and antiliberal. There is no dissent, only heresy. Individual human rights and freedom of thought do not exist. Indeed, radical Muslim thinkers regard democracy as blasphemy.

All this also applies to Communism, especially in its Stalinist form. But from a doctrinal point of view, Stalinism never quite divorced itself from its intellectual base—the Enlightenment, secularism, the ideals of the French Revolution. It claimed to be rational in inspiration and was, of course, antireligious, in contrast to fascism, which paid at least lip service to religion. Like fascism, radical fundamentalism is a populist movement, based on social tensions and the misery and resentment of an underclass that has not benefited from modernization but instead feels left out or marginalized. It has a pronounced egalitarian streak and is directed against those better off.

The rioters in Algiers and Egypt, stoning new cars and squatting in new buildings, are as much inspired by resentment and envy as by deep religious feeling. Underneath the "holy rage" resides frustration and old-fashioned class struggle. The recruits to the plebeian storm troopers in Germany in 1932/1933 had a good deal in common in regard to motives and mentality with the thugs of Teheran who became the backbone of the mullahs' movement.

The Islamic revolution in Iran was supported by its society's dissatisfied elements, of which there were a great many: the old middle class, or the *bazaris*, small traders and craftsment who felt left out and rejected by modern influences and developments. They could not obtain credit from the banks and felt threatened by modern stores and high-technology imports. A new, modern middle class existed, but the shah's regime, fearful of independent initiatives, did not permit it to organize. The movements that led to both European fascism and the Islamic revolution consisted of disparate groups with conflicting class interests. But class interests were not decisive, especially in the later phases. Instead, the new regimes were integrative, promising to reconcile class interests in the name of higher values. The *bazaris* were told to return to their traditional occupations, and Khomeini announced that his glorious revolution was not based on the high price of melons.

Under fascism the state party is the main instrument of rule, and under fundamentalism the religious organizations are paramount. Such organizations may have charismatic leaders such as Khomeini, but usually they have a collective leadership. In the Shi'ite system, the clerics play a central political role, less so among the Sunni fundamentalists. In all these movements, however, the clerics are never far from the seats of power. This applies to radical rabbis in Israel, the Sinhalese monks in Sri Lanka, and clergy elsewhere. Like fascism, radical political religion attracts many students and the younger generation in general. This has to do with the failure of alternative ideologies, with the resentment of Western ways, and with the frustration of unemployment and the absence of opportunities for students to follow a career commensurate with their training.

Historical fascism and clerical fascism share an economic doctrine or, more accurately, an absence of an economic doctrine. They both reject materialist socialism but favor a "just social order." They are against Western-style capitalism but do not oppose the ownership of private property. Since they do not trust the markets, they dabble in state capitalism. In Nazi Germany, the SS and individual Nazi leaders established major corporations, such as the Hermann Goering Werke. In Iran, the ruling clergy, having amassed billions of dollars, have established holding companies and foundations controlling a substantial part of the Iranian economy. The mullahs discourage ostentatious spending but are quite willing to tolerate private luxury if it is discreet.

Finally is the crucial issue of violence. The radical Islamic view of human nature is grim: Unless people are frightened, they will become sinners. Indoctrination alone is not enough—hence the need for coercion—and this applies as much to enemies as to followers. The use of terror is widespread both at home and abroad. Although Nazis and fascists (and of course Stalinists) also tried in peacetime to kill their enemies abroad, they did so relatively rarely, and they always tried to cover their tracks. But radical Islam engages in such practices openly, as demonstrated by the demand for the murder of Salman Rushdie and of the Bengali writer Tashima Nasrin. Apostates and renegades must be punished; otherwise, their example might be followed. One would expect that hundreds of fanatic believers would only be too eager to undertake this holy duty, since a place in paradise is promised to every martyr. But the distrust of human nature has impelled the mullahs to make the inducement even more attractive, by promising a prize of more than $1 million for killing an apostate.

Islamism is not a religion but an ideology based on religious elements who see as their main function a revolt against the West and modernity in general. Islamism is rooted in the resentment felt by Muslims against the dominant position of the West politically, culturally, and economically and the stagnant state of Muslim societies. Western values are rejected because they undermine and subvert the traditional Muslim order and way of life, because they lead to the gradual marginalization of religion and the clergy. In principle, this ideology is as much opposed to China, Japan, and Russia as it is to the West. But since the contact and the collision were historically mainly with the West, most of the fury is directed against this part of the world rather than the other Satans.

Such ideological "anti-Westernism" has much in common with the traditional attitudes of the extreme Right in European intellectual history, which paved the way for fascism and have been amply documented.[5]

According to some analysts, the fundamentalist revival occurred because of the failure of nationalism and the national state in the Arab and Muslim world, because of the arbitrary borders drawn between Muslim countries. But this is true only in part. Borders may be artificial, but they are unlikely to change. In any case, Arab secular nationalists were also opposed to the previous borders. The conflict between secular nationalism and Islamism is not absolute: Nasser and Saddam Hussein were fervent nationalists but at the same time, believing Muslims, who appealed to *jihad* in their campaigns against the West. They were largely supported by the Islamic radicals despite the fact that they suppressed the Muslim Brotherhood, Shi'ite sects and other radical groups.

The rejection of liberal–secular values, including human rights as understood in the West, and their replacement by an Islamic order need not be elaborated in detail. Some Western advocates of cultural relativism have claimed that there are no conflicts but merely misunderstandings based on the traditional prejudices of Christianity against "militant Islam." Some of them argue that in the East words do not necessarily mean what they say (for instance, "holy war") and that, in any case, there is a great distance between Muslim dogma and Muslim practice. These arguments are not entirely wrong, inasmuch as all ideologies must make concessions to reality, to human imperfections and frailty. They must adjust to economic and technological change, and like historical fascism and Communism, Islam is subject to routinization. It is also true that the Arabic language tends toward hyperbole. But these apologies are still misleading because they make radical Islam appear more moderate than it actually is. Chinese Communists were not just "agrarian reformers," as some well-meaning foreigners believed in the 1930s and 1940s. And Muslim radicals are not just pious believers preoccupied with prayer and good deeds; their main preoccupation is the punishment of the nonbelievers. If a *fatwa* has been issued calling for the "punishment" of a writer who has criticized the Prophet or his teaching, if the death penalty is demanded for a Muslim woman who has complained about the treatment of her sex in Islamic society, it means precisely what it says. If Christian clergy are killed in Iran and Central Africa, or foreigners are murdered in Algeria or Copts in Egypt, this is not the result of a misunderstanding.

Concerning the elitist character of the fundamentalist political regime and the need for a dictatorship, differences can be found between Shi'a and Sunni Islam. The Shi'a is based on the expectation that the twelfth imam, who mysteriously vanished a long time ago, will reappear one day and that only then will legitimate (state) authority exist. In the meantime, Muslim believers need guidance, and since the mass of believers does not have the necessary knowledge, the Koran must be interpreted by the religious dignitaries known as *mujahids*, the highest of which are called *ayatollahs*. This can be one person, such as the late Khomeini or his successor Khameni, or a collective leadership of ayatollahs (*sura-ye rabbari*).

The Muslim Brotherhood in Egypt and elsewhere has been more liberal in this respect. Its chief guru, Sayed Qutb, who was executed under Nasser in 1966, stated that the leadership in a Muslim country need not be in the hands of those who wear the turbans. It was sufficient if the state accepted the *shari'a* (Koranic law) as the law of the land replacing the secular constitutions and legal codes.

But Islam has no comprehensive legal system. Only a small part of the Koran deals with laws and society, just as Muhammad left no instructions as to who should succeed him. Many aspects of society are not discussed at all in the Koran or are mentioned in an unclear or contradictory way. In brief, interpreters of the Koran are still needed; such guidance cannot come from kings and presidents, however religious they may be. On the other hand, Arab leaders such as Libya's Mu'ammar Gadhafi, have emphatically rejected such claims by the clergy, demanding for themselves the right of interpretation and dismissing the extremists as "charlatans and heretics" who should be eliminated like animals because their aim is to ruin Islam and to split the nation.

In clerical fascism, the role of the mass party is fulfilled by the community of the faithful, who are mobilized into giant demonstrations, people's militias such as the *pasdaran* in Iran, and elite units. The population is closely supervised by a system of resident supervisors not unlike the Nazi *blockwart* system.

When the clerical fascists are in the opposition, in countries such as Algeria and Egypt, their terrorist organizations operate to undermine the authority of the state, by murdering key government officials, foreign residents and tourists, and members of native national minorities. Clerical fascists in North Africa and the Middle East have, to date, carried out more acts of individual terrorism than did the Nazis and fascists before they came to power. In Germany during the three years before the Nazis' rise to power some three hundred political murders were committed, not all of which by the Nazis, whereas in Algeria between 1992 and 1994 many thousands of people were assassinated.

Violence is common to fascism and clerical fascism and includes severe punishment meted out to all enemies of the regime. Allah may be merciful, but his fundamentalist representatives on earth are not. In contrast to old-fashioned dictatorships (and also Asian tyrannies), radical Islam demands total obeisance. It controls not just the political activities of citizens but all their activities, including their leisure time. The private sphere is reduced to a minimum, being in many respects more totalitarian than European fascism ever aspired to be. Opponents to the regime are liquidated, imprisoned, or forced to emigrate. The number of those killed in Iran under Khomeini and his successors runs into tens of thousands. Emigration from Iran and Algeria, legal and illegal, has been considerably greater than that from Nazi Germany after 1933 (350,000, including Jews) and infinitely greater than from Fascist Italy. Clerical fascism is a conflict not just between political regimes but between two societies, one modern and the other antimodern, hence the much higher number of those forced to flee.

Finally, political Islam is aggressive. It arose as a defensive reaction against modernity and the Western world. But early in its development it staked claims to world leadership: The West was not only morally but politically bankrupt; its end was near; and the only force capable of establishing a new world order was political Islam. The West was shrouded in a deep moral and cultural crisis, a *Sinnkrise*, ever since it had jettisoned religion as a guiding principle. Islam, on the other hand, had not undergone a reformation or an enlightenment and was willing and able to take over where Christianity had failed.

Such claims are not original, as they were voiced in the 1950s by left-wing radicals such as Frantz Fanon, who also passionately advocated the use of violence against the putrid West. But all Fanon and his friends could offer in return was some mythical (and artificial) Third World ideology, whereas the fundamentalists reflect the feelings of many millions of believers motivated by the same resentments and fears; it is a movement with a traditional feeling of universal mission.

The turn to aggression probably also has other reasons: Unless Western civilization is destroyed, Western rationalism, Western science, and Western profanity and entertainment will overwhelm Islam and drag it down to perdition. Since it is impractical—and useless—to build a wall to shut out Western cultural influences, the only way to stop the rot is to destroy the source of the evil, thus the need to Islamize Spain and France, followed by the rest of Europe and eventually the whole world.

What are the sources of support for the Islamists, and what their weaknesses? Islam's appeal is rooted above all in the rise and domination, political and cultural, of the West. Once a high culture and one of the greatest powers in the world, Islam is now poor and weak. Its attemps to copy Western institutions and customs in the nineteenth and early twentieth centuries failed. This led to the revolt against the West under the banner of Arab (and North African and Persian) nationalism, but this was not successful either. What remains is Islam, traditionally a political religion that has become the second stage of the revolt against the West. Earlier, in the late 1930s, fascism pure and simple had a certain following in the Muslim world. Ahmad Hussain's Misr al Fatat (Young Egypt) Party drew its inspiration from European fascism, and so did, to a considerable extent, Antun Sa'adeh's Social Nationalist Party in Syria and the pan-Arab Ba'th Party which subsequently split into a Syrian and an Iraqi wing bitterly fighting each other, even though the doctrinal differences between them are minimal.

Two generations of Arab military men, including Nasser and Sadat, as well as later on Saddam and Assad, were influenced in their younger years by European fascism or its derivatives. But their parties were not specifically Islamic in inspiration, and Christian Arabs numbered among the leading figures of the Ba'th Party. However, when the Axis powers were defeated, their image of fascist strength and inexorable victory vanished, and their admirers in the East had to look for inspiration in other directions: Communism, left- or right-wing populism, and ultimately Islam. The first fascist wave in the Middle East failed but was followed by a second, the rise of Muslim radicalism.

We have mentioned the connection between the socioeconomic misery of many millions of people and the rise of Muslim radicalism. The countries that face the gravest political challenges are the ones with the most severe economic problems. Sudan and Bangladesh are among the poorest countries in the world. Sudan has for many years shown negative economic growth, and Bangladesh has suffered major natural catastrophes. The Algerian economy has not grown for many years; its per capita income has fallen; and its unemployment rate is 50 percent, even higher among the young. Millions have no proper housing. The economy of the former Soviet Muslim republics has sharply declined (with the exception of Kazakhstan, where, however, inflation was running at 150 percent in 1993); Tadjikistan's economy has virtually collapsed. At the same time the birthrate in countries such as Algeria and Sudan is over 3 percent. In 1974 Algeria had 16 million inhabitants, and now it has 31 million. In the same period the population of Sudan doubled, from 18 million to 35 million, as did the population of Iran (from 30 million to 60 million). Although birth control was introduced through the back door, it arrived too late to have an effect in the forseeable future. At the end of World War II, the city of Algiers had a population of 300,000; today it has 2 million. Teheran (plus its suburbs) has grown from 1 million to 10 million.

Algeria and Iran are oil-producing countries that earn considerable income from oil and natural gas. But the Algerian oil revenues were squandered under Houari Boumedienne's "socialist" regime, and although Iran made substantial economic progress during the 1960s and 1970s, the revolution of 1979 and the ensuing events put an end to it. Unemployment in Iran is now nearly 50 percent, and per capita income has declined.

If Iran were developing fairly rapidly under the shah, how could a theocratic dictatorship have come to replace it? The answer is that expectations among the population, especially the middle class, were even higher. However, the opposition to the shah's dictatorial regime fought under the banner of freedom rather than the rule of the ayatollahs. That is, the democrats and the revolutionaries of the Left paved the way for a regime they had not wanted and that quickly suppressed them far more effectively and brutally than the shah's government had.

These observations regarding economic and social problems apply to some extent to all Muslim countries, except only the major oil exporters such as Saudi Arabia and the sparsely populated rich Gulf emirates. They are true even with regard to Pakistan and Turkey, which have had a slight increase in output and per capita income, but accompanied by a high inflation rate (Turkey) and various nonproductive commitments, such as high defense spending in both Turkey and Pakistan.

With large sections of the population living in poverty and little hope for substantial improvement, a large army of the unemployed can be mobilized by populist movements promising salvation through the propagation of faith. It is reasonably certain, however, that the masses will not indefinitely put up with regimes that promise so much and accomplish so little. First comes passive resistance and then active opposition.

In times of grave crisis, political Islam is a serious contender for power in the Muslim world. But the radicals aim even higher: They believe that they have a universal mission that everyone should eventually accept. Their dreams of global mission may not come true; even a poor and relatively underdeveloped country can become a major danger to its neighbors if it acquires modern weapons.

Iran has taken a leading part in terrorist activities in many parts of the world, through the establishment of training camps, arms supplies, and the logistic support of terrorist groups in Lebanon, Egypt, and other parts of the Middle East and Africa. It has been involved in bombings and assassinations in Europe, the Americas, and Asia. The long-term benefit derived from activities of this kind is dubious, but in the short term such actions have certainly enhanced Iran's nuisance value. North Korea would have been ignored but for its nuclear program, and the same is true with regard to Iran, which is also engaging in a buildup of long-range missiles, a nuclear-weapons program, and the acquisition of other means of mass destruction, both biological and chemical. Neither terrorism nor the possession of such weapons will make Iran into a world power; conversely, the use of such weapons would result in its destruction.

The rulers of Iran have not shown suicidal tendencies in the past; rather, they seem to want to acquire the capacity of mass destruction mainly to establish their country as a dominant power in the Middle East. Their policy is based on the assumption that the smaller Middle Eastern countries will not be able to follow the Iranian example. This assumption could be wrong, and it does not take into account the possibility that a crisis provoked by Iran may get out of hand or that disasters may occur accidentally.

Western critics are aware of the weaknesses of their societies, without the benefit of Islamic advice. The joylessness of Shi'ite Islam and the other radical sects, with their strong emphasis on ritual (including masochist practices) such as the five daily prayers, the ablutions, the fast during Ramadan, and the *haj*, is not likely to find enthusiasts among people in the West thirsting for a spiritual message rather than the observation of rituals. Islam, which is premodern, has been praised by some because of its revolt against the Enlightenment and against reason. But if the West (or the East) needs a dose of fundamentalism, it has its own religions to fall back on, not to mention the various esoteric New Age cults.

The strength of radical Islam is that of a populist system that appeals not to the educated but to simple people. It provides certainties, however primitive, in a world of dangers and uncertainties. But the weakness of a political religion is that its claims and promises are mainly of this world. Therefore, it cannot plead mitigating circumstances when things go wrong. It must show distinct achievements. By cutting itself off from modern civilization, radical Islam has also cut itself off from modern science, the present source of power and wealth. Islamic dignitaries do believe that if modern science is properly Islamized, it can be safely used in an Islamic order. This implies lagging behind others, nor is it certain whether competent application is possible in a theocratic system.

Fifteen years of fundamentalist rule in Iran has little to show to its credit. Despite substantial oil revenues, only stagnation and decline have resulted. There is no reason to believe, therefore, that if the radicals came to power in Algeria, Egypt, or another Muslim country, the results would be different.

What happens when prophecy and promises fail? Liberalization is a theoretical possibility, and it is true that all along, a greater measure of freedom has prevailed, especially in Teheran, than should have been the case. Minor transgressions of the Islamic code have been ignored, and the corruption of the officials has attenuated the rigors of Islamic orthodoxy; just as the Soviet system was never quite like Orwell's *1984*, neither is radical Islam.

But as the regime faces growing difficulties, it cannot liberalize itself without endangering its very existence, and so it is likely to become even more radical. Even if Islamists came to power in one or more other countries, they could offer little benefit for the mullahs in Teheran. They could not provide substantial financial help, and their leaderships would be challenged. The most that they could hope for would be a small "fundamentalist International" temporarily acting in unison, coordinating political action and terrorism.

Much has been made of the suicide missions against which, some believe, there is no defense; the same was once said about the kamikaze pilots. In fact, there have been few candidates for suicide missions, and there is no reason to assume that there will be more than a handful in the future. In the past, the Iranian leaders were careful to reject charges of state terrorism as wholly unfounded. But if their situation should get desperate, the theocrats will not abdicate without a struggle. The relative restraint (and the dissimulation) that prevailed in the past may be shed.

The weaknesses of radical Islam are obvious. It has no viable alternative economic, social, and political system to compete with those of the rest of the world. The aims and the style of the rulers and the joyless existence in a fundamentalist society—black Shi'ism with its mourning processions and self-flagellation—collide with the temper, the hopes and aspirations of the majority of the people. Fanaticism may be welcome in an emergency, but it cannot feed the hungry or alleviate boredom. In our age, a closed society cannot be sealed off from the forbidden entertainments of other countries. If the shah's regime were undermined by the cassettes of Khomeini's speeches, the ayatollahs' rule is being undermined by the television programs that millions of Iranians watch through their satellite dishes.

Fascism understood better than the Islamists that the masses ought to be entertained. The ayatollahs offer neither *panem* nor *circenses*, only rituals; like fascism, they can mobilize the masses, but for how long can they keep them mobilized? Two other basic mistakes ought to be mentioned: Radical Islam should have realized that for their cause to succeed and to grow strong, they need a middle class of entrepreneurs and intellectuals. These segments of society are more difficult to manipulate than the masses, but without their cooperation, radical Islamic regimes are doomed. Finally, the radicals have been preoccupied with the great Satan in the West (as the Soviet Union was for many years) while ignoring the fact that other global centers of power have emerged. For example, instead of cultivating the goodwill of India, they have threatened it. At the same time, China has shown as much concern as Russia has about radical Islam. In brief, the clerical fascists have thrown down the gauntlet not just to America and Europe; they are regarded as a potential enemy by all other political forces in the world. Even if Islam were united, such behavior would be foolhardy. As it can count on the support of a minority only, it is suicidal.

The boast of the Iranian rulers that a billion Muslims or more are waiting anxiously to join the struggle at their side is a fantasy. The most populous Muslim countries, such as Indonesia, Pakistan, and Turkey, have no wish to become involved in a cause in which they do not believe. Even the fundamentalist groups in these countries are not impressed by the Iranian example. Although they may accept their money and their weapons, they do not want to emulate the rule of the ayatollahs.

Radical Islam has expanded mainly into Central, West, and East Africa, where the number of Muslim believers has doubled within the last generation. The strategies followed in these backward countries have been similar or even identical. During the first phase, mosques are built, and Islamic schools and centers are established. Newspapers and radio and television stations are opened, with the purpose of making converts. An attempt has also been made to replace French and English with Arabic. At a later stage, once a sizable community of believers exists, political parties are founded, and guerrilla fighters are trained. A campaign follows, to turn the country into an Islamic republic based on the *shari'a*. Armed groups are the main tool for the conquest of power. Initially their main aim is to liquidate rivals such as Christian missionaries and to destablize the state when the authorities are reluctant to make concessions to radical Islam.

This has been the common pattern from Mali and Niger in the west to Somalia and even Tanzania. Such religious imperialism is greatly helped by the country's economic backwardness and the low cultural level of the population. In Africa south of the Sahara—the Sahel countries—Islam has become the religion of the poorest of the poor and the most backward elements.

Radical Islam's progress has been hampered, however, by a lack of unity among its crusaders: The Saudis, their most active and most generous paymasters do not coordinate their activities with the Iranians and their Sudanese allies—who concentrate their efforts on East Africa—or with Gadhafi, who, furthermore, preaches a kind of Islam unlike that of the orthodox clerics. Furthermore, radical Islam must contend with the old problem of the specifically African character of Islam, with its cult of saints and animistic elements. These elements are particularly evident in the most important African Muslim countries, such as Senegal and (northern) Nigeria. The fundamentalists of the north might tolerate an "African road to Islam," but other elements neither the Iranians nor the Saudis can accept, such as the much higher role accorded to women in African Islam than in the Arab world and Iran. Such internal divisions, even if profound, do not however, affect the overall importance of the trend that we have noted, namely, radical Islam's invasion of Africa.

Islamism (not Islam per se) is today the only major force in the world that openly advocates expansion, hegemony, and the export of revolution and that calls for a jihad, a holy war, against internal and external enemies. In this war—in the struggle against other cultures—there can be no compromise. The jihad is the starting point and the central issue of radical Islam.

Some have tried to explain the jihad as a purely spiritual concept that holds only as long as radical Islam does not consider itself prepared for full-scale jihad. Obviously, it cannot engage at the same time in an attack against the whole world and also its internal enemies. The "Islamic threat" is therefore sometimes overrated in the West, not because it is described as more fanatical and aggressive than it really is, but because of its innate weakness. Islamic radicalism resembles Fascist Italy, a colossus on feet of clay, rather than Nazi Germany. Its ultimate fate thus must be that of Mussolini's Italy, but it may last for years and cause a great deal of suffering. Neither the Croatian Ustasha state nor the clerical fascists in Slovakia in World War II had access to missiles and nuclear devices. The combination of fanaticism and the means of mass destruction that now confronts humanity holds dangers that did not exist in the past.

Although clerical fascism is the most fascinating of the new varieties of fascism in the Third World, it is by no means the only one. Iraq's Saddam

Hussein was called a fascist by President George Bush at the time of the Gulf War, and although one should not attribute undue importance to epithets of this kind, especially if used in the heat of the battle, there is more to this designation than mere rhetoric. The Iraqi political system is not just a military dictatorship or a one-party system. It has been striving for totalitarian rule, with a massive use of terror and propaganda, the cult of its leader, unbridled nationalism, and military aggression that have taken it as far on toward full-fledged fascism as most European fascist regimes and movements did in the 1930s. Repression in Iraq was considerably more severe than that in Nasser's Egypt twenty years earlier, and if Hussein nevertheless found much support, especially among Arab intellectuals in the Middle East, this was because of his intense anti-Westernism and the pan-Arab slogans.

Before World War II, fascism outside Europe was usually dismissed as "false fascism," and not without reason. Fascism presumed a certain degree of development, an infrastructure, and a capacity for effective rule, for without them, fascist dictatorship was not possible. Since then, conditions have changed, and fascism outside Europe has become a possibility and, in some cases, a reality. The Iraqi and the Syrian regimes have pronounced fascist features, even though they are secular rather than clerical in inspira- tion, and are ruled by politically ambitious officers rather than religious dignitaries. Both the Iraqi and the Syrian leadership belongs to the Ba'th Party, an elitist, pan-Arabist group that arose in the 1930s partly as a result of the rise of fascism in Europe.

The postwar Ba'th Party had no intention of copying the prewar fascist regimes, however. It realized, correctly, that its chance to come to power was by means of a military coup rather than a mass movement, and it looked for recruits and sympathizers among the younger army officers. Before Saddam Hussein and Hafiz al-Assad became leaders of their respec- tive countries, military dictators had followed one another in rapid succes- sion in Baghdad and Damascus. To make their governments last longer than those of their predecessors, the new rulers had to establish new and more ruthless mechanisms of control, not old-fashioned military or police regimes, but more modern ones in which terror and propaganda would be used to paralyze the opposition.

Since the mid-1970s, both Iraq and Syria have moved a long way toward becoming nationalist–socialist regimes, despite certain differences. Although both regimes have violently suppressed undesirable ethnic groups (the Kurds and Shi'ites in Iraq), the leadership cult is more pro- nounced in Baghdad than in Damascus. In fact, the cult of Saddam Hussein has been as intense as the cult of the leader in Stalinist Russia or Maoist China. Both regimes have been eager to expand their territory, but Iraq has been more recklessly aggressive than Syria. The Iraqi attacks against Iran and Kuwait ended in defeat. But such was the hold of the dictatorship that Saddam managed to hang on to power. Saddam has even become a cult figure among German neo-Nazis, Le Pen's followers, and the Russian neofascists. This was not an accident: Saddam symbolizes everything they admire: leadership, brutality, aggression, and anti-Westernism.

Both Iraq and Syria are ruled by nationalists who distrust the fundamentalist endeavor to abolish Arab nation-states and create an Islamic supergovernment transcending the current borders. At the same time, while suppressing domestic opposition from these quarters, Saddam and Assad support a general Islamic revival. Although this may not be sufficient to pacify the radical clerics in the long run, it has defused any conflict for now. The Iranians and the various Muslim liberation fronts in other countries know, of course, that the former Ba'athists are not orthodox Muslims at heart but, instead, want a secular state. Both sides practice what is known in Shi'ite theology as *katman* (deception). Both sides know that the pronouncements of the other are not genuine, but as long as both are isolated and under pressure, such professed support is preferable to open enmity.

The soul-searching of Arab and Muslim intellectuals between secularism and fundamentalism and between Communism and fascism has been as tortuous as it has been fascinating. Even though there has been strong resistance against the ambitions of political Islam in countries such as Turkey, Egypt, Pakistan, and Bangladesh, and although elsewhere, such as in Algeria and Iran, the intelligentsia has voted with its feet, there has been a substantial Islamic resurgence in some circles. Many former Marxists have discovered a kindred fundamentalist spirit, and when Saddam Hussein invaded Kuwait, he had the support of a majority of North African and Middle Eastern intellectuals, even though they had few illusions about the true character of his "republic of fear."

Are these fundamentalist or pan-Islamic leanings genuine? We do not know whether the people's identification with Saddam and his regime is rooted in free-floating anti-Westernism solidarity with their fellow Arabs (or Muslims) or whether Saddam's anti-Westernism is merely part of deeper sympathy with a fascist weltanschauung. Or is it simply an intellectual fashion with roots no deeper than those of their earlier attachment to Marxism–Leninism? Perhaps, as in the case of the Russian right, these intellectuals feel that in the last resort they belong to the West (and secularism) rather than to an Asian world, whose true essence has never been defined. But they feel not completely at home with the West and therefore resent it. There might also be a good part of opportunism involved, the wish not to be excluded from a powerful, contemporary trend.

It could well be that motivation varies from country to country and from individual to individual.

Most of the comments on radical Islam so far refer to Shi'ite Islam as practiced in Iran. But there have been similar movements elsewhere, identical in some respects, different in others. Militant Sunni Islam movements have engaged in propaganda and mass action as well as terrorism. These movements also contain fascist elements, and they aim at the establishment of dictatorial and aggressive regimes. At the same time, they contain, by necessity, modern features—indispensable in the age of television, computer, and fax.

The Origins of Sunni Fundamentalism

Islamic fundamentalism originally surfaced before World War II in Egypt and India, as a movement seeking a religious revival or a cultural revolution. The decision to turn to politics came in the Middle East and North Africa only in the 1960s, more or less at the same time that Khomeini and his followers had reached similar conclusions. In Pakistan, the politicization of Islam had, by necessity, come even earlier, when the subcontinent split after gaining independence. A majority of Muslims wanted their own state (Pakistan) but not a theocracy. Accordingly, the chief advocates of Pakistan and its early leaders such as Muhammad Ali Jinnah and Liaquat Ali Khan were confirmed secularists.

The politicization of Islam has been explained as the consequence of the failure of secular nationalism. But this does not account, for instance, for its development in Egypt. Hisham Sharabi, a leading Arab-American expert, wrote in 1966 that "in the contemporary Arab world Islam has simply been bypassed." The statement shows little foresight, at the time it seemed quite apt and was shared by many observers. During the 1960s, Nasserism was riding high, and its gospel was spread through the Cairo-based Voice of the Arabs, from the Atlantic to the Indian Ocean. Under Nasser, the Muslim Brotherhood was violently suppressed and so had no influence. It gained notice only under Nasser's successors, when Islam became Egypt's state religion (1971) and the Islamic radicals were given a great deal of freedom (including much time on radio and television).

In Algeria the Islamists became an important factor following the Arabization of public life. As they did in Egypt, the Islamists turned against the authorities who had done so much to support their activities. Egypt's Anwar Sadat was killed in 1981, and Muhammed Boudiaf, Algeria's president, was murdered in 1992. The Israeli issue (that is, the inability of Muslim countries to eradicate the Jewish state) did not play a crucial role in these countries' radicalization: In the two countries in which political Islam made most progress, Iran and Algeria, Israel was a side issue.

The radicalization coincided with the liberalization of the economy, when income and standards of living were becoming increasingly unequal. This also took place at a time of growing resentment against the West as the old elites were showing signs of exhaustion.

This development was most obvious in Algeria, where the old leadership of the National Liberation Front (FLN), victorious in the struggle against the French, had little to show to its credit after thirty years of rule. The population explosion (as in Iran and in Egypt) resulted in a high percentage of young people, literate but not well educated, without employment and without hope. Millions streamed from the villages to the cities but failed to find work and shelter. In the 1980s the radical Islamic Salvation Front (FIS) was founded in Algeria. It includes a more liberal wing that sees itself as the successor of the early leadership of the Algerian revolution of the 1950s, advocating an "Algeria First" rather than pan-Islamist policy. But it also contains a more radical wing (the Salafiya, led by Sheikh Ali ben Jah), fighting for scriptural Islam.

The Algerian government made far-reaching concessions to the Islamists but no real effort to reach an agreement with the more moderate wing of the FIS when this was still possible. In addition, the government promised free elections at a time when it could least afford them, and then, when the electoral tide was turning against it, declared the elections null and void. The dilemma facing the Algerian government is insoluble. If the Islamists had gained power through victory in a free vote, these would have been the last free elections. According to the teachings of the radical Islamists, Shi'ite and Sunni alike, democracy is a mortal sin against God and religion. Therefore, with the victory of the radicals, the political rules would have been changed.

The FIS set up a countrywide network of branches, and initially received considerable financial support from Saudi Arabia and other Gulf states, on the mistaken assumption that the wealthy Arab rulers could buy their goodwill, or at least immunity from attack. The Algerian authorities, especially Boumedienne in the 1960s, had also provided help to the radicals. Afraid of the strong position of the extreme Left in the universities, they had given much assistance to the Islamists as a political counterweight. This put the Marxists on the defensive, and they were ultimately squeezed out by Islamic radicals, who promptly turned against those who had made their success possible. The rout of the Left in Algeria—and also in Egypt and other North African and Middle Eastern countries—was a result, too, of the collapse of the Soviet Union and world Communism. It was the organizational and financial support by the government, however, that played a crucial role.

The basic failure of the Algerian rulers was their inability to cope with the country's economic and social problems. In 1988 Algeria produced as much food as it had thirty years earlier, but its population had doubled. This was aggravated by a false strategy against the wrong enemy. After the arrest of the FIS's political leaders, the movement was weakened and lost some of its electoral support. As a result, the initiative passed to the Islamic terrorists, the Groupes islamistes armés (GIA) under Abdel Hak Layada, who later escaped to Morocco. This radical group has been active on a small scale since the 1970s, independently of the armed wing of the FIS, the MIA under "General Chebouti."

An assassination campaign has been launched against foreigners and also against supporters of the regime and intellectuals who do not support the Islamic extremists. Another chief target is the school system, with school buildings being bombed and teachers assassinated. These attacks have resulted in thousands of victims, and the inability of the authorities to suppress terrorism has discredited the regime.

The Algerian protest movement has certainly been religious in its expression, and it has been violent in its opposition to modernity and fanatical in its opposition to the authorities. But the deeper motivation is not as obvious as it is in Iran, for the clergy in Algeria has not played a role comparable to that in Iran. Most leading positions are taken by laymen. If the masses turned to the Islamists, it was more because of a feeling of having been betrayed by the old leadership, of poverty and resentment. It was the consequence of excessive expectation and a lack of elementary self-criticism, that is, an inability to understand that the failure of Algeria after liberation was by no means the fault of imperialism and modernism but the responsibility of leaders and masses alike.

The roots of Islamic radicalism in Egypt date back to the 1930s, but its political influence has been limited. Egypt has the same social tensions as Algeria does, but Egypt also has a tradition of greater tolerance that works against the preachers of fanaticism. Egyptian nationalism is also older and more deeply rooted. Various terrorist groups were active in the 1970s and 1980s, with a following among students, junior officers, and some professionals. But essentially, Islamic radicalism originated in particular geographical regions, such as the Assiut and Ninyah districts of Upper Egypt, and among the poor of Cairo. The radicals have not done well in the elections; the attacks against foreigners have been on a smaller scale; and the popular reaction has been unfavorable. The radicals have killed some leading representatives of the hated regime, but without seriously under-mining it.

Virtually all key positions in the radical movement in Iran are in the hands of clergymen, as they are in the Hisbollah, the Lebanese Shi'ite group that is a political party, militia, and terrorist organization all in one. Among the Sunni radicals in Egypt and Algeria, such direct intervention by the clergy has not been the rule. Sheikh Kish in Egypt was the most effective propagandist of fundamentalism (through the state radio and television), and in Algeria although religious dignitaries played an impor-tant role, it was not even remotely comparable to Khomeini's. These radical Sunni movements did not try to achieve a theocracy all at once. In the state they planned to have clergymen (the "doctors of Islamic law") as the advisers to the leaders, the ultimate arbiters but not the holders of power. In this way, the clerics would not immediately be made responsible for any setbacks. Despite all these brakes on their progress, however, Sunni radicalism does share with the Shi'ite's certain fascist traits, espe-cially the demagogic populism and the uncompromising rejection of de-mocracy and of free institutions in general, as a matter of religious princi-ple. The Sunnis are less totalitarian than the Shi'ites, but the Sunnis' fanatic belief in violence is not notably weaker than in Iran.

Some defenders of radical Islam in the West have argued that this anti-Westernism extends only to pornography and other excesses of free speech, not to political freedom per se. But Islamic radicalism opposes democracy because it tries to take away from Allah (and the *ulema*, his only rightful interpreters) what belongs to them by right and give freedom to the people, who are in no position to understand and exercise it. Such intolerance is incompatible with any form of political freedom. Radical Islam must prescribe and supervise every aspect of social life. Such intoler-ance extends to minorities (such as the Copts in Egypt) and foreigners in general. It leads to a belief in giant conspiracies against Islam directed by Christianity, other religions, and infidel political forces, and it also leads to a hatred of the Jews, not as Zionists but as a race. Radical Islam is a new religion characterized by an absence of love and true piety that have been replaced by the strict observation of religious rituals.

This trend is no more authentically Islamic than the fanatical sects of the Middle Ages were truly Christian or the Jewish fanatics truly Jewish. But the radical Islamists have attained greater power and political importance than any of these ever did in modern times. Despite being the most rigid and orthodox of the great world religions, Islam has also been, for long stretches in its history, the most tolerant and adaptable. This attempt to reinterpret it radically has little to do with religious authenticity but, rather, with the social, cultural, and political tensions prevailing in many Muslim countries and the political ambitions of the theocrats. It is a religious revival as much as a political upsurge, using religious language and motives and based on deeply rooted traditions.

The Islamists must realize that the seventh-century desert of Arabia can no longer serve as a model. Although it may still inspire fanaticism for at least a while, it cannot provide guidelines for life in urban surroundings, and it certainly cannot create places of work and housing. The ayatollahs need an elite to run state and society—military and police officers, scientists, physicians, and many others who have to be given equal status and at least some measure of freedom. Thus Islamic radicalism contains the seeds of its own destruction, and the more extreme its manisfestations are, the more complete its breakdown will be. Even though the seeds of clerical fascism exist in many parts of the world, the prospect that they will ever bloom is dim except in the Middle East and North Africa. The prospects are even less favorable in South Asia: Maududi, the principal Islamic thinker in Pakistan, always stressed that the methods of an Islamic state should not be totalitarian and that it should not be ruled by the *ulema*. And the bloody civil war in Afghanistan was much more about power and ethnic and tribal strife than about religion.[6] The same is true with regard to the re-Islamization in the former Soviet republics of Central Asia.

The emergence of radical Islam as a dominant factor in Central Asia, expected by many after the breakdown of the Soviet Union, has so far not materialized. In all the Central Asian republics the old elite, which had a leading position in the Communist regime, has stayed in power. It is not easy to describe this elite. Under Brezhnev, it was not Marxist–Leninist, and it certainly is not now. Instead, it is secular and nationalist in outlook and prescribes an authoritarian rule, a mixed economy, and, above all, the preservation of its privileges. This elite is challenged by an opposition consisting of various counterelites, some of them liberal in outlook (mainly the local intelligentsia) and others more nationalist and authoritarian (and anti-Russian) than the incumbents and also the Islamists. But these Islamists are not as radical as the Iranian (or Algerian) variety. The opposition to them has been strongest in Tadzhikistan, where a civil war has been raging since 1989. The Iranians have made considerable efforts to make inroads in Tadzhikistan, which, alone among the Central Asian republics, speaks Persian (but belongs to the Sunni rather than the Shi'ite creed). The Iranians have not had much success, and the Central Asian Islamists have always maintained that they do not want to force an Islamic society on a country. It is uncertain whether such statements reveal genuine moderation or are motivated by a feeling of weakness and a lack of popular enthusiasm. The religious revival in Central Asia and the Caucasus has not been much more intense than that in Russia. The warnings by the leadership in the Central Asian republics of a major "fundamentalist threat" were exaggerated, intended mainly to gain support for their rule from Moscow and, above all, the West.

The Central Asian republics will face enormous difficulties in the future, which may lead to either a new rapprochement with Russia or to further disintegration and chaos. Even though the emergence of clerical fascist regimes cannot be ruled out, it seems more likely that nationalist authoritarian regimes will maintain the upper hand.

The Russian extreme Right has been divided in its attitude toward Islamic radicalism. Some regard it as a major threat to Russian territorial integrity and national interests in Central Asia (where Russians are systematically expelled), in the Caucasus, and in the Balkans. But others dream of an alliance between Russian fascism and Islamic fundamentalism. In the words of Alexander Dugin, a prominent spokesman of the Russian parafascists:

> The Eurasians believe that fundamental Islam, with its anti-materialism, its rejection of a banking system and of international usury, and its rejection of international economics as a system, is their ally. . . . The only geopolitical enemy of Russians and Muslims is the United States with its liberal, cosmopolitan, antireligious and anti-traditional system.[7]

Such eccentric views should not, however, be taken too seriously, for the aspirations of these two extremist movements collide on most basic issues: Islamic radicals want full freedom (including separatism) for the Tatars and other Muslim minorities inside Russia much more than the abolition of "usury" or the banking system. The idea of a Moscow–Teheran ideological axis is far fetched, to say the least. And the Russian extremists of the Right who advocate an "Islamic orientation" also support their Serbian brethren in their endeavor to exterminate Muslim Bosnia, one of the many contradictions in their policy.

Political Religion

Political religion has played a disturbing role in various geopolitical conflicts; it certainly has not been among the peacemakers in Yugoslavia. The Serbian Orthodox Church has supported the struggle for a Greater Serbia, considering Catholics and Muslims as its sworn enemies. Moreover, the Catholic Church has never apologized for the Croats' massacre of hundreds of thousands of Orthodox Serbs during World War II and has fully supported the intransigent demands by the Croat leadership. In the words of neutral observer: "Idols of Nazism and fundamentalism have escaped control like an evil genie, and now the Church is confronted with idolatry."[8] When Alija Izetbegovic, the current president of Bosnia, was in prison in 1970, he wrote an essay entitled "The Islamic Declaration," in which he declared that there could be neither peace nor coexistence between the Islamic religion and non-Islamic social and political institutions, that once the Muslims made up more than 50 percent of any population, the country should become an Islamic republic. But when Bosnia became independent, such views were not the official doctrine. Gradually however, under pressure from Serbs and Croats, exclusivist Islamic policies have prevailed.

The fact that the churches in the former Yugoslavia gave unreserved support to nationalist passions contributed to separation and the outbreak of war. Although they did not identify with fascist doctrine and practice, they nonetheless paved the way toward dictatorship and genocidal acts and thus to the creation of a political climate in which fascist policies were accepted as a matter of course.

Kemal Atatürk's secular reforms in Turkey in the 1920s provoked Islamic opposition from the very beginning, and in Turkey in the last decade there has been a spectacular resurgence of the Welfare (National Salvation) Party, proclaiming Islamism on its banners. Although support for political Islam is stronger in the countryside than in the big cities, the party did win control of Istanbul and Ankara in 1994.

Even during World War II, there were parafascist groups in Turkey, usually in a pan-Turanian guise. More recently, right-wing radicalism has appeared in both religious organizations and nationalist parties. During the 1970s, Turkey was the site of almost constant armed violence between the far Right and the extreme Left. More recently, the terrorism—especially against intellectuals—has been the work of fascist and religious fanatic groups supported by Iran and/or Arab radicals. The fact that these extremists' money, weapons, and usually also ideas have come from abroad, has not increased the popularity of their cause. The other main source of support for the extreme Right has been the Turkish diaspora, mainly in Germany, where the cultural clash between the traditionalists and Western civilization has led to radicalization.

Even though the heirs of Atatürk have retreated and made many concessions to the Islamists, it is still true that Turkey's modern sector is more deeply rooted than in other Muslim countries. Even Turkish fundamentalism, a small fringe, is not extreme measured by the standards of Iran and the Islamists in the Arab countries. Minorities have been persecuted in Turkey, but not because of their religion. Rather, nationalism is the crucial plank of the official Turkish ideology, and this makes a fascist break-through unlikely. Furthermore, the traditional extreme Right in Turkey has not been fundamentalist.

The extreme Right and the fundamentalists have collaborated in the past, but their leaders' conflicting ambitions and basic doctrinal differences have prevented so far a truly close and lasting cooperation. And anti-Westernism is no longer a monopoly of the parafascist forces, which makes it difficult for them to outflank the center from the right.

The secular state has come under attack in many parts of the globe, with those attacking it differing in both direction and motivation. There is no "fundamentalist International," just as there was no Fascintern. Religious fundamentalists in the United States battle secular humanism, and the lunatic fringe engages in acts of terrorism against physicians performing abortions. But even the most fanatical evangelicals do not dream of estab-lishing fascist organizations. Rather, their belief is based on despair, the assumption that the last judgment is near, that an immense disaster will occur, and that Christ will choose the elect, take them away from earth, and then return to build the Kingdom of Heaven. In this view of the world there is no room for storm troopers and Blackshirts.

In Russia there has always been a deep fundamentalist streak in the Orthodox Church, as the church has never undergone reform and remains fundamentalist to this day. But even the most extreme preachers of chauvin-ism, fanaticism, and the persecution of other religions and minorities—even those identifying themselves with the extreme Right, such as the late Metropolitan Ioann of Petersburg and Ladoga—do not openly advocate fascism. Ioann and his followers may give their blessing to those working to establish an aggressive dictatorial regime. But their ideal is the Black Hundred of 1906, not a modern fascist state.

The most militant fundamentalist group in the Russian church is the Union of Orthodox Brotherhoods. One of its leading members is Valeri Skurlatov, a figure with a rich political past. A prominent young Commu-nist, he subsequently became a spokesman of National Bolshevism and paganism and a popularizer of the pre-Christian mythical book of *Vles*. In the 1960s, he wrote a "moral code of behavior," widely regarded at the time as *fascisant*. His religious conversion could be genuine, but it is equally possible that like many other national Communists he came to regard the church as a political haven and recruiting ground.

On the whole, the church leadership has given support to the extreme Right and even fascist groups, within the limits of political prudence. It has defrocked democratic priests but has not reprimanded Metropolitan Ioann and those like him, even in cases of blatant racial incitement. The Russian Orthodox Church has always respected power, and it reached the conclusion long ago that all ideological considerations aside, the "patriots" were stronger than the democrats.

A Russian observer commenting on the demonstrations of orthodox fundamentalists wrote:

> Some call themselves patriots, others openly admit that they are fascists, yet others are still loyal to the Communist slogans. It is a great mystery what kind of new Russia is this going to be—portraits of Stalin in one corner and the last Tsar in the other, the banners of proletarian revolution side by side with the gonfalons of the religious processions.[9]

Some leading members of the Russian far Right have zealously advocated a common front of Russian Orthodox and Islamic fundamentalism. Even under Brezhnev, the "progressive character" of the Khomeini regime (that is, its anti-Western attitude) was welcomed. Such speculations, shared by some princes of the Orthodox Church, ignored the antagonism toward Russians in the Central Asian republics, which resulted in the expulsion of hundred of thousands of Russian residents. Nonetheless, the Orthodox Church still regards Catholicism as its implacable enemy and Islam as a potential ally.

Since the 1960s, there has been an upsurge of Jewish fundamentalism in Israel and parts of the diaspora. It has taken a variety of forms—messianism; a revival of orthodox religion; extreme anti-Zionism; the emergence of all kinds of charismatic rabbis, with some of them performing miracles; and aggressive racialist chauvinism among part of Israel's religious establishment. After the 1967 war, religion became politicized to a much greater degree than ever before. But the movement remained divided, with the Sephardic rabbis generally taking a more moderate line than their Ashkenazi (European) colleagues. This politicization of religion has been the bane of Israeli politics. Although the religious parties are small, given the multiplicity of political parties, their influence is considerable. However corrupt, their goodwill must be bought by their senior partners. This has strengthened their position, resulting in the imposition of religious commandments by administrative fiat and also undermining whatever respect there might have been for political religion outside the clerical camp.

At the fringe of this movement, there have been terrorist as well as openly racialist groups aiming at "ethnic cleansing"—before the term gained wide currency elsewhere. In extreme cases, the inspiration is apocalyptic—the redemption is near, but the coming of the Messiah could be hastened through a provocation such as blowing up the mosque on the Temple Mount in Jerusalem, and thus bringing about Armageddon, a general (final) war between Jews and Muslims that would lead to the coming of the Messiah. This belief is in contrast to fascism, whose main article of faith is that the Messiah had already arrived in the person of the Führer and the Duce.

Given the explosive nature of the Middle Eastern situation, even the action of one person, or a small group of madmen, could have horrible consequences. Religious fanaticism is one of the mainsprings of communal violence in many parts of the world, including Northern Ireland and the Indian subcontinent: It shares with fascism its intolerance, aggressiveness, and disregard of human rights and democratic institutions. But in contrast to fascism, religious fanaticism is regressive.

Buddhism has been traditionally the most tolerant, cosmopolitan, and antinationalist of the major world religions. For a long time, the image of Buddhism in the West was shaped by the nonviolence preached by Gandhi and before him by Aurobindo, Vivekenanda, and other religious thinkers. But Gandhi was assassinated; so was Indira Gandhi, Rajiv Gandhi, her son, and a Sri Lankan prime minister. Since independence, South Asia has been the scene of ethnic strife and communal riots as often as, if not more often than, other parts of the world. Since the early 1980s, there has been a growing aggressiveness on the Indian subcontinent on the part of ethnic and religious groups. This revival, however, has been more nationalist than religious in character. The extremist Hindu movements, the RSS, and the Jana Sangh Party (later the BJP) made great strides in the elections of the 1980s, emerging as the leading opposition party in the country and a partner in governing coalitions in several states in north and west India.

The BJP seeks a great India rather than the export of Buddhism. If the party's members consider the Muslims inferior, it is not so much because of their religion but because they believe them to be culturally backward and intolerant. The Hindu far Right is attractive to the lower middle class outside the big cities. Indeed, its youth organization has been compared with the Hitler Youth (a comparison that must seem far fetched to those familiar with Nazi Germany), and some leaders of this party have not been offended by this comparison with Nazism. Anti-Westernism and a disdain of democracy are prominent in these circles, as is the resentment against having to use the English language. But the real victims of such intolerance are the minorities, like the Muslims.

As the Right sees it, the Muslims should not be expelled, but they should not enjoy equal civil rights, either. According to RSS–BJP doctrine, the Indian nation is an organic unit; its national soul reveals a divine purpose; class differences must be reduced; and national solidarity must be restored. All this strikes chords familiar to students of fascist ideology in Europe. True, there are differences, inasmuch as the cult of the leader is not encouraged in India as it was in Europe, and politicians in general are not held in high esteem. The true inspiration for a religious–nationalist revival would be spiritual, and the total revolution would be cultural, not political. However, once the RSS–BJP became more active in politics, these lofty principles were often disregarded.

In regard to Tamil–Sinhalese relations, it is likewise nearly impossible to discern where religion ends and nationalist inspiration begins. Cultural–social factors have been decisive in fueling the ethnic conflict. Most Sinhalese consider Tamils to be evil, and vice versa. Far from acting as an inhibiting factor, religion has contributed to hatred and violence. The killers of the Tamil Tigers have more in common with Pol Pot's legions in Cambodia than with any known religion.

In the case of the Sikhs (few in number, 13 million in all of India but very active in every respect), the situation is even more complicated. Ethnically the Sikh are Hindu, and the victims of Sikh terrorism have been moderate Sikhs as well as Indians. The Sikhs' violence has been said to be defensive in character, based on a desire to preserve their traditional way of life, their weapons, their unshorn hair, and their foreskin, and not to be "enslaved" by the Hindus. But as in the case of fascism and of radical Islam, "righteous killing" is not just permitted, it is a sacred duty.

These and some other movements have been capable of stirring up religious and nationalist frenzy, causing communal rioting and even civil war. But popular support has often been less than overwhelming. The ascent of India's RSS–BJP was halted in the 1990s. Islamic fundamentalists, being a minority of just over 10 percent in India, cannot possibly hope for a theocratic state. Pakistan underwent Islamization in the 1970s, but political power has still not passed into the hands of the Jama'at, the chief religious organization. Furthermore, the presence of many sects has prevented the emergence of a true Islamic mass movement. In Bangladesh, the politicians have appeased the Islamic radicals in various ways, but the masses have shown no great enthusiasm for them, since the message of radical Islam does not resonate with Bengali culture.

The emergence of fascism in Iran and India has been explained against the background of social and economic trends—as mainly a movement of revolt by the middle class, the Bazar in Iran, and the shopkeepers in India (the BJP has frequently been called a party of shopkeepers).[10]

These groups are said to have felt threatened as the result of rapid industrialization and rapid social change in general (hence the parallels with pre-Nazi Germany). The Iranian merchants felt threatened by price controls and the arrests in the 1970s, whereas the Indian merchants, on the contrary, felt menaced by the abolition of controls by a government that had previously protected them. It is true that the Bazar made common cause with the radical clerics in Teheran and that the attempts by the

Indian Congress to improve the position of the scheduled castes such as the Untouchables, who constitute more than half of the population, upset many Hindus. The Congress's action had a direct impact on the chances of Hindu graduates for employment in government, and it could explain the growth of opposition to the Congress and the emergence of an authoritarian movement whose purpose is to preserve the rule of the present elite. But since the Muslims are the principal enemy of the Indian far Right, this explanation is not persuasive. The Indian merchants must know that communal riots are not good for business, except perhaps for glaziers and carpenters; indeed, extremism in any form is not good for business. Rather, Indian business prefer a regime both nationalist and protectionist, which has been the policy to a greater or lesser degree of every Indian government since 1948, and so there is no need for a fascist or any other extremist regime.

Likewise, the mosque in Iran was a natural ally of the Bazar, but only during the transition period, before and after the ousting of the shah. The kind of regime installed by Khomeini, though protecting the Bazaris from foreign competition, harmed them in other ways. In brief, although economic and social trends do, of course, play a role in the rise of fascist movements, they are seldom the most decisive factor; the interests of Iranian and Indian shopkeepers could also have been served by nonfascist political movements. Nationalist–religious beliefs and passions have a momentum of their own; the underclass in the big cities of the East has its own agenda and is not a force easily given to manipulation. In India, movements resembling fascism have primarily political and cultural causes, not economic grievances or religious ones. Even the saffron, a quasi-uniform of sashes and caps adopted by the Indian far Right, originally the symbol of religious asceticism, has become a nationalist military cultural emblem.

A review of the global resurgence of religious fundamentalism reveals a number of features it has in common with fascism, such as the rejection of modernism and secularism. All the fundamentalist movements are populist, claiming to strive not just for purity and adherence to the holy writs but also for social justice. Some movements are more aggressive than others, believing in a holy mission to impose their way of life and also to export it to other countries. Some fundamentalists are inspired by nationalism, even if they are not always aware of it or have combined radical religion and nationalism, whereas others reject political borders as arbitrary. Some believe in full-fledged theocracy, and others accept a government of politicians who are not clerics, provided it is based on religious law. Some clerics openly express contempt for the masses ("more benighted than cattle"). Khomeini and Mottahari, his pupil, belong to this school: The masses need benevolent rulers since they do not know what is best for them. Other Islamists have been extremely suspicious of clergymen in politics. In sum, if there are many doctrinal differences among the various fundamentalist sects, there are even more in practice.

Strong affinities exist between the more radical varieties of fundamentalism and national socialism, in the insistence by fundamentalists on active participation rather than passive acceptance of the new order. This participation refers to the hostility to Western democracy and the Enlightenment, the subordination of the individual to the "community," the belief in a divine mission, and the wide and intensive use of terror and propaganda. It refers to the obligatory censorship and the relegation of women to an inferior or marginal place in public life. Radical fundamentalism offers no freedom for religious and national minorities. Like fascism, radical fundamentalism is a movement of young males, in the Middle East as much as in Sri Lanka and elsewhere.

This list of common or similar features could be continued. That there are historical and cultural differences between prewar fascism and contemporary radical fundamentalism is obvious. But substantial differences existed even in European fascism in the 1930s.

The means of indoctrination, social control, and repression are much greater now than in the Middle Ages. But at the same time the temptations of the secular world are infinitely greater. Radical Islam has had considerable political impact in various parts of the world, but it is doubtful whether the Iranian model will find many more imitators. In any case, it will be subject to considerable routinization, the necessity of making compromises, the erosion of faith, and the growing disparity between religious teaching and reality. At the same time its inability to cope with the economic and social problems of the modern world has perpetuated the crisis which has made the rise of this movement possible. What will happen if political religion fails? There is an almost endless number of possibilities, ranging from an anticlerical backlash to the emergence of newer and even more radical political religions.

In the contemporary world, the means of repression in the hands of a resolute dictatorship are such that it can maintain its hold for a considerable time, even though its moral and political bankruptcy may be apparent, provided that it does not engage in war and does not lose its self-confidence. All this means that for a long time to come there will be a breeding ground for new varieties of fascism.

But why fascism, why not religious fanaticism or populism or radical political religion or militant fundamentalism? All these various phenomena are related, some more closely than others, and in the modern world all extreme manifestations of radical politics are bound to end up to some degree within the fascist orbit. Despite its affinities with other radical movements, Communism cannot fill this void whereas national socialism can. Secular political religions, such as fascism, and nonsecular ones, such as radical Islam, do, of course, have differences. They may fight each other, but students of politics know that populism can turn left or right with equal ease according to economic and social conditions, cultural traditions, and the general political climate. Two or three generations ago converts to Marxism frequently had an orthodox religious upbringing; more recently we have witnessed the opposite trend, of Marxists attracted to radical religion.

Communism is changing, and in a new guise, stripped of its atheist elements and nationalist rather than international, it could again be a serious contender in the struggle for power in various countries. Such Communism reborn would be similar, however, in many respects to a revived fascism or to radical religion.

What are the underlying reasons for the upturn in the fortunes of political religions? Studying the timeless messages of Buddha, Jesus Christ, and the Prophet Muhammad is of little help in this context. The teachings of the great religions can be interpreted in a hundred different ways, and what the fundamentalists have selected out of the Bible and the Koran for their purposes has much more to do with present conditions and moods than with the holy writ. Religious longing, transcendental belief, utopianism—secular and religious—and the need for order are as much part of the human condition as are violence, envy, and aggression. It has been argued that all religion involves violence, but it is also true that beyond a certain stage of human development, violence needs religion, political or secular to justify it. Deprivation, frustration, and holy rage all have been used to explain violence, but this is not of much help in explaining why some societies have been less violent than others and why fascism (or terrorism or radical fundamentalism) has prevailed in some places but not in others. Why frustration and rage? Is it because a society is a victim of oppression or because its members are less gifted, work less hard, are less conscientious, or are less capable of putting their house in order? Social conditions play a role, but Germany in 1933 was not the poorest and most disadvantaged country. Ambitions, resentment, and a feeling of superiority are necessary ingredients, but it is difficult to account for them. What Hitler wrote in *Mein Kampf* about the role of hatred in all great upheavals was the instinctive recognition of a bitter truth.

The *Sinnkrise*, the general cultural crisis affecting many societies for two centuries or more, is an important factor, and it has resulted in all kinds of panaceas, ranging from New Age to religious fundamentalism. They serve as ersatz religions, as the time of true, spontaneous, spiritual belief seems to have passed with the ancient and medieval world: The devil's temptations in the modern world are too pervasive, and there are too many man-made technological miracles. Although fundamentalist religion in the contemporary age should mean withdrawal from the world, this is not a viable option. We are left therefore with nationalist–religious upsurges in backward and poor countries, with guerrilla warfare and terrorism. But this the Communists in Asia also achieved, at least for a while.

Political religion obviously answers certain needs and longings, some positive and some destructive. If it did not, its appeal would have been more limited. Political religion also imposes order and discipline and provides a common bond. But fundamentalism, Islamic and other, still has a impossible task: Economic and social developments cannot be unmade, and education cannot be limited to the religious sphere. Hence it needs to adopt techniques of rule that in the past were used by fascism. Such a fusion of political religion, nationalism, and fascism can fanaticize the masses, but whether it can do so for any length of time remains to be seen.

Russia

The prospects of the extreme Right in the former Soviet Union and Soviet bloc seem better than in most other parts of the world. A political and ideological vacuum was created by the demise of the old order; the roots of democratic institutions are weak; and all these countries face major social tensions and economic difficulties. In Russia, as in Germany after 1918, there is a strong nationalist resentment following the loss of empire and of territories that had been an integral part of Russia for hundreds of years.

True, there are also countervailing factors: The Communist regime was in important respects quite similar to a fascist regime, with its one-party system, official doctrine, central role of propaganda, and political police. But the old system was unpopular, and although many people may favor a strong government, even a neo-Communist one, they do not want the excesses of leader worship, terror, and propaganda.

Pure Nazism has even less appeal than pure Stalinism. The Nazi attack on Russia in 1941 caused untold losses. The Poles and other Slavic people have no reason to be grateful to the Nazis and their racist theories of eastern *Untermenschen*. As a result, there are few outright neo-Nazis in Russia and Eastern Europe, and most of the far Right's leaders recognize that in the post-Communist era, different approaches and new ideas must be used. Furthermore, the consequences of Communist rule cannot be ignored, as certain attitudes inculcated by Communism are deeply ingrained and so have to be embraced by the extreme Right. The majority of the population shuns radical movements; it wants peace, order, and prosperity even more than national glory.

Russia has a prerevolutionary, prefascist tradition, that of the Black Hundred, which was formed around the turn of the century. Some of its basic ideas have endured until today. The Black Hundred was not exactly a fascist party because it greatly depended on the church and regarded its support for the monarchy as its main task. But the Union of the Russian People (its official name) was one of the first political mass movements in Russia, in contrast to the small elitist groups of the extreme Right that preceded it. Its propaganda was populist, denouncing liberal–Jewish capitalism as well as the corrupt administration that prevented the tsar from communicating directly with his subjects. It was xenophobic and racialist and believed in a global Masonic–Jewish conspiracy (*zhido-masonstvo*). It consisted mainly of the urban lower classes, with a sprinkling of aristocrats. The union was stronger in southern and western Russia than in the north and east and received financial subsidies from the government. The Black Hundred hated liberals as much as socialist revolutionaries and all ethnic minorities. It was no accident that the *Protocols of the Elders of Zion*, the bible of modern anti-Semitism, was concocted by Russians of this persuasion in the 1890s, even though it achieved wide publicity only after the revolution.

Vladimir Purishkevich, a flamboyant rabble-rouser and the Black Hundred's most gifted leader, was regarded by latter-day historians as the first Russian fascist. But the Black Hundred were by no means alone in spreading messages that were later taken up by modern-style fascists. Certain leading members of the Russian Orthodox Church, such as Jon of Kronshtadt, broadly sympathized with their ideas and propagated them in their sermons and writings, with an emphasis on the evil doings of Satan rather than the blessings of God. With the Russian Revolutions of 1917, the Black Hundred ceased to exist, but the tradition of the extreme Right survived among Russian émigrés.

Many early Bolshevik leaders were Jews and foreigners, and this fueled the belief among anti-Communists of an anti-Russian conspiracy and the need to combat it by violent means. By 1935 most of the "alien elements" who had participated in the revolution had been thrown out of positions of Communist leadership and been replaced by a new native elite. This undermined to a certain extent the arguments of the Russian far Right. But on the other hand, fascist impulses were renewed by the upsurge of national socialist movements all over Europe. Fascism seemed the wave of the future, hence the sympathies for such parties among Russian émigrés, particular the younger generation. Their mission was made more difficult, however, by Stalin, whose policy in crucial respects resembled that of the fascist leaders. The one major exception was ideology. In theory, Communism was still internationalist, but in fact it reintroduced nationalism through the back door and made "cosmopolitanism" a deadly sin. Furthermore, Stalin made Russia a more powerful state than it had ever been in its history.

All this complicated the task of Russian émigré fascists, and it is no surprise that some of their leaders recanted at the end of their lives or even chose to return to the Soviet Union. Seen in retrospect, the ideas developed by the Russian émigré fascists in the 1920 and after were less important than some of the postwar trends inside the Soviet Union, such as the emergence of Soviet (Russian) patriotism, "anti-Zionism," and eventually the rise of a "Russian party." Despite the customary genuflections before Marx and Lenin, beyond them lay a new ideology of national Bolshevism. This Russian party had its own literary journals and cultural associations, and even though from time to time, it was called to order by the authorities for having strayed too far from the official party line, it had powerful protectors among the party leadership, the KGB, and the army command.

This development was interrupted by *glasnost* and *perestroika*. Without Mikhail Gorbachev's reforms, this new ideology might indeed have gradually replaced the old regime, and the Soviet Union would have become in theory what it had been in practice for a long time—a national socialist dictatorship. There were, of course, differences between the pre-1987 Soviet Union and the historical fascist regimes: The economy was in the hands of the state, and there was virtually no legal private sector. Religion was barely tolerated, and in view of the Soviet Union's multiethnic makeup, there could be no openly racist doctrine, whatever the Communist leaders might privately think on this subject.

This, then, in broadest outline was the situation when *perestroika* was introduced in 1985/1986. The first and loudest group with clearly fascist leanings to emerge was Pamyat (Memorial), which had in fact been founded as a cultural club a few years earlier. In the prevailing climate, it could not reveal its true aims but limited its activities to lectures on cultural topics and the restoration of historical monuments. It was led by a former actor and photographer named Dimitri Vasiliev, whose dramatic appearances in public meetings soon alerted the media, both local and foreign, that a movement quite unprecedented had arrived on the Russian political scene. Vasiliev, who described himself as a "nonparty Bolshevik," savagely attacked "Zionists" and Freemasons who, as he put it, were responsible for all of Russia's misfortunes. He frequently quoted the *Protocols,* and for good measure he also attacked American-style discotheques, alcoholism, and satanism. His followers—of whom there were no more than a few hundred—wore black uniforms, jackboots, and various insignia, some dating back to the Tsarist period and others newly created.

Vasiliev did not openly attack the Communist authorities, and the party organs preferred to ignore Pamyat. Right-wing intellectuals did not join Pamyat, but they also did not dissociate themselves from it. As they saw it, some of Pamyat's activities were constructive and deserving of support.

Vasiliev's appearance was often open to ridicule, and despite his professional training as an actor, he was far less accomplished a performer than Vladimir Zhirinovsky, who made his appearance a few years later. Vasiliev had no great aspirations and lacked both education and organizational talent. He made grotesque statements that shocked the unsophisticated but were merely derided by the educated, however sympathetic they might have been to Pamyat. With no political instincts, Vasiliev could never quite make up his mind whether he wanted to lead a cultural association, a political party, or a popular movement. Furthermore, his performances were too repetitive: If one had attended one or two Pamyat happenings, there was no need to go to a third. In 1989/1990, as Soviet rule weakened, Pamyat gradually broke away from national Bolshevism and joined the camp of the church and the monarchists.

Vasiliev was frequently asked about his feelings toward Hitler and Nazism, but his replies were always contradictory and ambiguous. Yes, he approved of various aspects of fascist policies, but no, they were not applicable to contemporary Russia. He was not too well informed about the subject. Thus if there were similarities between Pamyat and some prewar fascist groups, it was not because Vasiliev had copied them.

Even earlier, Pamyat had undergone a series of internal divisions, so that in the end half a dozen Pamyats existed side by side. To some people, Vasiliev was not radical enough but seemed to constitute a loyal opposition to Yeltsin. Others had doubts about his qualities as a leader. The other Pamyat factions fared no better. Although some of them continued to exist, they were outflanked on all sides. Finally, Pamyat was overtaken by various right-wing organizations, and while Vasiliev continued to gatecrash the meetings of other patriotic groups, he became an embarrassment to those he wanted to embrace.

Seen in historical perspective, the role of Pamyat is that of precursor: It was the first in a field that quickly became crowded. Many future leaders of the parafascist groups that appeared in the 1990s had started their political career in this organization. But all of them left when Vasiliev did not succeed in transforming himself in a respectable leader and his group into an acceptable political movement. This was clearly beyond his abilities and vision. Pamyat was too old-fashioned in content; the post-Communist groups of the extreme Right needed something better to advance their cause than a rehash of the Black Hundred and the *Protocols*. Although these had been sufficient in 1910, they had only a limited appeal eighty years later; Pamyat seemed almost irrelevant in the new situation.

To understand post-Communist fascism, we should remember that under Stalin and his successors, fascism and Nazism had been forbidden subjects in the Soviet Union. Accordingly, these movements, their ideology, their social origins, their leaders, their propaganda, and terrorist methods were never seriously studied. In the Brezhnev era a few thrillers and television series appeared about the (fictional) exploits of KGB agents who had infiltrated the Nazi leadership during wartime. But this was about all the average Soviet citizen knew about Nazism, unless, of course, he or she had had a personal encounter with Nazi rule in the occupied territories. Furthermore, the term *fascism* was used indiscriminately. According to Stalin's famous definition, the Social Democrats were fascism's left wing, and Wall Street was fascist or at least controlled the fascists. But a veil of silence was drawn over the real fascism, not so much because the Soviet rulers were afraid that Hitler and Mussolini, decades after their demise, would attract many followers in the Soviet Union, but because there were so many similarities between the two systems. A book on the Nazi Party could easily be read as a veiled critique of the Communist Party, and a study of the Gestapo could be interpreted as a discussion of the KGB. Both regimes were stridently nationalist; both opposed cultural modernism; and both systems adopted a new *nomenklatura*.

In brief, even a purely descriptive account of fascism would have shown that the Soviet system had more in common with it than either had with "bourgeois democracy." It could always, of course, be argued that these similarities were purely superficial, since the Soviet Union was the state of workers and peasants. But it is not certain that this explanation would have satisfied everyone and might even have prompted people to ask awkward questions. Thus the Soviet public, even the educated, were quite ignorant of Nazism, except that they knew that it was a barbarous regime that had attacked the Soviet Union in World War II and caused millions of deaths and much damage.

Early manifestations of profascist feelings under *glasnost* were limited to small groups such as Pamyat, with an emphasis on anti-Semitism, military training, hatred of the intelligentsia, chauvinism, and the adulation of the old tsarist regime and its symbols and key figures. In addition, there were gangs of young people playing "SS and Gestapo" rather than robbers and detectives. All this naturally did not amount to fully fledged fascism. But in a variety of ways, through many dozens of journals, the tradition of the Black Hundred was revived. The émigré literature on the Judeao–Masonic conspiracy against the Russian people found readers in Russia, as did the writings and speeches of Hitler, Goebbels, and Alfred Rosenberg.

This appeared inexplicable, if not perverse to most observers: The Nazis had been, after all, the enemies not just of the Communists but also of the Russian people. So how could Russian nationalists find their new idol in the Third Reich? But such a reaction was by no means unique. Hitler had despised African Americans, and yet Louis Farrakhan and some other black leaders had more than a little admiration for some of Hitler's policies. Even a few French and Dutch neo-Nazis admired the Third Reich—there is no madness that will not attract at least some people, including victims of aggression. Furthermore, only a few of Hitler's admirers in Russia and Eastern Europe suggested copying Nazism to the letter. Rather, they were intrigued and attracted by the concept of a strong leader, of a dictatorship that got things done, of the appeal to aggressive nationalism and other "healthy instincts." They were fascinated by the marching columns in uniform, the anti-Semitism, the belief in conspiracy theories. Other aspects of Nazism they simply ignored.

Furthermore, the thinkers of Russian fascism took their cue as much from the (French) New Right as from historical fascism, and they also drew heavily on native Russian traditions. And last, a so-called instinctive fascism attracted people who were not particularly interested in the history or doctrine of the Nazis and who did not care greatly about the Black Hundred, either, but to whom extreme nationalism, the idea of a single-party dictatorship, propaganda, and violence came naturally. To some degree, this had always been the case; that is, democracy was an innovation that seemed not to work in Russia. Thus new political groups appeared in Russia that had pronounced fascist features, even if those concerned were not quite aware of it. Like Molière's bourgeois who had always talked prose without being aware of it, those on the extreme Right in Russia had always believed in something akin to fascism without knowing it. The main difference was that now, for the first time, they could openly express their thoughts and longings.

An assessment of neofascist and parafascist doctrines and movements in post-Communist Russia is difficult because there are not always clear divisions between the conservative "respectable" Right and the extremists and between the far Right and the neo-Communists. After the initial liberal–democratic upsurge in 1989/1990, Russian politics shifted to the right. At the same time the growing polarization found its most striking expression in the attempted coup against Gorbachev in 1991 and again in the storming of the White House in October 1993. Although there were obvious differences between the mainstream conservatives and "patriots" (such as

Baburin and Aksiuchits) and the wild men of the far Right, they also cooperated; each needed the other against their common enemy.

There were even more disagreements between the neo-Communists and the Right. A figure like the academician Igor Shafarevich, a well-known mathematician who had devoted most of his life to denouncing socialism, could not regard with enthusiasm the revival of Leninism among his patriotic allies, the paeans of the October revolution, and the achievements of seventy years of Soviet rule.

And yet a rapprochment has taken place between the anti-Communist Right and the neo-Communists, on a doctrinal level and also for practical reasons. The extreme Right recognized, albeit a bit reluctantly, that if it opposed liberalism, democracy, and capitalism, it would have to advocate a state-controlled economy and perhaps even state ownership, such as under Communism. The Communists, on the other hand, quickly realized that they had to drop the internationalist character of their ideology and to opt for national socialism. Both the extreme Right and the neo-Communists wanted a strong Russian state. Above all, they faced a common enemy and understood that they would have to join forces in order to prevail in the political struggle. Many differences remained, but between 1991 and 1995 the Right became more socialist (or at least collectivist) and the Left more nationalistic. The dividing lines began to blur.

Of the many right-wing extremist groups that appeared with the advent of *glasnost*, most have been short lived and limited to one or a few localities. They split, merged, changed their names, disappeared, and reappeared again under a different name. They published perhaps two hundred newspapers at one time or another, which came out at irregular intervals. But a handful of them, such as *Molodaya gvardiya, Nash sovremennik*, and, above all, Prokhanov's *Den*, which was banned after the events of October 1993 and reappeared under the name *Zavtra*, have a sizable readership. The extreme right wing is, however, hopelessly divided on ideology as a result of its leaders' conflicting ambitions, but altogether, it is not a negligible force. Gradually, though, the number of these groups has declined as its members have joined bigger organizations.

The extreme Right's most important party has been Vladimir Zhirinovsky's Liberal Democratic Party, and its sudden success was striking. The history of the party is the biography of its leader, as in the case of Hitler and Mussolini. One of six children, Zhirinovsky was born in Alma Ata, Kazakhstan, in 1946. His mother was a White Russian; his father, a Jewish lawyer from Lvov. His early years—he left Alma Ata at age eighteen—were a time of frustration and a lack of love; Zhirinovsky describes this period openly and in revealing detail in an autobiography published in 1993 (*Poslednyi brosok na yug*). Zhirinovsky studied Near Eastern languages in Moscow, and served in the army in the Caucasus. Later he also studied law and worked for a Moscow publishing firm.

Zhirinovsky's first venture into politics under *glasnost* was tentative, but he knew that he wanted to found a new party and be its leader. He appeared on the fringe of various democratic and oppositionist groups— even for a while among Jewish activists—and he took part in various initiatives and coalitions. In 1989 he failed to be elected to the Moscow City Council, and when his party was registered in early 1991 he had difficulty finding five hundred signatories in eight republics. His break-through came later that year in the Russian presidential elections, when 6 million Russians voted for him. Zhirinovsky's greatest success came in the general elections of December 1993 when more people voted for him than for any other single party.

This was a phenomenon without precedence in Russian history and has few, if any, parallels in any other country. It was, above all, a personal success; true, he had a "shadow cabinet" as well as a "supreme council," some of them army officers, a few economists and engineers, two law-yers, a physician, two journalists, and several businessmen. However, these deputies were not nationally known; only Zhirinovsky was fetching the masses. Zhirinovsky called for the reunification of the old Soviet Empire, including the Baltic republics and possibly Poland and Finland. ("We must force our republics to return"). He reasoned that if Russia stopped trading with them, they would collapse and beg to be readmitted to the empire. But in the future, they would be mere provinces. He was willing to release the Caucasian and Central Asian republics because he felt there was no profit in keeping them. Moldova and the Baltic repub-lics, he declared, would be reduced to the size of Liechtenstein, and the Ukraine would have to surrender all its eastern and southern regions. If economic measures were not sufficient, nuclear waste would be buried along the borders of the Baltic republics so that all the people would die of radiation and disease. Two weeks after Zhirinovsky became president of Russia, the Baltic republics would cease to exist—their lights would be switched off. The Caucasus had been a wilderness before the Russians had come, and it would again become a desert if they left, because the locals would kill one another, as they had in Central Asia. The survivors would come running, begging for district status in the new Russian Empire.

The future of Europe and the rest of the world, as Zhirinovsky envisions it, is briefly as follows: Poland will be divided between Germany and Russia; the Czech Republic will become part of Germany; Slovakia will be incorporated as part of Russia; Bulgaria will take over Macedonia and parts of Greece; and Russia will establish bases on the Indian Ocean littoral and incorporate Turkey, Iran, and Afghanistan in order to save the world from the Islamic danger. Zhirinovsky particularly resents Turkey, where he was kept in prison for a time, and would like to see it disappear.

Zhirinovsky dislikes America ("Our greatest problems are the Americans and the Zionists"). But, he predicted, America will be overrun by blacks and Latinos; American factories will close; medicine and food will disappear; and Americans will emigrate to Europe, Japan, and Russia. But it is not readily clear why Americans would emigrate to Europe, since Zhirinovsky also predicted that in ten or twenty years "all will be over for France and Germany," and the Turks will be in charge there. Furthermore, he would nuke Britain and Japan if they made so much as a peep.

We should add in fairness that occasionally Zhirinovsky has expressed slightly different views. That is, when he was in Poland he stated that the Polish borders were inviolable. While invoking the Islamic threat he has also praised Muslim fundamentalism; he has always welcomed Saddam Hussein as "Russia's most reliable ally." Zhirinovsky is a great admirer of the North Korean regime. Russia, according to Zhirinovsky, possesses weapons far more effective than nuclear devices which could destroy the whole world in an instant. He would solve Russia's shortage of food by ordering 1.5 million Russian soldiers to invade Germany, brandishing nuclear arms. Within seventy-two hours there would be sufficient food in Russia.

Zhirinovsky believes that the executive power must be strengthened, that all political parties, including his own, must be dissolved, and that an iron fist will be needed for at least two years, to enable Russia to survive. But he always stresses that he would never stage a coup but come to power only legally: Accordingly, in October 1993 he did not join the Right in the uprising against Boris Yeltsin but followed a "third way." Why risk military confrontation if time were working for him?

It is unlikely that many Russians voted for Zhirinovsky because of his foreign political views, and on domestic and economic issues he has been more cautious. He has never made it quite clear whether he favored a state-controlled or a mixed economy, whether he opposed Communism or wanted to revive it. But he left no doubt that he wanted a strong army (every officer would receive an automobile) and that he would hang or shoot the gangsters and destroy the Mafia and most of his enemies ("perhaps 100,000 of them").

Zhirinovsky's speeches make entertaining reading, but they reveal only some of the reasons for his party's success. He seems to have an uncanny understanding of what the masses want to hear—in particular the less educated and less advantaged who cannot afford to buy the luxury goods now freely available and who lost their jobs as the result of reform; the pensioners who felt that they lived better under the old regime; and the Russian patriots who resent the loss of empire and superpower status. Although antialcoholism has been a sacred principle of the Russian far Right—in theory, if not always in practice—it has never been popular, and so Zhirinovsky shrewdly discarded it, promising the masses to make available vodka at a much lower price.

Zhirinovsky started his career as a fighter for human rights but soon realized that these issues were of little interest to the public he wanted to reach. So he dropped them from his agenda and became a fighter for law and order. The liberal media treated him as a clown, and the nationalists and neo-Communists tried to ignore him. But for years they could not prevent his seemingly unstoppable rise on the political firmament. Despite the other pretenders on the Right, only Zhirinovsky succeeded in attracting millions. He seems to have realized early in life that even negative publicity is better than none, hence his clowning, grandiose promises, and bloodcurdling threats. Wherever Zhirinovsky goes in Russia or abroad, he creates a scandal and thus attracts the media.

We may never know how much of his scandal mongering is calculated and how much is genuine, spontaneous outbursts. Some of his closest collaborators, who later defected, claim that Zhirinovsky has been a KGB agent all along, and others maintain that he is temperamentally unsuited to be anyone's agent for any length of time. Yet others compare him with the priest Gapon, who had played an important role in the revolution of 1905, originally a creature of the tsarist political police, the Okhrana, who pursued at the same time a policy of his own, so that in the end no one, including himself, knew for certain for whose benefit he was acting.

Zhirinovsky's success can partly be explained with reference to good organization. He traveled frequently and widely, keeping in touch with supporters and trying to find new ones all over Russia. A geographical breakdown shows that he was doing less well in certain parts of Russia than in others, but the differences are not very significant. His movement was truly nationwide, in contrast to other opposition parties, except the neo-Communists. He had ample funds, but others on the extreme Right, such as Aleksandr Sterligov, a former KGB general, initially had even more funds at his disposal and yet did not remotely do as well. Virtually all leaders of the Russian extreme Right have been accused by both their enemies and their rivals of being KGB agents. Such indiscriminate charges have frequently been made throughout Russian history, but they still must be taken seriously. For it is also true that the tsarist secret police, as much as the KGB, financed agents on every segment of the political spectrum.

Most groups mentioned in this brief survey probably did receive support from the KGB, the old Communist Party, or some of its front organizations. But whether this made them obedient servants of the donors is a different question altogether.

Much information has become available confirming that all the more substantial groups on the extreme Right have received financial assistance from major Russian banks, investment and holding companies, and other business interests. Some patriotic business leaders have supported them because they want to keep foreign banks out of Russia. Others have done so as a means of reinsurance. Although they gave money to key figures in the Yeltsin administration, they had no wish to keep all their eggs in this one basket. These patriotic businessmen were afraid of foreign competition and were accustomed, moreover, to working within a monopoly framework.

Zhirinovsky has, nevertheless, remained highly vulnerable. Everything in his movement depended on him; there was no single person (let alone committee) who could replace him. His great success came at a time when the Right was deeply divided and many of its leaders were in prison. But once conditions had changed, he could not repeat his success.

The attitude toward Zhirinovsky of the "respectable" Russian Right and also of the other extremists has been mixed. They rejoiced in his victory inasmuch as it weakened and frightened the liberals and compelled Yeltsin and his colleagues to move to the right. From time to time, the Russian Right interviews him in their journals but seldom enthusiastically, and they probably would not invite him to their meetings and "unification initiatives." Zhirinovsky was an unlikely leader for the Right, and not only in view of his mixed racial origin. Few Russian nationalists dared speak out openly against him (Aleksandr Solzhenitsyn was a rare exception). One does not easily pick a quarrel with a man for whom so many Russians voted. But privately they would say that he was clearly no statesman but a vulgar, shadowy demagogue, lacking dignity and seriousness. He seems to be a Dostoyevskyan hero, not a positive one but a caricature.

For his part, Zhirinovsky has tried to ignore his rivals from the far Right. They lack the common touch; they are dignitaries without a popular following, such as Aleksandr Rutskoi, who is part of the former establishment; and their appeal is far more limited than his own.

Zhirinovsky has never clarified his attitude toward Nazism and fascism. When compared with Hitler, he has noted that Hitler was an uneducated corporal, whereas he, Zhirinovsky, is a reserve officer, has two university degrees, and can converse with world statesmen in their own languages. Like most Russians, Zhirinovsky is not particularly well informed about

Hitler and not much interested in Mussolini. What he does know seems to appeal to him; the dynamism of Nazism, its appeal to violent emotions, its aggressive foreign policy, and its militarist bent. At the same time Zhirinovsky seems to be aware that merely copying Nazism would not generate much political capital. Unlike some other groups on the far Right, Zhirinovsky's publications have ignored Hitler, for he feels that he cannot learn much from the Germans. He has established contacts with neo-Nazi groups and personalities in Germany, Austria, the Balkans, and the far Right in France. Some of his new friends have come to Russia to address the conventions of the "Liberal Democrats," but these "foreign relations" seem not to have figured high on his agenda.

Far closer to the Nazi model is Aleksandr Barkashov's "Russian National Unity Group" (RNE are the initials in Russian). "I am not a fascist; I am a Nazi," Barkashov stated in one of his interviews. The RNE is a much smaller organization of activists undergoing military training, with the swastika as their symbol and a Heil Hitler–like greeting with the right arm raised. Founded in 1990, the RNE claims to have members in some 250 cities, but this cannot be verified. There is a substantial RNE presence in some of the major Siberian cities. The group sees itself as the avant-garde of the coming national revolution and considers the major organizations of the extreme Right (including Zhirinovsky's) to be too tame. It publishes several news sheets (*Russky poryadok* claims to have a circulation of 150,000) but has only limited ambitions in the field of ideology and propaganda, which it leaves to other groups of the extreme Right. It prides itself to be the only doers among a multitude of idle talkers.

Barkashov was born in 1953. His grandfather was one of the "purgers" in the wave of terror in the 1930s. His parents, however, did not belong to the *nomenklatura*, and he grew up in a working-class family. An electrician by training and perhaps the only figure on the Russian Right without a higher education, Barkashov served in the army as a karate instructor. The full members of the RNE are called Soratnik (comrades in arms), and Barkashov is the chief comrade in arms. They receive combat training at locations near Moscow, and many earn their living as security officers and armed guards. Their social background is predominantly working class, and accordingly, the RNE has been in close contact with some of the new trade unions.

Barkashov's own writings and speeches (which are few) do not reveal anything original or radically different from the doctrines of similar groups. He believes in a giant conspiracy ("total genocide") against the Russian people that is trying to destroy its "racial core" ("genotype"). Hence the demand to introduce eugenic principles into the future Russian state and the virtual ban on mixed marriages. There will be two classes of citizens, Russians and non-Russians, with the latter being mere inhabitants and not sharing citizens' rights. The propagation of democratic, humanist, and internationalist values will be a crime.

The RNE is ultranationalist and critical of the Russian Orthodox Church except for its most radical representatives. It claims that although religion originally played a positive role in the development of the Russian nation, it later gravitated toward "internationalism." The RNE considers the church's current leadership to be Zionist and Masonic, and it opposes the restoration of the monarchy, since this system is out of touch with the spirit of the times. The RNE considers itself a revolutionary rather than a restorative force, very much in the tradition of European fascism. There is a strong mystic element in Barkashov's thinking, with references to an "explosion of popular mysticism," the "meaning of the soul," and the "spiritual victory in heaven," the meaning of which is not clear.

Until the great showdown in October 1993 the former karate instructor and his followers were not taken seriously by the Russian right-wing establishment, in view of Barkashov's intellectual shortcomings and mindless activism. But his prestige rapidly rose when it appeared during the critical hours of fighting near the White House that Barkashov was the only leader who could mobilize at least a few dozen of his followers. Since then he has gained the admiration of Aleksandr Prokhanov, the editor of *Zavtra*, and he has been joined by Eduard Limonov and Aleksandr Dugin, two of the extreme Right's chief propagandists. While on the run in October 1993, Barkashov was injured in a shoot-out in Krasnogorsk, possibly between rival gangs. This has made him a martyr and further added to his prestige.

A few of Barkashov's followers have seen military action in the Caucasus and Yugoslavia, and well-wishers in the police and the army have provided arms and logistic support to his organization. Barkashov has followed a double-track strategy: He registered the RNE with the authorities as a legal, law-abiding political organization. At the same time, he formed a secret organization that has its own intelligence and counterintelligence service, arms dumps, and communication network. Nevertheless, despite all this activity, Barkashov does not have the qualities of a political leader, and his movement appeals only to males of a particular age group and social background.

Even though the RNE has received more publicity than any other pro-Nazi organization, it has had no monopoly. Among the other, similar groups is Viktor Yakushev's National–Social Union (NSS) which wants to establish a "national state," an economy emphasizing Aryan values, and is fighting to prevent the Zionists from establishing hegemony over the whole world. According to Yakushev, all Masons were and are homosexuals, all inferior races have one fewer chromosome than the superior races do, and Jews are "biorobots" programmed to commit suicide.

To the right (or left) of Barkashov is Nikolai Lysenko's National Republican Party, based in St. Petersburg and claiming ten thousand members. Like Zhirinovsky and Pamyat, Lysenko, a youngish biology teacher of Siberian origin, did not take part in the armed insurrection of October 1993 but, on the contrary, strove to give his party a moderate image and was elected to the Duma, the Russian parliament. The party even dropped its erstwhile racialist program, which would have restricted (or ousted) all non-Russian citizens from Russian political, cultural, and economic life. It opted instead for proportional representation, which would achieve more or less the same goal without exposing it to accusations of racism. Unlike the RNE, the National Republican Party has established close relations with the monarchists and church circles. Although it maintains an armed branch, this has not figured prominently on its political agenda. Despite all this the Lysenkoites have a hidden agenda and have not dropped their SS-like emblem.

There are some twenty other illegal groups, the most prominent of which were the Werewolves, which was planning a series of terrorist attacks when their leading members were arrested in July 1994 by the Russia's federal intelligence. Headed by a Russian native of Estonia named Andrei Anokhin, who—like Lysenko and Barkashov—served his apprenticeship in Pamyat, the Werewolves were acknowledged Nazis. They did not, however, believe in mass action but felt that terrorism should be the main instrument of destroying society and seizing power. For example, when the Werewolves committed a series of murders, the victims were defectors from their own ranks. Some of the Werewolves' members were sent to fight in Yugoslavia, not, however, with their Serb "brothers," but with the Croats, apparently in recognition of the Croat fascist tradition dating back to the 1930s. The Werewolves bitterly attacked Barkashov and his followers, and Barkashov retaliated by calling them "provocateurs." Following the arrests in 1994, Werewolves' organization ceased to exist.

Besides these sectarian groups are some regional organizations such as the National Democratic Party, the People's Social Party (both based in St. Petersburg), and the Center of Russian National Resistance (Yekaterinburg). There is also a fairly large camp that subscribes to some, but not all, of the basic tenets of fascism. This camp includes the Russian National Sobor, headed by Aleksandr Sterligov, a KGB general turned businessman, and the Vozrozhdenie (Renaissance) group led by Valeri Skurlatov, a veteran of Russian right-wing politics who graduated from propagating paganism to an important role among the lay people in the Orthodox Church. To a greater or lesser extent almost all these parties belong to the National Salvation Front (an umbrella organization founded in 1992).

The National Salvation Front claims that they are, first and foremost, Russian patriots who desire the restoration of a strong Russian state. If this can be achieved only through the adoption of fascist means, so be it: Russian power and greatness are crucial as far as they are concerned, but freedom and human rights are not. Even members of Yeltsin's government are among those who have responded in this way.

Such views reflect the political and psychological reaction to the loss of empire, and the eradication of 250 years of Russian history, and the resentment against the separatists and defectors within the former Soviet Union. They also mirror the anger at Russia's not being treated as an equal by the West. Indeed, to ignore such feelings is to underrate the reservoir of support for movements pushing for a nationalist dictatorship. They have an almost unlimited demand for "order," a regime that would stamp out crime, stabilize the Russian economy, and restore to Russia its past power and grandeur. Such a dictatorship would certainly be antidemocratic. Whether it would be in the authoritarian mold of Franco or Pinochet (a hero of the Russian Right) or more extreme and pronouncedly fascist, cannot be predicted. Those concerned are not eager to spell out such details.

Attempts have been made to look for common denominators, and no one has been more active in this direction than Aleksandr Prokhanov, the far Right's unofficial minister of propaganda. He is the editor of the most widely read weekly, *Zavtra,* and has tried indefatigably to bring together fascists, monarchists, clerics, pagan sectarians, and plain patriots, provided only that they be willing to fight against the current liberal "occupation" regime.

Prokhanov began his literary career as the protégé of democratic writers and journalists. During the war in Afghanistan he discovered his inclination toward romantic (or exotic) imperialism and thus acquired his nickname "the nightingale of the General Staff." The style of *Zavtra* resembles Zhirinovsky's speeches, with the same extreme verbal aggression, ludicrous exaggeration, open incitement, utter lack of tolerance, and total negativism. *Zavtra* consists almost entirely of attacks against enemies, real and imaginary, and is permeated with paranoia—plots and conspiracies everywhere. Despite invoking the great national idea and "spirituality" (*dukhovnost*) (*Zavtra* calls itself the organ of the "spiritual opposition"), it has in fact never made clear what these spiritual values are.

Such national socialism derives a substantial part of its inspiration from the ideology of a bygone era. It is united more by hatred of a common enemy than by a common vision of a future Russia.

Such aggression should not have come as a surprise, as the writers and speakers of the extreme Right were trained in the Communist school, where they learned these attitudes. But in some respects, the extreme Right outdid Communism, which did, after all, at least pay lip service to humanist values and the preference of peace to war. Although these incantations were usually not sincere, they did impose certain limits on the Communist propaganda, whereas the Russian fascists and parafascists could disregard such inhibitions and go to any extreme. This refers, for instance, to their persecution mania. Hitler, Goebbels, and their acolytes were brazen liars. But these were "holy lies," deliberate untruths, that had to be spread for the good of the cause. In the case of the Russians, the impression is sometimes gained that they sincerely believe many of their lies.

The extremists have enjoyed complete freedom in propagating their views, including even incitement to murder—not to mention criminal libel—which would be severely punished in other countries. In fact, the situation now in Russia has frequently been compared with that of Weimar Germany. Such comparisons are often tenuous, but in some respects there is an uncanny resemblance, including the impotence (or unwillingness) of the state to defend itself against its detractors, even when they violate the law.

In response, the Russian authorities explain that the existing laws concerning incitement or libel, like all other laws, date back to the Soviet period and therefore cannot be applied. This is not a plausible excuse, because other laws are still in force. Rather, Russia has become a lawless state by choice, and everyone may propagate his or her views with impunity.

The extreme Right has a more or less consistent foreign policy: the reestablishment of the Soviet Union through the incorporation of the republics that have seceded or, at the very least, the establishment of a Russian sphere of influence, something like a Russian Monroe Doctrine. They assume that the basic goal of the West, especially America, is to weaken and ruin Russia and to keep it totally dependent. The West is innately hostile to all things Russian, hence the pervasive idea of Russophobia. Most rightists believe in an Eurasian orientation that turns its back on Europe and directs its policies toward Asia. The drawback of this concept, which was first suggested by the Russian émigrés in the 1920s, is that it is divorced from political reality. Not Japan or China, not the Muslim world or India or Afghanistan has any wish to enter a close alliance with Russia or perceives any common interests with it. Some on the extreme Right dream of an European (anti-American) axis "from Dublin to Vladivostok," but others want a close alliance with the new Germany, which they claim is at heart as much opposed to democracy and other Western values as Russia is. Yet others propose reviving pan-Slavism.

The extreme Right's economic and social policies are only vague ideas. They oppose capitalism and fulminate against the few exploiters who have amassed great fortunes while the masses starve. Many of the right-wing extremists originally were fanatical antisocialists but subsequently found redeeming features in the old Soviet system. All want to smash the Mafia (a term used quite indiscriminately in contemporary Russia) and foreign deal- ers, be they American bankers or Azerbaijani vegetable sellers in Moscow markets. But most also realize that a return to the old system is impossible, even in agriculture. So they have reluctantly accepted a "national bourgeoi- sie," national banks, and a mixed economy.

With regard to the monarchy and the Orthodox Church, the rightists' opinions sharply diverge. Most of the extreme Right do not want, for a variety of reasons, to join the monarchist camp. Some have dissociated themselves from the Orthodox Church, whereas others openly advocate a return to the pre-Christian Slavic gods or a quasi-Indian religion (Vedism). The majority prefer neutrality in religious affairs, just as Hitler and Musso- lini did.

Various occult sciences, especially astrology, have played a central role in the thinking of the extreme Right. These include a belief in magic numbers, good and bad, devils and demons, and all kinds of fads and superstitions. If the Ariosophists of Germany and Austria had a presence in the early days of Nazism (until Hitler purged them), the purveyors of occultism have assumed an even greater role in the genesis of Russian fascism and the extreme Right.

Typical of the Russian extreme rightists is the unshakable belief that all of Russia's misfortunes can be blamed on foreigners. Whatever goes wrong has nothing to do with anything that ethnic Russians have done or have not done. Without the machinations of foreigners, Russia would be great, prosperous, and powerful. A spirit of honest self-criticism is totally absent from their ranks.

All right-wingers believe in grand conspiracies, an assumption that has always been strong in Russia and reached its apogee under Stalin. Some Russian fascists have gone even further than their predecessors. Not only were Marx and Trotsky Jewish—a fact that has never been doubted—but so were Lenin, Stalin, Beria, Hitler, Goebbels, Eichmann, and virtually the whole Communist and Nazi leadership. If they were not full Jews, they were at least half Jews or married to Jewish women. The purpose of this exercise is not entirely clear: If everyone is or was a Jew, and/or Mason, what is the purpose of pointing it out? Sometimes one suspects a black sense of humor behind the grotesque fantasies. But the fanatics of the extreme Right lack a sense of humor. They know that the last judgment is at hand, that the Russian people are about to be exterminated. People in such a frame of mind are not likely to engage in frivolous jokes.

To what kind of men or women are doctrines of this kind likely to appeal? They attract especially those not benefiting from the social changes taking place and, equally, to members of the lower echelons of the party and state administration who have lost their jobs, those who did have a certain position, however lowly, in the old regime. There are among them members (or former members) of the army and the security forces; in many army districts, Zhirinovsky won overwhelmingly. Those working in the military—industrial complex, together with their dependents, number in the millions. Under the old regime they were well paid and esteemed members of society. But as the danger of war receded, the armed forces were cut; military production was reduced or discontinued; and some of the internal security forces were disbanded.

By no means was a material self-interest the only reason that people joined the ranks of the extreme Right. They also had an acute fear of the future, resentment of Russia's diminished status in the world, and, on the other hand, anger about the new rich, flaunting luxury goods. Above all, they longed for certainty. Under the old regime, the state had somehow taken care of everyone. Even though, more often than not, it had been a miserable existence, people did not have to worry about a roof over their heads (however small) and bread and other staple goods. There had been less crime under the old regime, or, to be precise, crime was not publicized. In brief, there is now a great deal of uncertainty, and for decades Russians had been unaccustomed to living without security; those in authority had made the decisions for them.

But democracy is uncertainty writ large, hence the Russians' willingness to do away with the new freedoms and replace them with strong leadership. In most essential aspects the ideology of the present-day Russian extreme Right is a rehash of the doctrines of similar groups in late tsarist Russia, except, of course, that more than seventy years of Communism have made certain adaptations necessary. Therefore, the Right and the national Bolsheviks were able to create a rapprochement.

Avant-garde thinkers of the extreme Right, such as Aleksandr Dugin ("geopolitician and metaphysician," in his own words), have attempted to update their doctrine. Russian fascists and parafascists missed out on all the prefascist and fascist thinkers in Europe, and so they now, together with the French Nouvelle droite, have been introduced to the Russian public. They include Haushofer and his school of geopolitics; Giulio Evola; Central European conservatives like Spann, Spengler, and Sombart; the German "national revolutionaries"; and various advocates of dictatorship and the "friend–foe dichotomy" such as Carl Schmitt. Even the concept of *mondialism* had a short-lived popularity in Russia (a global conspiracy engineered by finance capital with Jews and Masons playing a subordinate role only).

The French New Rightists were for a while honored guests in Moscow, but it soon appeared that what they had to offer was unsuitable for Russian conditions. For example, the French New Right would not have dreamed of featuring pictures of Himmler and other Nazi idols in their publications. Indeed, they carefully hid their views on race behind a smoke screen of "ethnopluralism." The French New Right's "third way between capitalism and Communism," their anti-Americanism, and other such features should have endeared the French to the Russian extreme Right. But their arguments were unnecessarily philosophical and complicated, well beyond all but a handful of Russian intellectuals. Something more intelligible and tangible was needed. A mixture of Mussolini and Dostoevsky, of de Benoist and Leontiev, was indigestible. To sugar the pill, Dugin tried to introduce these foreigners as great admirers of Russia and the "Russian idea," but this conclusion was simply not true and would not have made much difference anyway.

The fact that Evola and the French New Right made no secret of their hostility to Christianity did not help either; it was an unnecessary provocation of the Orthodox Church. What remained in the end was the common denominator of "conspiratology," on which there was full agreement between the Russian extreme nationalists and the neo-Stalinists, between the open anti-Semites in the Orthodox Church and those preaching paganism, between advocates of economic freedom and those in favor of collectivism.

Believers in demonic plots can be found at all times and in most parts of the world, not only on the extreme Right. But in Russia in recent years such fantasies have strongly appealed to more people than elsewhere: Whenever a leading fascist or anti-Semite died, he was inevitably believed to have been killed (preferably by means of ritual murder) by satanic forces. This refers not only to the present time but also to the past. For example, the alleged assassination of the poet Sergei Essenin in 1925 (and of Aleksandr Blok and Vladimir Mayakovsky) remains a favorite topic in the fantasy world of the extreme Right, even though there is no good reason for such suspicions.

Besides the right-wing extremists and parafascist groups, there is the much larger camp of "patriots" (and national Communists) and *gosudarstvenniki,* who are advocates of strong state power in broad sympathy with some of the basic views of the extremists but are critical of certain exaggerations and manifestly absurd allegations. This camp includes a considerable part of the old and new *nomenklatura* and people in all walks of life. They are probably more numerous outside Moscow and St. Petersburg. For this "respectable" Right, the extremists are useful allies in the struggle against the liberals. But they also know that the liberals and democrats are not very numerous and lack influence. Furthermore, the verbal excesses and violent actions of the extremists give nationalism and the Right a bad name and complicate relations with the outside world. If they could, the respectable Right would prefer to keep the extremists at arm's length. But the right-wing establishment does not have the foot soldiers it needs; its members are pillars of society and cannot be expected to take to the streets and man the barricades. For this purpose, militants in black uniforms are needed. But again, once the genie is out of the bottle, it tends to develop a will of its own, as the German Right learned to its detriment when it made common cause with Hitler. Fascism was not the running dog of monopoly capitalism, and Russian fascism is not an instrument in the hands of the right-wing establishment that can be easily manipulated to be produced at will and to be withdrawn from circulation when no longer needed.

Conditions in Russia at the present time are auspicious for an upsurge of authoritarian movements. It is unlikely that the political situation will stabilize soon and that prosperity and social harmony will prevail in the near future. On the other hand, crucial factors inhibit the growth of a strong fascist movement. One is the internal dissent between the national Bolsheviks and the ultranationalists; between radical populists and monarchists and the church; between conservatives and right-wing revolutionaries; between *gosudarstvenniki*, representing the old *nomenklatura*, and those who are riding the crest of the wave of working-class discontent. It would be exceedingly difficult to paper over the rifts among these various doctrines, interests, and ambitions of individual leaders unless the situation deteriorates rapidly and greatly, and the old leadership abdicates and a new one is not yet ready to replace it. Only at such a historical juncture could fascism have a chance that it may or may not be able to exploit. However, even at a time of acute crisis, the prospects of national Bolshevism and the "statists" seem much better than those of fascism: Stalin, after all, is closer to most Russians than is Hitler or Mussolini.

Eastern Europe

Eastern Europe had a mixed record in the prewar period with regard to fascism: In Romania, Hungary, Slovakia, and Croatia, Nazi and fascist movements were strong. Elsewhere, such as in Poland, Serbia, the Baltic states, and Bulgaria, it was weak, but authoritarian–military rule prevailed.

Later, two generations of East Europeans were educated in the spirit of Communism. This did not perhaps go very deep, because Communism was a foreign importation. National Communism in the Titoist fashion, however, was strong almost from the beginning.

The liberation of Eastern Europe in 1989 was widely welcomed as a national and democratic revolution. But it did not take long for the people to realize that the roots of democracy were still weak and that, given the economic difficulties and the social tensions, much of Eastern Europe was fertile ground for radical populist movements of the Right and the Left. True, unlike the case of Russia, they did not suffer a loss-of-empire syndrome, but on the other hand, the old national tensions resurfaced that had bedeviled Eastern Europe for so long and helped the spread of ultranationalist groups. Finally, politically immature people had unreasonable expectations, and when these were not fulfilled, they turned to protest and despair. Thus in the Polish presidential election of 1990 a totally unknown figure named Stanislaw Tyminski came in second, with 22 percent of the vote. He had allegedly made a fortune in the jungles of Latin America. In any case, his speeches were incoherent, and he appeared in public with a boa constrictor around his neck. The aims of his appropriately named Party X were equally unclear. Subsequently it was revealed that he had been in touch with shadowy figures of the extreme Left and Right and the political police; he also voiced anti-Semitic slogans. His party collapsed within a year, but the Tyminski phenomenon was by no means singular. Populist movements gravitating to extreme forms of nationalism—anti-Western, antidemocratic, and anti-Semitic—appeared in many Eastern European countries. Frequently, they were headed by political adventurers. The goals of these parties were as mysterious as their finances and their attitude toward Communism.

The upsurge of nationalism in Eastern Europe enabled the return of extreme right-wing parties. However, there was a basic difference between the genuine extremism in the tradition (as one example) of the Iron Guard, the Romanian fascists of the 1930s, and the protective coloring of other groups, mainly consisting of former Communists, who merely engaged in extremist rhetorics on the assumption that nationalist slogans would attract more support than would the doctrine of the old regime.

Poland

During the Soviet period, Poland was the quintessential anti-Communist country. The hold of the Catholic Church over the population was strong, and the rise of Solidarity in the 1980s made the Communists feel like a besieged minority even while Poland was nominally still Communist. But once Communism had been overthrown, its opponents proved incapable of providing effective leadership. In fact, Lech Walesa presided over the disintegration of Solidarity, the movement he had created and that had created him. The Catholic Church became involved in various controversial ventures through a conservative party it supported, the Christian National Union (CNU). The fact that it advocated religious censorship and a ban on abortion added to the growing political polarization.

In comparison with that of other Eastern European countries, the Polish economy has performed fairly well, but the social cost of economic reform has still been great. Large sections of the population have suffered, resulting in the electoral victory of two parties, the ex-Communist SLD and the peasant UD. It would be incorrect to define these parties as nothing but neo-Communist in inspiration, as they are led by younger people willing to accept the democratic ground rules. But it is equally clear that their election was a protest vote of large sections against the liberal democrats who have tried to build a Western-style system in Poland.

This, in broadest outline, is the background against which we should view the emergence of extreme right-wing groups. It is a confusing scene with almost a dozen factions competing. The most active and extreme is Boleslaw Tejkowski's Polish National Community–Polish National Party; it is also one of the smallest contenders. Its leader is a former Communist Party official allegedly connected to the secret police. The same is true with regard to a group headed by Janusz Bryczkowski, who defected from Party X and organized the visit by Zhirinovsky to Poland in March 1994. Tejkowski is opposed not only to the Jews but also to the Vatican and virtually everyone and everything else except Pamyat, Le Pen, and neo-Nazi organizations in North America, Libya, and North Korea. He was put on trial in 1992 and was examined by psychiatrists who found him normal. Not one of his candidates has ever been elected.

The Christian National Union (CNU) is a more substantial force, but it clearly belongs to the conservative camp, despite its forays into the populist field. "Christianity, Church, Fatherland, Honor" is its slogan. Another anti-Communist national party is the KPN, the Confederation of Independent Poland led by Leszek Moczulski. In the early days, it had close ties with the church but later turned against it. It regards itself a patriotic movement rather than a party of the Right and refused to take its seat in the Polish parliament on the extreme Right. The KPN's vision is the restoration of a historical Polish commonwealth including not only Poland but also part of the Ukraine, the Baltic countries, White Russia, the Czech Republic, Slovakia, Hungary, and perhaps even the Balkan countries. This bloc should serve as a counterweight to Russia as well as to the European Union.

Moczulski is a genuine anti-Communist who was arrested countless times under the old regime, whereas the anti-Communist record of the other parties of the extreme Right is dubious, to say the least. The KPN sees itself as the legitimate heir to Józef Pilsudski's authoritarian regime, and it recognizes the 1935 (Pilsudskian) constitution as the only valid one. At one time it polled some 10 percent of the total electorate, which subsequently declined to 6 percent.

More extreme is Andrei Lepper's Self-Defense Farmers' Union, which has engaged in spectacular extraparliamentary activities, such as storming town halls and blockading roads. Lepper, a former boxer and Communist believer in conspiracy theories, opposes the parliamentary regime. Although his party has some following in districts with high unemployment, it did not do well in the general elections.

Polish groups tending toward neofascism are led by shady figures. Virtually all had been either Communists or members of the Grunwald National Communist Circle—anti-Western, anti-German, and, of course, anti-Semitic. The National Party ("Poland for the Poles," "Down with Judaeo Solidarity") was headed by an Oxford graduate and professor of forestry. This was one of the few groups that attracted some young people, mainly skinheads. Indeed, skinheads were involved in the murder of a German truck driver in Nowa Huta. This incident threatened to create international complications, and it was one of the few instances in which the authorities meted out strict punishment to the perpetrators. Generally, the Polish extreme right-wing groups have enjoyed a great deal of freedom of action but still have failed to make major inroads into Poland's political life.

Hungary

Hungary had a fairly stong fascist movement in the 1930s, was an ally of Germany during World War II, and had for a while, under German occupation, a native Nazi government. Political developments after the overthrow of Communist rule were much like those in Poland: A center–right government headed by the Democratic Forum was replaced in May 1994 by the Hungarian Socialist Party, led by former leading Communists such as Gyula Horn, who had been prime minister in 1989.

The former Communists, however, seem to be *bona fide* converts to social democracy and a belief in a mixed economy. They are not opposed to privatization and agrarian reform and have joined with foreign investors. Extreme right-wing leanings did appear in the ranks of the Democratic Forum, whose best-known representative was Istvan Csurka, a playwright and a member of its presidium. Eventually, Csurka left the Forum and established the party of Hungarian truth (Justice and Life Party), which had at one time 11 members (out of 386) in parliament. Csurka is a populist, and describes himself as a proponent of national radicalism. His enemies are liberals (mainly the media), former Communists, and Jews, although he has been careful not to single out Jews as the main culprits. Csurka has demanded a new constitution and has attacked the government for selling out to foreigners and for not giving Hungarian interests priority in its policy. He has been a staunch defender of the rights of ethnic Hungarians living outside Hungary, against Slavs (in Slovakia), and against Romania.

Csurka's party is in the tradition of Hungarian right-wing populism rather than of fascism, as is true with regard to another party, Jozsef Torgyan's (ISCP), which has its roots mainly in the countryside. It is one of the successors of Hungary's leading historical parties, the Smallholders. Torgyan's party claims to have more than sixty thousand members, which would make it Hungary's largest party. But in fact, it did not do at all well in the 1994 elections. Both Csurka and Torgyan have some working-class and farmer support, as they stand for a national Christian Hungary and a "third road" between capitalism and socialism. Note, however, that the "third road" has also been all along the official slogan of the Democratic Vorum. And if Csurka demands more living space for Hungary and refers to the "lost territories," we should remember that most Hungarian parties have been ambiguous about Hungary's current borders.

The great national movement envisaged by Csurka and Torgyan has not come to pass. In the elections of 1994, their parties received 1.5 percent of the total vote, and not one of them was elected to parliament. Beyond the respectable Right, a variety of extreme groups have emerged, some openly neo-Nazi, self-styled followers of the Arrow Cross who ruled Hungary in 1944/45. They have such names as the Hungarian National Socialist Action, National Popular Rule Party, Hungarian Coordinating Society 1956, and Popular Will Society. None of them has more than a few hundred members. The Action Group, which later changed its name to the National Socialist Action Group, is based in the city of Gyoer, and its leader, Istvan Gyorkos, was given a one-year sentence fo racial incitement. The National Popular Rule Party is headed by Albert Szabo, who spent the previous seven years as an émigré in Australia. The neo-Nazi groups maintain close ties with like-minded circles among Hungarian émigrés abroad and other neofascist groups, especially in Austria and the United States. The leader of yet another neofascist sect is an émigré who returned from Canada.

Isabella Kiraly, originally a member of parliament for the Democratic

Forum, was expelled, and even Csurka's party found her views too radical. She then became the patron of the Hungarian skinheads, of whom there are several thousand, wearing black uniforms and jackboots. Not all of them are militants of the extreme Right, but those who are see their idol in the Arrow Cross of the 1930s. Their journal is called *Kitatas* (Perseverance), which was the greeting slogan of the Arrow Cross. Kiraly founded a political group named the Hungarian Interest Party specifically for the political education and defense of the interests of the skinheads. She denies the fascist character of her group, but the contents of their publications are unequivocal: struggle for a greater Hungary, "pure Hungarianism," and the removal of all aliens and foreign interests.

The main target of the skinheads is foreigners from Third World countries and especially gypsies, whom the skinheads want, as one of their songs says, to destroy by means of flamethrowers. They have a favorite football team, Ferencvaros, Budapest, and at the home matches the usual slogans are shouted and symbols displayed. But it is also true that attacks against foreigners are by no means limited to skinheads, who have been blamed on some occasions for attacks committed by other "non-political" groups.

Gypsies constitute 5 to 6 percent of Hungary's population, and only a third of them are thought to be literate. If Hungarian Jews are attacked by the extreme Right for being too rich and clever, the gypsies are thought to be "inferior" and mainly criminals. The Jews are attacked as Communists, but the gypsies are not identified with the old regime, although this does not help them with the far Right. The Communist authorities tried to settle the gypsies in new housing projects in the suburbs, but they soon turned into slums and new tensions arose between them and their neighbors. Only a small percentage of Hungarian gypsies were affected by the Nazi policy of extermination, and their number is now probably greater than it was before World War II.

Because of their low position in society, the gypsies are a target of skinhead attacks, but they cannot possibly provide the raison d'être of a political party. There is only limited support for the extreme Right in Hungary, and the more responsible right-wing politicians have tried hard to dissociate themselves from the extremists. There still remains, however, much discontent: Unemployment among workers is relatively high, and broad segments of the population, perhaps as much as three-quarters, have not yet benefited from the economic reforms. This nationwide resentment dates back to the Treaty of Trianon, in which Hungary lost its former empire, part of which was settled by Hungarians. Most Hungarians feel that their compatriots in Romania, Slovakia, and the former Yugoslavia are treated as second-class citizens. Accordingly, there is a reservoir of support for a nationalist and populist movement, even though it is unlikely to be in the mold of the Arrow Cross.

Romania

The break with the national Communist past has been less pronounced in Romania than in any other Eastern European country. President Ion Iliescu is a leading former Communist (Central Committee secretary for propaganda and education), and the other main figures of the regime—the National Salvation Front renamed the Party of Social Democracy—belong to the same category. Economic reform has been very limited, and the political struggle took place predominantly within the governing elite and between this elite and forces even further to the right, such as the Romanian National Unity (PRNU) and the Great Romania Party (GRP). The far Right favors a return to the policies of Marshal Ion Antonescu, who was an ally of the Nazis in World War II. The more extreme elements sympathize with the Iron Guard, the openly fascist movement of the 1930s and 1940s. Antonescu eventually suppressed the Iron Guard, and the military dictatorship turned against the most radical fascist movement in Europe.

The extreme Right in Romania has not been able to make stronger showing in recent years, for two reasons. First, the economic situation has continued to deteriorate since the overthrow of Nicolae Ceauşescu. But since it was bad even before, the right-wing opponents cannot refer to the "good old days." Second, because the orientation of the ruling party is very much toward nationalism rather than democratic reform, it is difficult to outflank it from the right.

Nevertheless, the Party of National Unity (PRNU) has made progress in recent years, and since the ruling party has no majority in parliament, it has to rely on support from the PRNU. The PRNU was created in 1990 from a cultural association named Vatra Romanesca, and it was originally centered in Transylvania, where Romanian nationalists felt under pressure from the Hungarian minority, campaigning for equal cultural and educational rights. Although the party made a poor showing in the nationwide elections of 1990, it did well in Transylvania, where its base was the underclass of peasants who had recently moved there in the wake of industrialization.

The PRNU represents itself (as did the fascist parties of the 1930s) as a broad national movement, not a group seeking partisan interests. It is vague on social and economic specifics, always stressing the national interest and solidarity. It opposes Communism (which had been imposed on the country by foreigners) but views with favor Ceauşescu's legacy.

Gheorghe Funar, the PRNU mayor of Cluj, the biggest town in Translyvania, became the leader of the movement. His campaign was financed by the Romanian business and administrative elite in Transylvania. Under him the party has continued its antiforeign campaign: The Hungarians should be deprived of their cultural rights, and foreign capital should not gain a foothold in the Romanian economy. Given the state of the Romanian economy, the danger of excessive foreign investment is not great. But such attitudes are still interesting as a feature common to all extreme right-wing parties in Romania (and, to some extent, to all such parties in Eastern Europe): a fear not so much of "foreign rule" but of modernization as a whole, and the defense of the "national bourgeoisie," however ineffective. The PRNU became involved in the questionable dealings of a holding corporation named Caritas that promised investors an eightfold return within three months on their investment. More than 3 million Romanians were taken in, but the company, not surprisingly, became insolvent.

The PRNU opposes the excesses of a liberal democracy and the media, advocates an "iron-fist government," with the military in a leading position. It wants to get rid of the gypsies through administrative or other means and has engaged in anti-Semitic propaganda. But the anti-Hungarian issue is more central to the concerns of this party than its other preoccupations are, in contrast to those parties even farther to the right, such as the Greater Romanians (GRP) headed by Corneliu Tudor.

This group originally came from the same stable as the PRNU did, and there is reason to assume that it was established with the help of the ex-Communists and the secret police, who saw it as useful in protecting its right flank. This, to a certain extent, both these groups have accomplished, but whereas the PRNU has behaved with more restraint, the Greater Romanians have been more radical and outspoken in their approach. This has made them an unreliable ally and, at times, an embarrassment for the ruling party, which denounced the GRP's "intolerance, xenophobia, and antisemitism." After the GRP received 3.5 to 4 percent of the vote in the last elections the popularity of this party has declined, and the circulation of *Romania mare*, its popular weekly, fell from (perhaps) 400,000 to less than 100,000.[11] The GRP has increasingly cooperated with the Socialist Labor Party (SLP), a group of faithful followers of the late Ceauşescu. The SLP is headed by Ilie Verdet, who was prime minister during the Communist regime. Romania offers more striking examples of "Red–Brown" coalitions than any other Eastern European country.

Yet further to the right are several smaller groups such as the MFR led by Marian Munteanu and the PNR led by Radu Sorescu. Some of these groups are parliamentarian, and others advocate an armed uprising. They all want to return to the fascism of the 1930s and the 1940s and if they have differences, they are rooted in the conflicts among Romanian fascists at that time.

Antonescu, the military dictator who was executed for war crimes, has been more or less rehabilitated as a result of much pressure from the moderate right-wing parties and wide circles of Romanian society. President Iliescu opposed the rehabilitation but faced dissent in his own ranks. A Bucharest judge finally decided in a libel case that Antonescu had been one of Romania's greatest military and political leaders and that those opposing the rehabilitation lacked any feeling for the people and the nation.

Antonescu, however, opposed the fascist Iron Guard and had many of its leaders and followers killed in a bloody massacre in 1941. Reconciling the differences between Antonescu and the radical fascists is therefore not easy, but their present-day admirers have found a way. According to their version, true Iron Guardism ended with the murder of Corneliu Codreanu, its historical leader, in 1938. His successor, Horia Sima, who died in exile in 1993, was a deviationist who engaged in terrorism, pogroms, and general lawlessness and eventually brought about the ruin of his movement, whose destruction was approved even by Hitler. Not all neofascists have accepted this version of events, denying any deviation after 1938, and thus the present-day admirers of the Iron Front are divided between "Codreanists" and "Simists."

The extremists want to put certain sectors of the economy under military control, to have criminals whipped in public, and to establish an "ethnocratic" corporative state from which unassimilated minorities would be excluded. They would pursue an aggressive line against Hungarians and gypsies. The extremists oppose the European Union and dream of a restoration of the wartime alliance with Germany and Japan.

As in the case of Hungary, extreme right-wing circles among Romanian émigrés have made an important contribution to the resurgence of neofascism. Thus Constantin Dragan, who began his political career with the Iron Guard, emigrated after the Communist takeover, made a fortune abroad, supported the national Communist regime, and eventually became the honorary president of Vatra Romanesca and the owner of the leading publishing house of the extreme Right as well as of several radio stations.

These parties, as well as a few others that are even smaller, have made some inroads among the younger generation, both students and the working class. But their overall impact has been limited.

The ideology of the Romanian far Right is complicated and contradictory. Thus Marshal Antonescu has been rehabilitated because he was the greatest anti-Communist in Romanian history. But this is a misleading claim, because the successors of the Iron Guard by no means regard Communism as their main enemy; in fact, they are quite willing to collaborate with former Communists. They appreciate the merits of Ceauşescu and his predecessor Gheorgiu Dej and oppose Communism only to the extent that it is not nationalist. As does the Russian extreme Right, they believe in a giant conspiracy against the Romanian people and its legitimate interests by virtually everyone—Russians, Americans, Romania's neighbors, and its "internal enemies."

Although there are hardly any Jews left in Romania, anti-Semitic attacks still have a place in neofascist propaganda, and efforts are constantly being made to prove that the Holocaust never occurred. (According to reliable estimates, some 300,000 Romanian Jews perished during the war, many thousand during one single Romanian pogrom in Iasi.) Romanian nationalism always staked claims to ethnically mixed territories, and as a result, after World War I, it had a little empire, by Balkan standards, that mostly consisted of national minorities. The Romanians' desire to hold on to these territories and either to assimilate the minorities or to engage in ethnical cleansing resulted in an intense and aggressive nationalism with all kinds of mythical and mystical beliefs in the eternal mission of the Romanian nation. This was also the main ideological plank of Romanian fascism and it had some support in all classes of the population.

The case of Romania shows that classifying aggressive and authoritarian nationalism as "extreme rightist" is true only to a point. Significant differences still exist among Marshal Antonescu, the National Communist regime (after the early 1960s), and many present-day politicians, in both the government and the opposition. They all want a greater Romania, and even though most of these regimes were dictatorships or, at best, very imperfect democracies, their popular appeal has been considerable. The chances of a truly democratic Romania at peace with itself and its neighbors are not great. However, since political and economic realities limit the ultranationalist ambitions of a small country, military aggression is ruled out, and because of its poverty, Romania depends to a large extent on the goodwill of the outside world, the prospects of radical fascism in Romania are less than brilliant. Although small oppositionist groups can engage—without fearing punishment—in unbridled attacks against the outside world and utter dire threats against their enemies on the domestic scene, the government cannot afford to do so. Thus, just as Antonescu prevailed over the Iron Guard, the conservative forces are likely to defeat their radical challengers.

The Former Yugoslavia

The former components of the Yugoslav federation are ruled by nationalist parties and leaders, with the intensity of nationalism differing from republic to republic. It is the least aggressive in Slovenia, but the drive toward nationalism is present everywhere and has resulted in war and civil war. Such nationalism creates obvious difficulties for ultranationalists and neofascists: It is difficult to outflank Slobodan Milosevic or Franjo Tudjman (of Croatia) from the right or left, though the attempt has been made. The Serbian Radical Party (SRS) headed by Vojizlav Seselj has 29 seats (out of 250) in the Serbian parliament and has challenged Milosevic by advocating even more energetic ethnic cleansing and an even greater Serbia. This stand has brought the Serbs into conflict with the West and has driven them into the arms of Zhirinovsky, who has been a welcome guest in Belgrade and has expressed full support for a Greater Serbia. The SRS has attacked democratic politicians at home, but in view of Milosevic's firm grip on the army and police, it has not been able to make much headway. The party's main support is outside the big cities and in Bosnia, and it has devoted more energy to building up its militias than to organizing as a political party. As in other civil wars, the various armed groups of the extreme Right have been reluctant to surrender their independence, hence the quarrels between Seselj (commanding the Chetniks) and Arkan, another commander of the extreme Right (the "Tigers") supported by the Serb military.

Croatia has a fascist tradition dating back more than sixty years, and the Croatian nationalist establishment led by Franjo Tudjman has made considerable efforts to deny it. If the Serbs strive for a greater Serbia, the Croats have traditionally wanted a state including Bosnia and Herzegovina, which perpetuates the conflict with Belgrade. Tudjman, a former general in Tito's army, with training as a historian, was purged as a Croatian nationalist. Eventually he became a conservative politician. In his book, entitled *Wasteland*, published in 1988, he argued that only 40,000 inmates, not 700,000, as claimed by the Serbs, were killed by the Ustasha in the notorious Jasenovac extermination camp during World War II. The truth could be somewhere in the middle between the two estimates. In fact, according to Tudjman, the Serbs and gypsies were killed (or, rather, were selected for murder) by the Jews who "have an inclination towards genocide." Later, Tudjman withdrew many, but not all, of his anti-Semitic attacks, mainly perhaps because of the unwelcome echo abroad, at a time when Croatia very much depended on Western help.

There can be no doubt about the political leanings of Tudjman and his party (the Croatian Democratic Community, or HDZ). They were pushed to the right—that is, toward a policy of greater expansion, by Croatian émigrés, mainly those in Canada. But the Herzegovina lobby was less enthusiastic about a state with a substantial Muslim minority and preferred either dividing Bosnia between Serbia and Croatia or giving it some autonomy.

Tudjman's policy on these issues was not radical enough to please some extreme elements, and it was to some extent inconsistent and contradictory, given to sudden switches. The extremists (the Croatian Party of Historic Rights, or HSP), mainly young militants led by Dobroslav Paraga, saw themselves as the heirs to the historic HSP, founded in 1861, the fount of Croatian nationalism and also of Ante Pavelic's Ustasha, the fascists who ruled Croatia during World War II. The extremists had their own paramilitary organization that was gradually absorbed into the Croatian army. There could be little doubt about the antidemocratic character of the HSP, which did not do well in the reasonably free elections but was still a force to be reckoned with in view of its members' militancy.

Tudjman and his comrades belong to the conservative–nationalist–authoritarian rather than the fascist tradition. Their party has split, with the moderates establishing their own movement. The moderates may constitute a genuine challenge to Tudjman, as they are concerned about Croatia's image abroad and fear that in a conflict with Serbia in the future, Croatia may need all the help it can get.

Slovakia and the Czech Republic

Between the two world wars, even democratic Czechoslovakia had a fascist movement, the NOF (National Fascist Community), although it never amounted to much. This was a party led by an ex-general, Rudolf Gajda. In 1935 it polled 2 percent of the total vote countrywide, but in 1939 it was disbanded. During World War II, the Czech regions were a *Protektorat* under German occupation. Slovakia attained an independence of sorts and was ruled by a clerical–fascist regime in which the church, the old Slovak nationalists, and die-hard fascists were more or less equal importance.

Following the division of Czechoslovakia on January 1, 1993, Prague again witnessed the emergence of a new party of the extreme Right in which certain fascist leanings could be detected, even though it claimed that its spiritual father was Tomáš Masaryk, the democratic founder of the first republic. This new party is the Republican Party, founded in late 1989 and headed by Miroslav Sladek, who worked as a censor under the Communist regime but later assumed the mantle of an extreme anti-Communist. With its eight members in parliament, it is more a curiosity than a real danger to Czech democracy. It engages in propaganda against the establishment and has been attacking the democratic leaders of Communist leanings, corruption, and ineffectiveness in fighting crime. The Republican Party wants foreign workers expelled and is the only Czech party not to accept the secession of Slovakia. Its style is similar in some respects to Zhirinovsky's. It has maintained contacts with parties of the extreme Right in other European countries, but on visits to the United States, Sladek appears as a pillar of Czech democracy. The support for this party comes from working-class youth groups, mainly skinheads, and the depressed regions with high unemployment in northern Bohemia and Moravia, where it scored better than it did in Prague.

Most observers regard the Republicans as a party of free-floating protest against social conditions and crime rather than of the extreme Right. A poll among party members showed that only half think of themselves as sympathizers with the Right. The Republicans want to abolish obligatory military service, but on occasion Sladek has called on his followers to appear armed with rifles at meetings and demonstrations. The Republicans see their idol not in the prewar Czech fascists but in the Agrarian Party, originally a democratic movement that later gravitated toward authoritarianism.

The strongest nationalist force in Slovakia is the Slovak National Party (SNP). It is the successor to a historical movement founded in 1870 that strove for Slovak independence and was restored after 1989. It is difficult to define the character of this party, partly because old Communists are strongly represented in its leadership, side by side with staunch nationalists, but also because it has undergone several changes of policy in recent years. It is not a monolithic party but includes moderates, conservatives, and even admirers of Zhirinovsky. It has cooperated with Prime Minister Vladimir Meciar's ruling party but has also opposed him. During the first year of Slovak independence, its rhetoric was strident, attacking Czechs, Hungarians, and Jews. The SNP's assemblies were often accompanied by acts of violence, and it made no secret that it derived much of its inspiration from the Hlinka guards, the fascist militia founded in 1938 and active during the war. Later, however, the party became more moderate, in order to gain respectability. Its share of the vote has varied between 7 and 11 percent. With the election of its leader, Jan Slota, the mayor of Zilina and a more charismatic figure than his predecessors, it has again veered toward a radical line. The party's program has remained deliberately vague. Nonetheless, the difference between Slota and Meciar is one of degree rather than substance and quality—"fascism with a human face," in the words of a political opponent.

Besides the SNP there are a few small groups, such as the Slovak Peoples Union, that derive their inspiration from the Tiso regime and work for its rehabilitation. (Tiso was executed as a war criminal.) However, unlike the situation in Romania, the authorities have resisted their initiative. To the majority of the population, the economic consequences of separation from the Czech Republic have come as an unpleasant surprise. They are therefore more concerned about their low standard of living than about the ideas of Tiso and Hlinka, which seem irrelevant at the present time. Blaming the Czechs for all of Slovakia's shortcomings and poverty has been the line taken by the nationalist groups, but as time passes, this argument becomes less and less convincing.

East Germany and Bulgaria

East Germany and Bulgaria are the two countries in which, for a variety of reasons, fascism as a political factor did not arise after the breakdown of the old regime. In the interwar era, Bulgaria was not more democratic than other Balkan countries; it had political parties, but the monarchy, the army, and other nonelected forces played a crucial role in its politics. But Bulgaria also has a tradition of relatively greater tolerance than do the other East European countries, except Czechoslovakia. There has been some tension with its sizable Turkish minority (about 10 percent), and pressure has been exerted on them to re-Bulgarize their names. But there has been no Turkish separatist movement. The Jews are well integrated into Bulgarian society, and although the gypsies (about 3.5 percent of the population) are not well liked, they are not persecuted. There was in Bulgaria a traditional "German" party, but this did not extend to embracing Nazism, just as the "Russian" party did not want to copy Stalinism. After 1989, Bulgaria again showed more political stability than did the other East European countries, even though its economic difficulties were no less severe than elsewhere in the region.

Bulgaria is the home of the IMRO (the Internal Macedonian Revolutionary Organization), which for a hundred years has been fighting for an independent state. Such a state then came into being following the breakup of Yugoslavia, but some Macedonian radicals still want to expand its territory. At one time, Bulgaria supported the IMRO, but the goals of the Macedonians are not now those of Bulgarian nationalism.

For a number of years, the tiny Bulgarian National Radical Party (BNRP) has existed and is the nearest to a party of the extreme Right. It has established relations with the usual partners abroad (Zhirinovsky and Le Pen's National Front). But it attracted not more than 1 percent of the vote in the 1992 general elections, and its aggressive leanings are limited to irredentist claims abroad and populist slogans at home. It has not rejected in principle a democratic system.

There has been considerable political violence in the former German Democratic Republic and the attacks against foreign workers attracted worldwide attention, even though the number of foreigners in East Germany is quite small in comparison with that in West Germany and other European countries. The reemergence of the right-wing skinheads on East Germany's streets in the 1980s has often been explained with reference to Germany's Nazi past. But since the overwhelming majority of the new fascists (if fascists they are) are very young and are not visibly influenced by former Nazis, we must look for explanations elsewhere.

Communist East Germany never made a real effort to come to terms with its Nazi past. The official line was that Nazism (and neo-Nazism) had nothing to do with the republic, that it had been sponsored by West Germany's finance capitalists and revanchists. Thus a new generation grew up with only scant knowledge of the Nazi era. In any case, it is by no means certain that anti-Nazi political indoctrination would have made staunch democrats out of the young hooligans roaming the streets and dominating the soccer fields. If Nazism has found admirers and emulators among them, this can be attributed to the tensions inherent in Communist society: boredom among wide sections of working-class youth, with aimless energy turned into violence, cynicism, and a lack of values and convictions.

As long as the Stasi was in charge, such outrages could be controlled. But as soon as the police state disintegrated, the unrest came out of hiding, with xenophobia as its main manifestation. The general mood in East Germany after unification was a feeling of disappointment: The East Germans had had unreasonable expectations with regard to a rapid and striking improvement in their standard of living. Although their economic situation did improve, it took much longer than most had assumed, hence the protest movement.

Given the political conditions in the united Germany and the stringent laws against neo-Nazi organizations, the potential support for an extremist movement of the Right will not turn into a political force. Those disappointed joined the PDS, the successor to the old Communist Party, which did surprisingly well in the elections, especially among the beneficiaries of the old regime. This left the skinheads out in the cold, and so they turned to *Neger Klatschen* (beating up foreigners, the equivalent of Paki-bashing in England), desecrating Jewish cemeteries with swastikas, and smashing windows. But they have neither the organization nor the leaders, direction, and ambition to become a political party.

The Baltic Countries and Ukraine

The successor states of the Soviet Union lack a democratic tradition and all face grave political and economic problems, so the prospects for the appearance of radical forces are favorable. The Central Asian republics have remained under national Communist rule, as they were for many years under Brezhnev and his successors. In Uzbekistan, under Islam Karimov (a deputy prime minister in the Communist regime), there has been hardly any change at all. Separ Murad Nijasov of Turkmenistan banned the old Communist Party in August 1990 and had himself elected for ten years by a majority of 99.5 percent. Askar Akayev, an anti-Communist and president of the Kirgiz Academy of Sciences during the old regime, was elected by 96 percent. Nursultan Nazarbayev of Kazakhstan was secretary of the Central Committee of the Kazakh Communist Party and is probably the Central Asian leader most willing to institute reforms—against the wishes of the local old Communists. Azerbaijan is ruled by Gaidar Aliev, a member of the Politburo under Brezhnev. In Armenia and Georgia, the struggle for power has been between the nationalist incumbents and the more radical Communist or right-wing groups. But because many former leading Communists can be found among the incumbents, any generalizations about them are impossible.

Ultranationalist movements exist in all these countries, but genuine fascist groups have not been able to organize. Power in Belarus also rests with the old Communist elite, and in view of the apathy of the population, its hold has not been seriously challenged.

This leaves the Baltic countries and Ukraine. The Baltic states tried democracy after World War I, but the experiment did not last long. In Lithuania it ended in 1926, and in Latvia and Estonia, in 1934. Authoritarianism, one-party rule based on the army and security forces (in Lithuania, also on the Catholic Church) under Karlis Ulmanis (Latvia) and Antanas Smetona and Augustinas Voldemaras (Lithuania), was fairly harsh, but under Konstantine Päts in Estonia, a little less so. In 1938, alone among the Baltic countries, Estonia restored a measure of democracy. The others took Mussolini rather than Hitler as their model.

During the Nazi occupation, the local population collaborated with the Germans, who were mistakenly welcomed as liberators from the Russian yoke. A confrontation with this awkward chapter in the history of the Baltic countries has so far been avoided. Considering that the Baltic countries had experienced democracy for only a few years, their record after regaining independence from Russia has been better than expected. All these republics were reluctant to give full civil rights to the Russian minority in their countries, but with some pressure from Russia and also Scandinavia and the European Union, they did make some concessions. The "Russian" problem is less acute in Lithuania, with only 10 percent Russians, than in the two other republics. There are a handful of right-wing extremists in the Lithuanian parliament, but the former Communist Party (now the Democratic Workers Party) won the general election in 1993. Aleksandr Brazauskas (a former first secretary of the Communist Party) became president of Lithuania in 1993, but even his opponents did not doubt that he and his party had undergone a true conversion.

Extreme right-wing groups exist in all three Baltic countries, receiving support from émigrés in the West, but only in Latvia do they constitute a serious political force. Among the Russian minority, many voted for Zhirinovsky and the Russian neo-Communists. Lithuania, Latvia, and Estonia know that their survival depends on Western and Scandinavian support and that right-wing extremism is bound to antagonize their well-wishers.

The OUN, the main force among the Ukranian émigrés in Poland and Germany before World War II, was strongly influenced by Nazism, but it changed its orientation when it appeared that the Germans would be defeated. Their successors in the Ukraine (the "integral nationalists") have always been much stronger in the western regions of Ukraine (Lviv-Lvov) than in the industrial east, which is heavily Russian. Power in the capital has remained firmly in the hands of Communist officials who, facing enormous internal and external difficulties, have carried out some modest reforms. At the same time, a swing toward fascism took place in the western Ukraine. This refers to the UNA (one of the successors of OUN) and its paramilitary arm, the UNSO. This movement declared itself the only incorruptible force in the country; became the proponent of a bellicose line vis-à-vis Russia; and published anti-American, antiliberal, antidemocratic, and anti-Semitic propaganda: Minorities were to be deported from Ukraine, and the Ukranian army (equipped with nuclear weapons) was to be strengthened. The UNA–UNSO also had a handful of representatives elected to parliament, including four in Kiev.

Although paramilitary formations were banned by government decree, this was not enforced in practice. Dimitro Korchinsky, aged thirty and the commander of the UNSO, claims 8,000 members; his journal allegedly has sold 100,000 copies. The UNSO's banner is black and red; its slogans are "War is our future" and "Provocation, revolt, revolution." However, according to reliable estimates, the fascist Right, including smaller organizations such as the Brotherhood of the Eastern Cross and the Legion of the New Order and even a National Socialist party, has a backing of no more than 3 percent.

Right-wing sentiments are widespread in Ukraine, among both Ukrainians and Russians, but profascist groups are only a fringe element, a situation that will probably not change even if the economic crisis deepens. Given the almost insurmountable problems that any Ukrainian government is likely to face, a victory of extremist, confrontational forces would inevitably lead to civil war and possibly to the disintegration of the country. Most Ukrainians are aware of the precarious situation of their country, and so they are unlikely to opt for a policy destined to end in disaster.

The reasons that make post-Communist Eastern Europe a fertile ground for political movements in the fascist tradition have been mentioned more than once in this book: The absence or lack of a tradition of democratic institutions (and of tolerance and other democratic qualities), without which democratic institutions cannot be successful; the economic difficulties and social tensions that will face these countries for a long time to come; and the prevalence of ultranationalism directed both outward and inward.

At the same time, the neofascist movements face many obstacles, and not just their internal divisions, which could be overcome by a charismatic leader. Rather, such obstacles also include the difficulty of finding the enemies needed by populist movements of the Right and Left: The Jews have disappeared, and even badly informed East Europeans cannot possibly believe that the gypsies endanger their national survival. A few intellectuals of the far Right have tried to conjure up the threat of the West, above all America. But it will be impossible to persuade Eastern Europeans that they should hate America, because for many of them it is paradise, at least a material paradise. It is equally difficult to play the anti-Communist card, for often the leaders of the extreme Right come from the same stable as do the ruling ex-Communists, and the economic social ideas of the neofascists are similar to theirs.

Yet another obstacle has not been mentioned: Interwar fascism in Eastern Europe and the parafascist military dictatorships were very much part of the zeitgeist. All the major continental powers except France abandoned democracy in the 1930s, and the French model was not widely admired. Thus it was no accident that during the 1920s, Eastern Europe decided to try democracy, admittedly without much success, and then in the 1930s, fascism and dictatorship became the norm.

Today, dictatorship and fascism have been discredited, even if nationalism is again acceptable. But if any Eastern European country defied the zeitgeist, it would have to pay for it. China may be able to ignore this trend, but small countries heavily dependent on the rest of the world cannot. The disapproval of the West did not, however, prevent the civil war in Yugoslavia. But Yugoslavia is a multinational country, and once Tito was gone, the country was bound to fall apart. All other Eastern European countries are now more homogenous than in the past.

Questions remain: Why did the Czech Republic and Slovakia divorce more or less harmoniously? Their history explains why an armed conflict did not ensue. Why has Hungary been more successful in its political and economic transition from Communism than Romania has? Again history, but not only the recent history of these countries under Communism, provides the answer.

The various obstacles on the road to fascism may well be insurmountable, even though as the difficulties multiply, the trend toward authoritarian rule will increase. But candidates other than the fascists can fill the void left by Communism and a democratic system that does not work; indeed, the ex-Communists know more about ruling a country than do right-wing extremists. Whatever their weaknesses, the ex-Communists are unlikely to engage in uncontrolled activities at home or abroad; most likely they will do little other than restore order, for which there is great demand.

What form will such authoritarian rule take? In some cases, it could be an enlightened dictatorship trying to steer the country through a difficult period, with the aim of creating greater freedom. In other cases, the authoritarian rule might be little better than fascism with a human face. And there are, of course, always unpredictable circumstances: What if there is a breakdown in one of the major Western European countries or in Russia?

There have always been exceptions to rules, and even if the age of fascism is over in Europe, individual aberrations are always possible. We have witnessed Communist regimes with an unparalleled cult of the Führer, but also with a collective leadership. There have been bellicose Communist regimes and others that basically want to be left alone. Contemporary China seems to have given up Marxism and is trying a transition to the market. Fascism could be equally adaptable: Hitler and Mussolini have been dead for fifty years, and so discussions of fascism should not focus on a specific variety that now belongs to history: Attempts to preserve or revive it will fail. The specter of historical fascism should therefore no longer haunt us, but others may come to take its place.

Conclusion

The Prospects of Fascism

Twice in the twentieth century, civilization was seriously threatened, by fascism, which was a European phenomenon, and by the ambitions of Communism, which spanned the whole world. Communism collapsed largely under its own weight, whereas a world war was needed to defeat fascism.

The temptation was great to celebrate victory, first in 1945 and again after the fall of Communism. But the moment of triumph did not last long—an interval of one or two years between world war and cold war, and an even shorter time after 1989 before disillusionment set in. But this anticlimax should not have come as a shock, because these two threats were at no time the only ones facing humankind. The conditions that made possible the rise of totalitarian regimes continue to exist, albeit in different forms and in other parts of the world. And so, near the end of the century that witnessed the great triumph and the short moment of relief, the question of a second coming of totalitarian movements is again on the agenda.

Democracy has never worked well; it has never generated as much enthusiasm as the modern dictatorships have. As the twentieth century draws to a close, the democratic system in many countries shows greater weakness than ever before. Outside Europe and North America, its roots were shallow, in any case.

The reasons for the crisis are known: the absence of strong democratic leadership, the weakness and lack of self-confidence on the part of the elites, the great majority's unreasonable expectations of what the state should and could do, the lack of cohesion in society, and the social changes creating ferment and uncertainty. With this weakening of the

center, ethnic separatism, the strengthening of individual and group interests over common bonds, there is a perception of impending collapse,
which may be quite false but which opens the door to various alternatives
to democracy.

In regard to their attitude toward the democratic system, the strategy of
the contemporary extreme Right is no longer that of historical fascism. The
open propagation of the idea of dismantling democracy is not thought
advisable, except in the more backward countries, where democracy barely
existed in the first place. A right-wing populist leader such as the Austrian
Jörg Haider is today influenced as much by the techniques of Ross Perot as
those of Adolf Hitler. Haider's future state will have "direct" rather than
representative democracy. Political parties will be largely replaced by citizens' initiatives, perhaps with an occasional plebiscite, and, above all,
strong presidential powers. The exploitation of modern technological and
social trends, such as telecracy, combined with the decline of public interest
in politics as well as the personalization of political issues, make it possible
to create the illusion of a "participatory democracy," a euphemism for the
manipulation of people unhappy with the political parties' performance.

These changes are not only tactical; rather, they reflect deeper changes
in world politics. Even the most extreme nationalists in Western Europe no
longer dream of wars of aggression against their neighbors: The new
European fascism is defensive rather than offensive, because even ultranationalists need allies to survive. Ideologically, most groups of the
extreme Right have become strong supporters of European solidarity
against common dangers such as a loss of identity, foreign influences, and
the influx of immigrants. This is the concept of fortress Europe, a Europe
of the Aryan race, an idea first proposed toward the end of World War II
when the tide had turned against the Nazis. But this new "Euronationalism"
is extremely fuzzy. The German neo-Nazis want to include all of northern
Europe, including Britain and France. The French want to keep the British
out, to gravitate more toward the south, and they have their doubts about
the Germans. The Italians are distrustful of the northerners, and the Russians are drawn to the Balkans and do not feel close to the Europeans,
whom they consider almost as decadent as the Americans.

The idea of the decadent West is even more central to the Islamists in
the Middle East and North Africa; but they are as divided among themselves as the European extreme Right is. Teheran has offered help and
cooperation from Khartoum to Algiers. The national and religious antago-
nisms continue to fester, however, and the perception of a common enemy
is not a sufficiently secure base for truly close unity.

All neofascist and right-wing extremist parties are nationalistic. International fascism is unthinkable, a contradiction in terms. But the character of

nationalism has changed as the role of Europe in world affairs has shrunk. Whereas the Nazis envisaged a strict hierarchy of races even inside Europe, this is no longer feasible today, or at least cannot be preached openly.

What has remained is the hostility to the ideas of freedom and to the rights of the individual and Western values in general, anti-Americanism, and the concept of a "third way." Hostility to the West, one of the basic tenets of historical fascism, was submerged during the cold war. Communism, after all, also was an enemy of the extreme Right and the neofascists, certainly on an ideological level. In practice, though, Marxism–Leninism hardly ever bothered them. Even during the cold war, these circles were inclined toward neutralism, and with the breakdown of the Soviet Empire, America (and the West in general) has become the main enemy, outside Western Europe even more than among the various European national fronts and "Republican" parties.

2

The debates about the future of neofascism, clerical fascism, and the populist movements of the extreme Right in Europe and beyond have begun, even though the discussions of historical fascism—its origins, characteristics, and consequences—have by no means ended. These debates encompass the revisionism of the Right and the Left and also the attempts to define and classify fascism—assuming always that there is such a thing as "generic fascism" on which the experts do not at all agree.

The two revisionist approaches start from entirely different viewpoints but reach conclusions that are remarkably similar. The revisionists of the Right believe that it is irrelevant to state that Nazism and fascism were evil. The reasons are that Hitler led Germany out of its economic crisis. He was a great modernizer and made Germany a powerful country. If it had not been for certain mistakes and excesses, he would have entered history as a great leader. In any case, the assignment of the historian is to understand rather than to judge. Unlike the neo-Nazis, these revisionists do not argue that Hitler and his movement should be idolized; they merely maintain that their crimes were by no means unique and that one should approach fascism with objectivity and detachment.

Fascism generated much enthusiasm among Germans and Italians. Many of its most ardent followers were idealists, and so it is a mistake to depict them as mere gangsters. One could have lived comfortably and relatively undisturbed in the Third Reich if one were not a Jew or a political dissenter and refrained from taking an active interest in politics, did not run afoul of individual Nazi dignitaries, and made the necessary concessions to the regime in daily life. The same is true, incidentally, with regard to Fascist Italy and even Stalinist Russia.

What should we conclude from these arguments? Less than the revisionists believe, for even if there was genuine enthusiasm in the summer camps of the Hitler Youth, fascism—and particularly Nazism—subscribed to a barbarous doctrine that caused the death of millions of people and the untold suffering of more. Even though not everyone was affected, the lasting achievements of the regimes were few, for which an inordinate price in devastation and ruin had to be paid. German nationalists may find it difficult to accept that the crimes of Nazism were unique, and it might indeed be true that other dictators caused even greater havoc among their own people or others. But crimes also must be judged according to time and place, and Nazism did not prevail in a distant age—or in Cambodia— but in twentieth-century Europe. Fascism, quite likely, will be subject to "historization" as the memory of the victims fades, the pain and awareness become dimmer, and other problems become more of a concern as time passes. But this does not mean greater detachment and objectivity; it merely means less interest in the tragedies of the past and greater difficulty for historians to understand what happened in an extraordinary time, so different from the experience of the year 2000, let alone 2100. Empathy and instinctive understanding will become more and more difficult.

Revisionists of the Left see no merit in the Nazi movement except perhaps that it helped modernize Germany's antiquated social structures. The same argument has been made with regard to Fascism in Italy. These revisionists attribute little importance to individual leaders and their ideological beliefs. If massive crimes were committed, they believe, it was the fault not so much of National Socialism but of capitalism and the bureaucracy. So they have decided not to pay too much attention to Hitler's motives and ideas but instead to focus on the structures that made fascism possible, not to concentrate on its well-known unique features that, after all, may not have been so important. If the revisionists of the Right want to put Nazism in historical perspective, those of the Left want to put it in sociological context. They see, in most respects, no decisive qualitative differences between Nazism and other capitalist and bureaucratic regimes. They believe that the fascist regimes were not really totalitarian in character, because there was chaos beneath a thin skin of strict order. Seen in this perspective, Hitler was not a strong but a weak dictator, had difficulty making decisions and did not know much of the time what was going on around him, because the bureaucracy was following its own agenda.

Similar arguments have been made with regard to Stalin's Russia. In both cases, they are not convincing and need not concern us here. But what would Hitler's place be in history had he called a halt to aggression in 1938, not invaded any more countries, not unleashed a world war? Would he and his regime not have entered history as great and effective, albeit somewhat flawed? On his own, Mussolini might have engaged in some colonial adventures, but certainly not in a world war. But a Hitler capable of stopping would not have been Hitler.

Hitler wanted war to restore Germany to its former greatness and, if possible, to make it even more powerful, and he succeeded at least temporarily. Naturally he had no detailed blueprint, because Hitler was an opportunist: Had he been confronted with strong military resistance in 1939/1940, he probably would have been satisfied with minor revisions of Germany's borders. But when Poland, France, and the others collapsed, he concluded that his enemies were paper tigers, that he could defeat all others, and thus he decided to take on the whole world.

Hitler wanted to destroy the Jews, whether by killing some and exiling the others to some faraway island, or by killing them all, or by starving or shooting or poisoning them. These details were decided only after the war had broken out. Nazi Germany was a totalitarian state, Hitler had only five years of peace. It is certain that he did not make every decision in the Third Reich and that the intrigues and tug-of-war between the leaders under him continued, as they did in Italy. Hitler had strong beliefs on a great varieties of issues, but like Stalin and every other powerful dictator, he nonetheless did have some constraints. But he still made all the important decisions.

Were Nazism and Fascism just dictatorships, more purposeful and violent, but essentially not different from other such regimes in history? The general pattern of dictatorship and tyranny is unchanging, but technical progress opened possibilities of propaganda and control that did not exist before, and the ideological motivation (as in the case of Stalinist Russia) was stronger than in earlier regimes. The quantity became a new quality.

In what way was Italian Fascism modeled on the Soviet regime (as some have asserted), and to what extent was anti-Bolshevism the central issue for the Nazi movement? With regard to Italian and other kinds of fascism, the answer is obvious. What happened in Russia had no impact whatsoever on the origins of Italian Fascism, and anti-Bolshevism played no role in Mussolini's policy, either. Anti-Communism was one of the planks of the Nazi movement, and the fear of the "Red danger" certainly contributed to its rise to power. But there is no reason to believe that Communism was ever the paramount factor in Nazi doctrine and action.

In what ways were Nazism and Stalinism similar? According to some, they cannot be compared, because fascism is capitalist, and the Soviet regime was socialist, because under Communism the means of production is not in private hands. This is a correct observation, but how important politically was it in practice? Capitalists had no decisive say in the shaping of Nazi domestic and foreign policy, and the toiling masses of the Soviet Union had even less of an impact on that country's policy. In addition, the Soviet regime had initially been internationalist, but as the years passed and the construction of "socialism in one country" proceeded, it jettisoned more and more of its internationalist baggage and became national social-ist in practice, and gradually also in theory. The one-party system, propa-ganda, terror, and other ingredients of totalitarian rule were no mere accidents but the concomitants of dictatorial rule in the twentieth century.

Despite all this, the important differences between Communism and fascism pertained to ideological motivation and the German, Italian, and Russian historical tradition. During the early days of the cold war it was customary to maintain that Nazi Germany and the Soviet Union were "essentially identical systems," as Hannah Arendt put it at the time. But after Stalin's death and particularly after the Twentieth Party Congress, it became almost sacrilege even to compare the two systems, which, accord-ing to a majority view, were radically different in character.

With the breakup of the Soviet Union, the pendulum has again swung back in the other direction. In recent books, François Furet and Richard Pipes noted that Lenin and Mussolini came from the same political back-ground and that Hitler and Stalin shared a moral nihilism and a cult of political power. Their ideology liberated them from all moral scruples, and so conflicts between nation and individual were no longer subject to the rules of Western civilization. In other words, mass murder became legiti-mate. But these writers, and some others, go too far in stressing the impor-tance of the lessons that Hitler allegedly learned from the Bolsheviks.[1]

Hitler did realize that Communism had become national socialist in its own peculiar way, and he was also aware that Jewish leaders in the Soviet Union had been removed from power and liquidated. In some ways and within limits, Hitler had a sneaking admiration for Stalin. But all this did not for a moment influence his decision to attack the Soviet Union in June 1941 in an attempt to destroy it.

3

We have mentioned the impossibility of defining fascism precisely. The term *fascism* has been used indiscriminately, for instance, with regard to the

Franco regime or prewar Japan. But even more careful use of the term leaves open many unanswerable questions about the prewar period and even more about neofascism. The MSI and the Italian neofascists were created by a group of admirers of the late Duce who wanted to continue the fascist tradition after 1945. But historical fascism was always a coalition between radical, populist ("fascist") elements and others gravitating toward the extreme Right. The same tug-of-war continued in the MSI in the postwar period. Sometimes the fascist orientation prevailed, and at other times the extreme right wing held sway, until 1994 the party even changed its name in order to dissociate itself from its fascist past. Thus for a purist historian of the MSI, the party was fascist in certain years (under Pini) but not in others (under Fini); and under Giorgio Almirante, its secretary-general for many years, it was sometimes fascist sometimes neofascist, and sometimes postfascist. Such hairsplitting is impractical and only causes confusion. Nor is a solution brought any nearer by the introduction of yet another label.

The two most important recent developments have been the domestication of neofascism in Europe and the appearance of fascistlike movements, usually under the banner of ultranationalism or fundamentalist religion outside Europe where they did not exist before. It is too soon to consider the domestication of fascism in Europe to be an accomplished and irreversible fact. It is possible that the major neofascist movements in Europe have been converted to democracy, even though they maintain their populist character and continue to be authoritarian in approach and outlook. But this is by no means certain. As for clerical fascism, particularly in North Africa and the Middle East, the similarities with historical fascism are striking in some respects but not in others. Characterizations of the political system in Iran do not necessarily fit other such movements and regimes in the Muslim world, and the new fascist and profascist movements in Russia and the former Soviet Union are so far too inchoate and changing too much to permit more than a tentative classification.

In brief, the fascist label will have to be replaced by one or several others at some future date, but until they are provided, it is preferable to stick to the old.

There are good reasons, however, not to be distracted for too long by searches for theories and definitions of fascism offering a magic formula that has escaped us so far. In any event, such a formula does not exist; reality is always more complex than theory; and anyway, it matters less than widely thought. Alexander Pope wrote: "Nature and nature's laws lay hid in night; God said let Newton be! and all was light." Such a Newton will not arise in the field of fascist studies.

4

Among the issues we have not discussed so far are extreme right-wing thought and action in North America. The historical predecessors are well known—the Ku Klux Klan and the John Birchers, Father Coughlin and Gerald K. Smith, the Silver Shirts, McCarthyism, and the Aryan National Congress, the Aryan Resistance, the Identity Church, and some of the Survivalists. These and other groups have been numerous and not uninfluential. Given the chaotic American party system, it has been relatively easy for small groups of determined people to infiltrate the major parties and be elected—for instance, Klan members and more recently Lyndon Larouche's followers.

Some of these groups openly advocate and use violence. They share with the Nazis their burning hatred of minorities, anti-Semitism, and a firm belief in gigantic conspiracies. But virtually none has turned to systematic political action, nor has there been a determined effort to gain power by means of armed violence. Whatever the misdeeds of Senator Joseph McCarthy, he never dreamed about a fascist America with himself as the leader. Most American extremist groups are defensive by nature; they believe themselves under siege and subject to relentless attacks by foreign groups, who want to undermine American traditions. They are backward looking, in the tradition of the vigilante and the posse. Alternatively, they believe that Judgment Day is near, that the cities will go up in flames, but that they will survive and build a new America. The bombing of government offices in Oklahoma City in April 1995 was carried out by a number of paranoiacs who thought themselves besieged by an all-powerful state. The perpetrators imagined they were engaging in an act of revenge. They were not even members of a quasi-religious sect like the Aum Shinrikyo, which in March had carried out indiscriminate poison-gas attacks in Japan. The chief weapon of terrorism is violence, and fascism is a firm believer in violence. It is also true that on occasion fascist movements have engaged in individual terrorism rather than mass violence. But terrorism is still no synonym for fascism, but merely an instrument, a means to an end, and the ends often are very different in character.

Since the mid-1970s, groups such as Louis Farrakhan's Nation of Islam, an organization for African Americans, have sprung up, and they have been more successful in gaining a hearing and attracting followers than have the white extremists in their communities. The belief in a Jewish world conspiracy is all-pervasive: Jews were the principal slaveholders; they exploited blacks; and they invented AIDS to kill blacks. The gurus of this movement deny that the Holocaust ever took place and, moreover, believe that Christianity was invented to keep blacks in submission. They also maintain that women are inferior to men and have no equal rights, that homosexuals and lesbians are evil, and that UFOs exist and should be paid due attention. According to them, America is the main enemy of the black person. The Nation of Islam has also admonished young people to improve themselves, to work hard, not to take drugs, and not to kill one another. But these initiatives take second place to the hate propaganda, which has a much greater appeal: It is always easier to put the blame for the current dismal state of affairs on outsiders than to call for self-criticism and hard work.

With the exception of a few sectarians such as George Rockwell, no one has claimed to be a Nazi or neo-Nazi. The fact is that the Nazi and fascist ideal would not have been attractive in America, except at the height of the Depression: America has not lost a war (except perhaps the Vietnam War); it has no territorial demands; it is not militaristic; it does not dream of an imperial mission; and in recent times, no one has wanted to conduct an aggressive war. America is not ethnically homogenous, and although there has been some resentment against new immigrants, this could not, until recently, have served as a political platform.

The mood in America has changed in recent years, but as in Europe it cannot seriously be claimed that the initiatives to limit immigration and to keep out illegal immigrants are fascist in inspiration. As one-third of Latinos and almost one-half of blacks and Asian-Americans voted for such an initiative in California in 1994, it cannot be argued that the motivation is racist.

The propaganda of black organizations such as the Nation of Islam, however strident and similar to fascism in inspiration or rhetoric, reaches only a limited audience. If it is fascism, it is the fascism of a minority that can only hope, at most, to cause damage to the state and society. But it cannot possibly aspire to conquer the country. Nonetheless, fascist trends among minority groups is a fascinating topic to which insufficient attention has so far been paid.[2] As the Million Man March on Washington in October 1995 has shown, some of the initiatives of these groups have an appeal well beyond their normal constituents. It recalls in some ways the reception given in Europe sixty years earlier to the idealistic slogans of organizations such as the Iron Front in Romania, which called for a national recovery, solidarity, rejuvenation, honesty, fatherhood, motherhood, and, generally speaking, a moral as well as a political rebirth.

5

The defeat of historical fascism and the lack of success of neofascism owe little to antifascism. Why did it have so little effect? With regard to the 1920s and 1930s, the answer is obvious: The opponents of fascism and Nazism vastly underrated the power of nationalism, which the fascists were quick to monopolize, whereas the democrats became the "lickspittles of the West" or simply "traitors." But could the old democratic parties have competed with the unbridled chauvinist demagogy of Hitler and Mussolini? A more resolute "patriotic" line would have made it difficult for the Nazis to win over the masses of the uncommitted, a fact freely admitted after 1945 by German Social Democrats such as Kurt Schumacher. The Communists vacillated between indiscriminate attack ("Schlagt die Faschisten wo ihr sie trefft"), which meant physical attack against rank-and-file Nazis—and collaboration with them. The Social Democrats had no fighting spirit and rejected all extraparliamentary action. Under the German constitution then in force, they had the right to use force against those trying to overthrow the democratic regime, but they did not dare use it. And so the fascist parties were outmaneuvered or defeated by right-wing autocrats such as Ion Antonescu, General Francisco Franco, and Admiral Philippe Pétain while the democratic leaders of the larger parties stood helpless and forlorn against this seemingly invincible new force.

Antifascism was discredited after 1945 because it was often misdirected and misused. In addition, the need for antifascist awareness was less urgent because there were no large fascist parties in Europe. Antifascism was misdirected because the term *fascism* was used too freely by those wanting to denounce their political enemies. The worst offenders were the Communists, especially in East Germany, with their continuous stream of propaganda denouncing conservatives, liberals, and even social democrats as fascists but showing little or no interest in genuine neo-Nazism. In fact, when the secret police archives were opened, the Stasi were revealed as having been instrumental in fabricating neo-Nazi and anti-Semitic incidents in West Germany to discredit their enemies.

After the demise of Communism, the exploitation of antifascism became a specialty of various Trotskyite sects, not because they believed in the existence of a major fascist threat or cared about it, but because they hoped to attract supporters by cashing in on a popular slogan. In the end, such "popular front" antifascism was always ineffective, because even those willing to collaborate with the Communists or Trotskyites on one particular issue, such as demonstrations protesting attacks against minorities, had no desire to embrace Leninist–Trotskyite doctrines.

This kind of antifascism did more harm than good. The overuse of the term caused confusion with regard to the identity of the real neo-Nazis and neofascists: If Germany's Konrad Adenauer and France's Charles de Gaulle were fascists, then the real fascists would be disregarded. As antifascism was discredited, fewer and fewer democrats felt inclined to participate in *bona fide* antifascist activities. Fraudulent antifascism, however, helped the fascists, sometimes by giving inordinate publicity to small sects and at other times by branding as "fascist" people and causes that had nothing to do with it. There is something akin to Gresham's law in contemporary politics.

But antifascism had yet another weakness: Men and women of goodwill assumed a spirit of internationalist altruism and self-sacrifice among their fellow citizens that simply did not exist. This refers to the idea that Europe would welcome without reservation the nonpolitical immigrants from overseas, even at a time when the South African government under Nelson Mandela was deporting each month some ten thousand illegal black immigrants, more than the number in all of Europe. This presumption showed a lack of awareness of the widespread concern about crime in the streets and similar issues. It was a repetition of the old mistake of the 1920s, of opening patriotism to aggressive demagogues. The antifascists of the 1980s and 1990s felt they represented a higher democracy and were entitled to force the majority to accept a way of life they abhorred, which played into the hands of right-wing extremists.

There was a widespread feeling even in the most permissive societies that open-arms policies had gone too far, that there was a danger of political as well as moral and cultural anarchy, and that at least some order and some of the traditional values had to be restored. The political parties, almost without exception, understood this mood and tried to adjust accordingly. But some of the intelligentsia did not agree, which explains, at least in part, why antifascism remained inconsequential.

6

What are the prospects for fascism in the contemporary world? The record of more than seventy years shows common patterns: Fascism arises at a time of economic, social, and political crisis, when the old order no longer seems able to cope with urgent problems. These are the preconditions for the growth of fascist and neofascist movements, but whether the fascists are able to exploit such a constellation depends on a variety of circumstances, such as the intensity of the crisis, the determination of the incumbents to resist the challenge, and the presence or absence of effective fascist leaders. A promising situation (that is, promising from a fascist point of view) may pass unused because the fascists are divided or lack effective leadership.

Fascism has always been a movement of protest and discontent, and the contemporary world contains a great reservoir of protest. The social basis of the new fascism has become more plebeian (in some countries more than in others) and more radically populist than historical fascism was. Outside Europe it has been strongest in those societies unable or unwilling to keep in step with the West, or even to overtake it, as the Asian–Pacific countries have done.

To assess the overall prospects of fascism and similar movements, we must consider several factors. If it is true that the cold war ended with the decisive victory of liberal democracy as the only remaining contestant in the field, as the ideal to which everyone—or almost everyone—was aspiring, the future for fascism is bleak. But the prospects for liberal democracy are not that rosy, for there is likely to be a backlash against conditions on the international and the domestic scene, which many consider as increasingly chaotic. Clearly, not every nondemocratic regime needs to be in a fascist mold. If a society has reached a relatively high level of development and the crisis facing it seems to be transient, a relatively mild authoritarian regime could resolve the problem. "Objectively," a harsh totalitarian regime may not be needed to confront contemporary (or future) challenges. But "objectively," fascism and Nazism were not needed in 1923 and 1933, either, and yet they prevailed because nondemocratic movements tend to have a momentum of their own. The deeper the crisis is, real or perceived, the greater will be the desire for an effective dictatorship that enables its rulers to pursue their politics unencumbered by pressures and opposition from below. Such a dictatorship must be firm and ruthless; it cannot tolerate an opposition, thus the need for repression. It also needs the support of broad sections of the population, hence the need for propaganda.

Europe and other parts of the world have witnessed enormous economic progress over the last half-century. But there is no reason to assume that this growth will continue to rise at the same rate. Real income in the United States has fallen since the mid-1970s and has stagnated in most West European countries. Unemployment—virtually unknown in the 1960s—is now endemic, with a rate in various countries in excess of 10 percent, and in some, such as Spain, over 20 percent. According to projections, a considerable part of the labor force, perhaps as much as half, will be working part time in twenty years from now.[3]

New investment has been directed more and more toward Asia and certain Third World countries where productivity is higher. Free trade finds fewer supporters, and indeed, many regard it as detrimental to their interests. Economic growth in Asia will be, in all probability, fast in the decades to come. Accordingly, this relative decline of the West may give rise to resentment and fear. Some argue that democracy and radical economic reform do not mix. True, the relative decline is taking place during a period of prosperity, if compared with the situation in the 1920s and 1930s. Industrial jobs are disappearing faster in Europe than new ones become available, but a social security safety net now takes care of those affected. Shelter, food, and medical assistance are provided for the needy.

But it is not certain whether even rich Europe can afford to spend so much on welfare for a growing underclass. Even some of the richest cities on the Continent find themselves on the verge of bankruptcy. And even if the countries can afford it, the social consequences of a dependence on welfare are dismal and politically dangerous. It means that millions of people are marginalized and no longer seek employment. Areas of decay and violent crime have been created in major European cities; in America they have existed for a long time.

Since the 1970s the gap between the rich and the poor has substantially widened, particularly in the United States, Britain, and the former Soviet Union. According to projections, this trend will continue, and although some countries, notably the United States, have shown tolerance so far of this rising inequality, elsewhere it is causing social and political unrest.

The underclass is still a minority, but the feeling of uncertainty among the majority of the employed, about the future of their workplace, is rising. In technical language this is known as *accelerated structural change* in the economy, and it affects white-collar employees as much as manual workers. If enough people develop such feelings of insecurity, they will turn into a political factor of paramount importance. If there are not enough jobs for everyone (or almost everyone); if the young for whom no work can be found in the first place are joined by those of early middle age who, having lost their job, cannot be reintegrated into the economy; and if there are no far-reaching schemes for work sharing, the social and political consequences may be serious. Such a situation can lead to populist and/or extremist movements, as it did in the past. Of all the factors that contributed to the rise of fascism in the 1930s, insecurity was one of the most crucial, and certainly the least understood and examined.

Part of the new underclass is native born, and part is of foreign origin: In Holland, for instance, 40 percent of Turkish and Moroccan immigrants are unemployed, but only 7 percent of the Dutch have no job. A similar disproportion exists elsewhere. Such inequality breeds hostility among the guest workers toward the "rich" natives with whom they come into contact daily. It also means resentment of the "parasites" by the native-born population and a growing reluctance to pay billions each year to provide social services, food, and shelter for the nonworking underclass. The impression takes hold that the situation is out of control. Ethnic strife and class conflicts increase, and the demand for a strong government grows.

7

Another aspect, perhaps more important, as far as Europe is concerned, is the crisis of parliamentary democracy. Wherever fascism grew strong in Europe, it was against a background of a loss of faith in democratic institutions. In part, it had to do with claims of corruption. But such claims were only one aspect, and not the most important one: There had been little corruption in Germany before 1933. Nazism and fascism did not gain power primarily because of promises to clean up corrupt regimes; rather, they promised to replace weak governments. There was, and is now, a need for a strong democratic government, but is it possible in the contemporary world? Even where it has deep roots, democracy has never been loved; the most it engenders is a belief that despite all their drawbacks, democratic institutions are the best in an imperfect world.

In the 1970s, as in the late 1920s, the feeling prevailed that the system had become unworkable and the countries ungovernable. In the 1980s, this feeling was submerged, only to resurface again in the 1990s. It refers to the belief that governments have become weak and even impotent as the result of growing pressures that cause governments to act not in the national interest but to safeguard their reelection. Instead of making difficult decisions, they try to be all things to all people. It refers to the growing importance of lobbies fighting for vested interests and of the media— responsible to no one but their owners—setting the national agenda, not in accordance with real, deeper needs but with the quickly changing exigencies of entertainment.

These perceptions are not exaggerated, but they are incomplete. The weakness of democratic leaders and institutions is paralleled by irresponsibility and apathy in society: the belief in the omnipotence of the state, the widespread and increasing feeling that it can deliver almost anything without a corresponding effort on the part of the people, that a state and a society are akin to a corporation with limited stakes, concerned with profits, privileges, and entitlements, with civic duties limited to a minimum of taxation. Thus the inclination is growing to support a new kind of leadership proposing quick solutions outside the democratic system.

In what circumstances do democratic regimes disintegrate? Governments lose their monopoly of force, because the constitution gives them little power, because they have such power but are reluctant to use it, or because the forces of law and order are no longer loyal to the democratic system. Electoral systems that do not create stability have been cited as an important reason for the breakdown of democratic regimes. But frequent changes in government (and even protracted periods of no government) do not necessarily lead to the victory of extremist forces. Legitimacy is a crucial factor, as is the readiness of the opposition to accept the democratic system and act accordingly. If there is no broad democratic consensus in society resting on shared values and goals, the prospects of democracy are dim. Support for democracy will erode if political change is blocked. This was the case in Italy and Austria after World War II. There was no democratic alternative to the leading party (or parties), which stayed in power without interruption. But once the cold war ended, the old system disintegrated.

8

The crisis of democracy accounts for the rise of Fascism and Nazism in the 1920s and 1930s in Italy and Germany. But it does not explain the rise of strong fascist movements in Hungary and Romania in the 1930s, because there was no democracy in these countries in the first place. Nor does it explain the emergence of strong parties of the extreme Right more recently in Eastern Europe and the former Soviet Union. The crisis of democracy is irrelevant to the rise of radical Islam in Iran, Algeria, and Egypt, or to secular totalitarian dictatorships such as that in Iraq.

It is precisely in the more developed countries of the Third World that a political doctrine and a political system in the fascist tradition seem to have the best chances at the present time. Whatever the shortcomings of parliamentary democracy in western, central, and southern Europe, it is difficult to imagine the return to power of movements as repressive, violent, and enthusiastic as fascism was in its heyday. The neo-Nazi, the neofascist sectarians should remain uninfluential. The more substantial populist ultranationalist parties have much better chances, but even they could not, in all probability, go beyond authoritarianism if they gained power. They might dismantle part of the democratic system, but they could not establish a fully fledged totalitarian regime. The European countries have been immunized to a certain extent against fascism, and Europeans and Americans are too rich and lethargic to put up much of a fight for such a system unless confronted by a crisis much deeper than any that can be envisioned at the present time.

The situation in Russia and Eastern Europe is less predictable. The collapse of Communism created a void that some hoped would be filled by democrats. But even though Communism had a bad fall, the Communist leaders had a soft landing and, within a few years, again found themselves in power in most countries. Attempts to introduce democratic institutions were less than successful, and so the ideological void was filled by some kind of national socialism. Could it have been different? Perhaps, but the chances were not very good because there had been no democratic foundations on which to build, and the transition was bound to be difficult and protracted. With all this, historical Communism cannot be put together again, so perhaps fascism and Communism will have to combine forces in a search for innovation and refurbishment. Perhaps they will return in the framework of a military dictatorship.

The first manifesto of such a regime can be envisaged without difficulty, for there have been many precursors: Corrupt and inefficient politicians will be denounced; threats of a breakdown of public order, inflation, unemployment and economic decline, and growing anarchy and separatism will be invoked—in brief, impending total disaster. In such circumstances, in the national interest, a strong government will be chosen to save the country. A state of emergency (or siege) will be declared for a limited period only. Such a dictatorship will be popular, at least for a while. The fact that the military has not been victorious in recent wars will not be a major impediment, for it can always be argued that they would have won the war if it had not been for the corrupt politicians. (Primo de Rivera came to power in Spain immediately after the army had been humiliated in Morocco, and Neguib and Nasser ousted King Farouk after Egypt's defeat in the war against Israel.) What matters is that the army and the security forces still function, even when the other state institutions have broken down.

Russia could have additional support for a regime of this kind because of the strong presence of various mafias and the widespread belief that only iron measures can eliminate them. Since the supreme military leadership is thought to be involved in the general corruption, the initiative for such a coup is more likely to come from the colonels than the generals.

Would this be a fascist dictatorship? Not in the traditional sense, but it could turn into one, because the army does not have the competence to carry out the purge, nor could it act as an instrument of terror and propaganda. To manage a modern society and economy, a coalition is needed between the military and at least some civilian leaders. The army needs a political movement as a transmission belt, in the same way that Stalin did and virtually all modern dictators have.

The situation outside Europe is different. The grave crisis in the Middle East, North Africa, and other more developed countries of the Third World has been aggravated by demographic pressures. The people also subscribe to beliefs, fanaticism, and a willingness to fight that no longer exist in the rich and lazy West. This part of the world has no historical experience of fascism, no revulsion to bloodshed, and fewer restraints on engaging in mass violence. The potential of fascistlike movements and regimes is particularly strong in countries with much accumulated resentment that can look back on a great past. Some of these countries can turn easily from an authoritarian regime to one more repressive and aggressive. Iran under the shah was a dictatorship but not a very strict one. On the contrary, the shah experimented with reform and thus exposed himself to acute danger. But when challenged by extremists he lacked the determination to use the force that was needed to save his regime. Likewise, in Algeria the crisis occurred not when the dictatorship was harshest but when it began to make concessions to the Islamic challengers; this coincided with the consequences of a ruinous economic and social policy becoming ever more apparent.

Paraphrasing President Calvin Coolidge, we can say that the business of the Pacific Rim is business. China, Japan, and Southeast Asia have made enormous economic progress, and there is reason to assume that they will eventually catch up with the West. As a result, their political power—their standing in the world—will also increase. South Korea, Taiwan, Singapore, and China have shown an annual growth rate of 16 to 20 percent since the mid-1970s, with Malaysia, Thailand, and Indonesia not far behind. The reason for this economic "miracle" is no secret: It is the old-fashioned virtues of hard work and high saving rates. As a result, the percentage of the population below the poverty line in these countries is now a fraction of what it was in the early 1960s.

Conversely, the national income of Middle Eastern and African countries has stagnated or declined, and because of the rapid population growth, the number of the very poor and unemployed has increased. Over the past decade, per capita income in the Muslim countries of the Middle East and North Africa has declined by more than 20 percent, the worst performance by any world region. This has generated even more frustration and hatred, which can turn inward but can also turn into terrorism and a political system such as clerical fascism. A democratic solution seems ruled out for the forseeable future. These countries have fallen behind the rest of the world, and the more frustrated the people are, the greater will be their rage and their desire to reassert themselves.

9

The early-twentieth-century European thinkers who paved the way for fascism were preoccupied with a cultural as much as a political critique of society. The parallels between their ideas and the situation, at the end of the century, which has witnessed the rise and downfall of fascism, are striking. Fascism appeared with the promise of a new synthesis of nationalism and socialism but also a halt to decadence, a regeneration and rejuvenation of society, and a restoration of faith and values. It also vowed to provide a more effective government than democracy was and to put the national interest ahead of the egotism of individuals.

European fascism was both a product of the *fin de siècle* of 1900 and a reaction against it. It is fascinating even in retrospect how a hundred years ago, literary cult figures such as Maurice Barrès and Gabriele D'Annunzio transformed themselves in record time from world-weary dandies engaged in the cult of the self and hyperaestheticism to advocates of superpatriotism and antiliberal ideas of war and dictatorship that came close to fascism. The career of Giulio Evola, from Dadaism to ultrafascism, proceeded on similar lines, and Martin Heidegger, prophet of nihilism, has become the guru of a later generation of nihilists.

Writing under Mussolini, thirty years later, Benedetto Croce, great philosopher and astute observer of the Italian scene, wrote that fascism was the new irrationalism and decadence, "including occultism and theosophy, with logical restraints removed, the critical faculties enfeebled, the responsibility of rational assent brushed aside." Croce's comments again sound highly topical. Taken one by one, the *fin de siècle* ideas were no more than entertainments, intellectual fads that would not have survived unless the political stage had been set for them.

The new fascists believe that the political stage may have been set for their message to be accepted as the result of the cultural and political crisis of the West, its drifting and general weakness. With the disappearance of the "Communist danger," there is only the threat of chaos, but it is a far more difficult challenge to cope with.

Decades of attempts to perfect democracy and to weaken authority have often resulted in bedlam. Concern has spread about the weakness or absence of leadership, about moral and cultural relativism and the fragmentation of society. Special-interest groups and ethnic minorities demand not just autonomy and equal rights but even preferential treatment. As a result, the pendulum is swinging back in strange ways to the mood of an earlier age, with the emphasis on the good of the collective rather than on that of the individual, from permissiveness to discipline, order, and authority. Fascism is neither the only nor, in many countries, the most likely form of this backlash. But is is certainly one contender eager to exploit the discontents of society. New messages may fall on open ears in some developed countries and especially in backward societies. But those hypnotized by a second coming of Nazism and fascism, in Western Europe, are looking in the wrong direction. The fashions, the symbols, and the rhetoric of the 1990s are not those of the 1930s, and those countries most likely to succumb to nondemocratic ideologies are neither Germany nor Italy. Rather, these new movements will be populist, with a strong religious element in some places or a conservative or national Bolshevist streak. Fascism may not have a thousand faces, but it certainly may have a dozen, some old and familiar and others that we have not seen before.

If microbes and pests have become resistant to the magic bullets and the miracle pesticides of the 1940s and 1950s, fascism has used evolutionary techniques to adjust itself to new conditions and outwit humans. And since democratic societies always tend to celebrate victory a little too early, discarding tools that were of some use in the past and removing its guards out of negligence, convenience, and the desire to make some misplaced and shortsighted economies, fascism, like the staphylococci, is making a comeback. There might be no wonder drug in either case, but at least there ought to be awareness that a threat still exists and that it might be premature to dispose with the injunction in the Bible calling for sobriety and vigilance.

Notes

Introduction

1. W. Kowalsky and W. Schroeder, *Rechtsextremismus* (Opladen, 1994), p. 7.

2. Ervand Abrahamian, *Khomeinism* (Berkeley, 1993), p. 17. For a critical review of recent attempts to define fascism, populism, and other extremist movements, see Stanley Payne, *Fascism: History and Interpretation* (Madison, 1995).

3. K. D. Bracher, *Turning Points in Modern Times* (Cambridge, Mass., 1995), pp. 149–50.

Part 1

1. The features that fascism and Communism seem to have in common gave rise to the debate about totalitarism. See my *The Dream That Failed* (New York, 1994). On the differences between historical fascism and Communism, see my "Post-fascism, Post-Communism," *Partisan Review*, July 1995.

Part 2

1. *Studium*, June 1928, pp. 324–28, quoted in Richard Drake, "Julius Evola, Radical Fascism and the Lateran Accords," *Catholic Historical Review*, July 1988, p. 411. See also Thomas Sheenhaus, "Myth and Violence," *Social Research*, Spring 1981.

2. This is described in detail in George Marshall, *Spirit of '69: A Skinhead Bible* (Dunoon, 1991).

3. For reasons that are not clear, certain prominent European clubs acquired at one time the reputation of being "Jewish clubs," even though the connection between them and Jewish players, trainers, managers, or supporters was either tenuous or nonexistent. Among them were the Austria Vienna, MTK Budapest, Ajax Amsterdam, and Tottenham Hotspurs. Other clubs were known—including, at one time, Chelsea and Leeds United—correctly or not, for the racism of their fans. The influx of hundreds of foreign players, including many blacks, into the European League teams at first made the situation worse. But eventually, there were so many of them on virtually every side that the issue lost some of its urgency. The aggression of the fans had to find other targets.

4. Needless to say, this statement does not apply to the former Soviet Union, the

Balkans, the Middle East, and that part of the Third World where conflicts among ethnic groups persist and constitute a potential source of strength for fascist and fascist-like movements.

5. Paradoxically, such a correlation had not existed with regard to the Jews and the rise of Nazism in Germany. There was, if anything, a reverse ratio: Nazis were strongest precisely in those regions, such as north and northeast Germany, in which there were the fewest Jews. In German university elections, the Nazis emerged on top well before their success in the general elections. But they were strongest in universities attended by few Jews, and in faculties in which Jews were hardly represented at all.

6. See R. Maurer, "Schuld und Wohlstand," in H. Schwilk and W. Schacht, eds., *Die selbstbewusste Nation* (Berlin, 1994), p. 73. In the same context, the author argues that there was no difference in principle between the doctors in a Norwegian prison who treated the famous writer Knut Hamsun after 1945 and the Nazi physicians in the extermination camps. Hamsun, an admirer of Nazism, had collaborated with the German authorities in his native country and, like the leaders of the Quisling party, was detained after liberation. But there was a difference, for Hamsun was released and survived.

Part 3

1. *Christliche Welt*, 1924, pp. 235–43.

2. Edgar Alexander, *Der Mythus Hitler* (Zurich, 1937), pp. 21, 223–25. Alexander quotes *Mein Kampf* (Munich, 1933), pp. 189, 379.

3. See E. Abrahamian, "May Day in the Islamic Republic," in *Khomeinism* (Berkeley, 1993), pp. 66–87. Originally, there was no clergy in the Western, Christian sense in Islam. What happened in Iran can be interpreted as the Christianization of Islam, according to Bernard Lewis.

4. See Said Arjomand, *The Turban and the Cross* (New York 1988), p. 209.

5. See, for instance, Aurel Kolnai, *The Revolt Against the West* (London, 1938).

6. But it is also true that the chaotic aftermath of the Afghan war and the unending and destructive warlordism produced the fundamentalist Taliban movement. The radicalism of the young *ulema* of Taliban went even further in some respects than did the Iranian mullahs, and they had sudden and unexpected successes in the fighting in southern Afghanistan during the winter of 1994/1995.

7. *Den*, 1992, p. 26.

8. Paul Mojzes, *Yugoslav Inferno* (New York, 1994), p. 134.

9. Alexei Malashenko, "Iz proshlovo v proshloe. Fundamentalizm Islama i Pravo-slavie," *Svobodnaya Mysl* 14 (1993): 69–83.

10. Pram Shankar Jha, "The Fascist Impulse in Developing Countries," *Studies in Conflict and Terrorism* 17 (1994): 229.

11. However, in view of the unstable position of the ruling coalition, it has become more and more dependent on the support of the extreme right. The PRNU entered the cabinet in August 1994, and even the Greater Romanians were brought into the alliance in January 1995.

Conclusion

1. The main authority of both Furet and Pipes for this argument is Hermann Rauschning, a local Nazi leader from Danzig who defected and published a sensational

book entitled *Conversations with Hitler* in 1939. But Rauschning is not a reliable source. Although his book contains some intelligent, and even prophetic, observations, they are not based on conversations with Hitler, who (it has been established) seldom if ever saw Rauschning. According to Rauschning, Hitler told him that National Socialism is what Marxism might have been if it could have broken its absurd and artificial ties with a democratic order. However, Rauschning makes it clear that in Hitlerian parlance, "Marxism" always referred to the Social Democrats, not the Communists. But this was no secret. Hitler had made it known much earlier (in *Mein Kampf*) that Social Democratic propaganda and indoctrination had impressed him well before 1918. Rauschning wrote this book partly as an exercise in anti-Nazi propaganda—an honorable enterprise—and partly to improve his personal finances; indeed, the book became a best-seller. What he did was a legitimate stratagem, but it is not legitimate to treat such a book as a primary source.

2. Marcus Garvey, the leader of the UNIA, the first major black nationalist (and separatist) organization, claimed in the 1930s that he had been the first fascist and that Mussolini had copied fascism from him. But this is true only in the vaguest sense. There was perhaps an inchoate desire in Harlem in 1917, the first stirrings of a fascist style, but not the capacity to make it a reality. The same is true with regard to the Third World in 1950. For a discussion of Garvey and the issue of fascism in underdeveloped countries, see A. James Gregor, *The Fascist Persuasion in Radical Politics* (Princeton, 1974).

3. B. Croce, *A History of Italy, 1871–1915* (Oxford 1929), pp. 242, 261, 268. The *fin de siècle* origins of fascism remain to be investigated in detail; the historical interest apart, this is a subject of topical relevance in the age of postmodernism. See W. Laqueur, "Fin de Siècle—Once More with Feeling," *Journal of Contemporary History*, January 1996.

Bibliographical Note

The number of books relating to fascism, neofascism, and the extreme Right can be measured in the hundreds of thousands. The literature covers European history from World War I to the end of World War II; the fascist ideology and movements; its leaders and institutions; its economic, social, and cultural aspects; its foreign political orientation; its attitudes toward religion; and many other aspects. These books include academic studies as well as memoirs, biographies, autobiographies, and, to a certain extent, also fictional literature.

So far there are not as many serious studies of neofascism and more recent phenomena such as fascism in the former Soviet Union and Eastern Europe and radical movements and clerical fascism in the Third World. These movements are too recent; they are constantly changing; and there is a natural reluctance to generalize on ongoing developments. Leaders and movements that rose meteorlike a year ago or two may have vanished by the time a book appears in print.

Among the most useful bibliographies are those by P. Rees, *Fascism and Pre-Fascism in Europe, 1890–1945* (Brighton, 1984); and *Biographical Dictionary of the Extreme Right Since 1890* (Brighton, 1990).

The relevant literature on fascism is discussed in a monograph by Stanley G. Payne, *Fascism: History and Interpretation* (Madison, 1995), as well as in two collective works by Stein Larsen, Bernt Hagtvet, and Jan Peter Myklebust, *Who Were the Fascists?* (Bergen, 1980); and in Walter Laqueur, ed., *Fascism, a Readers' Guide* (Berkeley, 1976).

Another significant work discussing one aspect of the literature is by Michael Marrus, *The Holocaust in History* (London, 1988). W. Wippermann, *Europäischer Faschismus im Vergleich, 1922–1982* (Frankfurt, 1983), is a comparative study, as is R. Griffin, *The Nature of Fascism* (London, 1990).

Important general works on Nazism include those by K. D. Bracher, *The German Dictatorship* (New York, 1970); and K. Hildebrand, *The Third Reich* (London, 1984). The question of Hitler's supporters is discussed by Jürgen Falter, *Hitler's Wähler* (Munich, 1991), as well as by T. Childers, *The Nazi Voter* (London, 1983); and R. Hamilton, *Who Voted for the Nazis?* (Princeton, 1991). The ideology and the doctrinal origins of Nazism are covered by George Mosse, *The Crisis of German Ideology* (New York, 1964); and M. Burleigh and W. Wippermann, *The Racial State* (Cambridge, Mass., 1991).

On Hitler, see Ian Kershaw, *The Hitler Myth* (Oxford, 1987); J. P. Stern, *Hitler*

(London, 1975); and the most detailed existing biography, Joachim Fest, *Hitler, eine Biographie* (Berlin, 1973). Alan Bullock's *Hitler* (New York, 1964) is also still useful.

Stimulating introductions to Hitler's goals and policies are those by S. Haffner, *Anmerkungen zu Hitler* (Munich, 1978); and E. Jäckel, *Hitler in History* (London, 1984). On Nazi propaganda, Z. Zeman, *Nazi Propaganda* (London, 1972), should be consulted as well as D. Welch, *Nazi Propaganda* (London, 1983). There is no multivolume history of the Nazi Party on a grand scale, but there are important monographs, of which the following should be singled out: K. Bracher, W. Sauer, and G. Schulz, *Die national-alsozialistische Machtergreifung*, 3 vols. (Frankfurt, 1979); and G. Schulz, *Aufstieg des National Sozialismus* (Berlin, 1975). For the structure of the Nazi state, see G. Hirschfeld and L, Kettenacker, eds., *Der Führerstaat, Mythos und Realität* (Stuttgart, 1981); and M. Broszat, *The Hitler State* (London, 1981). On daily life in the Third Reich, see D. Peukert and J. Reulecke, *Die Reihen fest geschlossen* (Wuppertal, 1981); and R. Bessel, ed., *Life in the Third Reich* (Oxford, 1978).

Among the most important works on Nazi foreign policy are K. Hildebrand, *Deutsche Aussenpolitik, 1933–1945* (Stuttgart, 1980); G. Weinberg, *The Foreign Policy of Hitler's Germany*, 2 vols. (Chicago, 1980); W. Michalka, ed., *Nationalsozialistische Aussenpolitik* (Darmstadt, 1978); and M. Funke, ed., *Hitler Deutschland und die Mächte* (Dusseldorf, 1976).

On Nazi terrorism, see R. Breitman's study of Himmler in action, *The Architect of Genocide* (New York, 1992); R. Gellately, *The Gestapo and German Society* (Oxford, 1990); and H. Krausnick and H. H. Wilhelm, *Die Truppe des Weltanschauungskrieges* (Stuttgart, 1981).

The German economy in the 1930s and 1940s is discussed in A. Barkai, *Nazi Economics* (New Haven, 1990); H. James, *The German Slump* (Oxford, 1986); and R. Overy, *The Nazi Economic Recovery* (London, 1982). Social conditions and social policies in the Third Reich are surveyed by Tim Mason, *Social Policy in the Third Reich* (New York, 1983); and N. Frei, *Nazi Germany* (Oxford, 1993). On the social composition of the Nazi Party and it leadership, see M. Kater, *The Nazi Party* (Oxford, 1983).

Among the leading works on the German resistance, two books stand out: K. von Klemperer, *German Resistance Against Hitler* (Oxford, 1982); and P. Hoffmann, *German Resistance to Hitler* (Cambridge, Mass., 1988).

The most detailed and authoritative work on German military policy and all aspects of World War II is *Das deutsche Reich und der zweite Weltkrieg* (Stuttgart, 1979–). Of the planned twelve volumes, six have been published so far. Detailed collections of source material on public opinion in the Third Reich are the Gestapo reports (17 vols.) *Meldungen aus dem Reich*, ed. H. Boberach (Herrsching, 1984), covering the years 1938 to 1945; and, from an oppositionist point of view, the multivolume *Deutschland Berichte* of the SOPADE (Social Democratic Party in exile from 1934 to 1940) (Frankfurt, 1980).

The main controversies concerning Nazi theory and the Third Reich are summarized in a number of books, including Ian Kershaw, *The Nazi Dictatorshibp* (London, 1985); and E. Nolte, *Streitpunkte* (Berlin, 1993); also W. Wippermann, *Kontroversen um Hitler* (Frankfurt, 1987). The most recent polemics, including the *Historikerstreit*, are reviewed in R. Evans, *Hitler's Shadow* (New York, 1989); and C. Mayer, *The Unmasterable Past* (Cambridge, Mass., 1988).

There is no biography of Hitler even remotely comparable to Renzo de Felice's six volumes (so far) about Mussolini. The first volume appeared in 1965. Given the central role of the Duce, they are also a history of the Fascist Party and state. A four-volume biography was written by Mussolini's admirers, G. Pini and D. Susmel (Florence, 1953–1955); a three-volume French biography by André Brisaud (Paris, 1983); and several biographies in English. Mussolini's collected writings, *Opera omnia*, have been published in thirty-six volumes (Florence, 1951–1953).

On the early days of the Italian Fascist Party, the following are of particular interest: R. Vivarelli, *Storia delle origini del fascismo* (Bologna, 1991); and E. Gentile, *Storia del partito fascista, 1919–1922* (Bari, 1989). The most important work in English and on the early period is A. Lyttleton, *The Seizure of Power* (London, 1973). The Italian economy under Fascism is reviewed in G. Toniolo, *L'economia dell'Italia fascista* (Bari, 1980). On Fascist modernization, see A. J. Gregor, *Italian Fascism and Developmental Dictatorship* (Princeton, 1979).

Italian foreign policy in the 1930s and 1940s is discussed by D. Mack Smith, *Mussolini's Roman Empire* (New York, 1976), and the later period is described and analyzed by Mac Gregor Knox, *Mussolini Unleashed, 1939–1941* (Cambridge, 1982).

On the last radical phase of fascism, the Republic of Salo, see G. Bocca, *La Repubblica di Mussolini* (Bari, 1977). On the purge after the defeat of Fascism, see R. P. Domenico *Italian Fascists on Trial, 1943–1948* (Chapel Hill, 1991); and L. Mercuri, *L'Epurazione in Italia* (Cueno, 1988).

The following books provide a starting point for the study of fascist movements and regimes outside Germany and Italy, and they also contain good bibliographical references: on Slovakia, Croatia, Hungary, and Romania, respectively, see Y. Yellinek, *The Parish Republic* (New York, 1976); L. Hory and M. Broszat, *Der kroatische Ustascha Staat* (Stuttgart, 1976); M. Szollosi Janze, *Die Pfeilkreuzbewegung in Ungarn* (Munich, 1959); A. Heinen, *Die Legion Erzengel Michael in Rumänien* (Munich, 1986); and R. Ioanid, *The Sword of the Archangel* (New York, 1990).

There is a considerable literature on fascism in France. For the early period, R. Soucy, *French Fascism, the First Wave, 1924–1933* (New Haven, 1986), is indispensable. For the later years, by way of introduction, see J. Plumyène and R. Lasierra, *Les Fascismes françaises* (Paris, 1963); and, more recently, P. Milza, *Le Fascisme français* (Paris, 1987). On fascist ideology, Z. Sternhell, *Neither Right nor Left* (Berkeley, 1986), is of particular importance.

On Spain, J. J. Campos, *El fascismo en la crisis de la segunda Republica* (Madrid, 1979), should be consulted, as well as the earlier book by B. Nellesen, *Die verbotene Revolution* (Hamburg, 1963); and S. M. Ellwood, *Spanish Fascism in the Franco Era* (New York, 1987). There is also much material on falangism in the two standard books on the second Spanish Republic: S. Payne, *Spain's First Democracy* (Madison, 1993); and M. Blinkhorn, *Carlism and Crisis in Spain, 1931–1939* (Cambridge, Mass., 1975).

Informative studies on fascism in minor European countries include L. Karvonen, *From White to Blue-and-Black* (Helsinki, 1988) (on Finland); and B. Pauley, *Hitler and the Forgotten Nazis* (Chapel Hill, 1981) (on Austria). For the fascist parties in other European countries, valuable references can be found in Payne, *Fascism;* and Larsen, Hagtvet, and Myklebust, *Who Were the Fascists?*

Two collections of contemporary and subsequent interpretations of fascism should be mentioned: R. De Felice, *Le interpretazioni dei contemporanei e degli storici* (Rome, 1970); and E. Nolte, *Theorien über den Faschismus* (Königstein, 1984).

General studies on right-wing extremism include the following: P. Hainsworth, ed., *The Extreme Right in Europe and the USA* (London, 1992); H. G. Betz, *Radical Rightwing Populism in Western Europe* (London, 1994) (with a detailed bibliography); Roger Eatwell and Neil O'Sullivan, *The Nature of the Right* (London, 1991); L. Chele et al., *Neo-Fascism in Europe* (London, 1991); M. Blinkhorn, ed., *Fascists and Conservatives* (London, 1990); W. Kowalsky and W. Schroeder, eds., *Rechtsextremismus* (Opladen, 1994); U. Backes and E. Jesse, *Jahrbuch Extremismus und Demokratie* (Bonn, 1991); F. Gress et al., *Neue Rechte and Rechtsextremismus in Europa* (Opladen, 1990); C. O. Maolain, *The Radical Right* (London, 1987) (a reference work); P. H. Merkl and L. Weinberg, eds., *Encounters with the Contemporary Radical Right* (New York, 1993); and W. Kowalsky, *Kulturrevolution?* (Opladen, 1991).

Among the many studies on the extreme Right in France are the following: Joseph Algazy, *L'Extrême Droite de 1965 à 1984* (Paris, 1992); Guy Birenbaum, *Le Front national en politique* (Paris, 1992); A. M. Duranton Crabol, *Visage de la Nouvelle Droite* (Paris, 1988) (Greece); N. Mayer and P. Perineau, *Le Front national à decouvert* (Paris, 1989); P. A. Taguieff, ed., *Face aux racisme,* 2 vols. (Paris, 1991); P. Milza, *Fascisme français* (Paris, 1991); J. F. Sirinelli, ed., *Histoire des droites en France* (Paris, 1992); and R. Badinter, *Vous avez dit fascismes?* (Paris, 1984).

On neo-Nazism and the far Right in postwar Germany, see K. P. Tauber, *Beyond Eagle and Swastika,* 2 vols. (Middletown, 1967) (by far the most detailed study on the early period); R. Stoess, *Die extreme Rechte in der Bundesrepublik* (Opladen, 1989); R. Stoess, *Die Republikaner* (Cologne, 1990); B. Siegler, *Auferstanden aus Ruinen* (Berlin, 1991); B. Schroeder, *Rechte Kerle* (Reinbeck, 1992); H. G. Jaschke, *Die Republikaner* (Bonn, 1992); H. J. Veen et al., *The Republikaner Party in Germany* (Washington, D.C., 1993); W. Benz, ed., *Rechtsextremismus in der Bundesrepublik* (Frankfurt, 1989); U. Backes and E. Jesse, *Politischer Extremismus in der Bundesrepublik Deutschland* (Cologne, 1989); and P. Dudek and H. G. Jaschke, *Entstehung und Entwicklung des Rechtsextremismus in der Bundesrepublik* (Opladen, 1984).

On Italy, see P. Ignazi, *Postfascisti?* (Bologna, 1994); P. Ignazi, *Il polo escluso* (Bologna, 1989); E. Santarelli, *Fascismo e neofascismo* (Rome, 1974); V. Marchi, *Skinhead* (Turin, 1992); F. Ferraresi, ed., *La destra radicale* (Milan, 1984); D. Della Porta, *Terrorismi in Italia* (Bologna, 1984); V. Marchi, *Blood and Honor* (Rome, 1993); G. Locatelli and D. Martini, *Duce addio* (Milan, 1994); P. Rosenbaum, *Il nuovo fascismo* (Milan, 1975); R. Chiarini and P. Corsini, *De Salo a piazza della loggia* (Milan, 1983); and E. Raisi, *Storia delle idee della nuova destra italiana* (Rome, 1990).

Among the studies of Giulio Evola, two should be mentioned: A. Romualdi, *Julius Evola* (Rome, 1971); and G. F. Lami, *Introduzione a Evola* (Rome, 1980).

On the extreme Right in other countries, see J. van Donselar, *Fout na de oorlog* (Amsterdam, 1991); S. Dumont, *Les Brigades noirs* (Brussels, 1983); M. Billig, *Fascists* (London, 1978); R. Thurlow, *Fascism in Britain* (Oxford, 1987); C. Butterwege and S. Jaeger, *Rassismus in Europa* (Cologne, 1992); S. Acquaviva, ed., *Le forme del politico* (Florence, 1984); M. S. Soler, *Los hijos del 20-N* (Madrid, 1993); R. Baehler, *Die rechtsradikale Szene in der Schweiz* (Zurich, 1993); and S. Taylor, *The National Front in British Politics* (Basingstoke, 1992).

On the far Right in Russia, there is not yet much literature, but see W. Laqueur, *Black Hundred* (New York, 1994).

On Eastern Europe, see RFE/RL Research Report, a special issue, *The Politics of Intolerance* (Munich, April 1994); and Paul Hockenos, *Free to Hate* (New York, 1993). G. Frazer and G. Lancelle, *Absolute Zhirinovsky* (New York, 1994), includes a selection from Zhirinovsky's writings and speeches.

In the absence of books, the periodicals of extreme right-wing and neofascist groups in West and East Europe are an indispensable source for these parties' activities. The essential sources are *Nation Europa* (monthly, Coburg), founded in 1951; *Zavtra* (formerly *Den*) weekly, Moscow; *Molodaya Gvardia* (monthly, Moscow) (originally a Communist monthly); *Nash Sovremennik* (monthly, Moscow); *Europa Rechts* (the organ of the parliamentary factions of the far Right in Brussels); *National Hebdo* (France); *Présent* (Paris); *Identité*

(London); *Il secolo d'Italia* (daily); *Il nazionale* (Rome); *L'Italia settimanale* (weekly); *Deutsche Stimme* (monthly, Vienna); *Neue Freie Zeitung* (weekly, Vienna); *Freie Argumente* (Vienna); *Schweizer Demokrat* (monthly, Switzerland); and *La nación* (weekly, Spain).

The Ministry of the Interior in Germany and the Federal Swiss Police Department publish annual reports on extremist activities in their countries that include much factual material. In Germany such reports (*Verfassungsschutzberichte*) are also published in each *Land*. On Switzerland, in particular, see Urs Andermatt and Hanspeter Kriesi, *Rechtsextremismus in der Schweiz* (Zurich, 1995). The occasional papers by the American Anti-Defamation League are relevant to the neo-Nazis' and right-wing extremists' activities in the United States.

On Islamic radicalism and fundamentalism, see S. Bakash, *The Reign of the Ayatollahs* (New York, 1984); M. Kramer, ed., *Shi'ism* (Boulder, 1985); B. Tibi, *Die fundamentalistische Herausforderung* (Munich, 1992); E. Sivan, *Radical Islam* (New Haven, 1985); E. Sivan and M. Friedman, *Religious Radicalism and Politics in the Middle East* (Albany, 1990); R. Mottahedeh, *The Mantle of the Prophet* (New York, 1985); A. Taheri, *The Spirit of Allah* (Washington, D.C., 1986); M. Wright, ed., *The Khomeini Revolution* (London, 1989); E. A. Abrahamian, *Khomeinism* (Berkeley, 1993); M. Juergenmeyer, *The New Cold War* (Berkeley, 1993); and M. Marty and R. Scott Appelby, eds., *Accounting for Fundamentalism* (Chicago, 1994). Also edited by M. Marty and R. Scott Appelby are *Fundamentalism and Society* (Chicago, 1993) and *Fundamentalism and the State* (Chicago, 1993). See also T. Meyer, *Fundamentalismus* (Hamburg, 1989); Montgomery Watt, *Islamic Fundamentalism and Modernity* (London, 1988); Ian Lustick, *For the Land and the Lord* (New York, 1988); G. Kepel, *Muslim Extremism in Egypt* (Berkeley, 1993); Fouad Zakariya, *Laicité ou islamisme* (Paris, 1991); A. Lamchichi, *L'Algerie en crise* (Paris, 1991); R. Leveau, *Le Sabre et le turban* (Paris, 1993); O. Roy, *L'Echec de l'Islam politique* (Paris, 1992); M. L. Ahnal et al., *L'Algerie par ses islamites* (Paris, 1991); A. Rouadjia, *Les Frères à la mosque* (Paris, 1990); Abed Charef, *Algerie: Le grand dérapage* (Paris, 1994); and G. Kepel and Y. Richard, *Intellectuels et militants de l'Islam contemporain* (Paris, 1990).

An interesting study about right-wing extremism in India is T. Basu et al., *Khaki Shorts, Saffron Flags* (Hyderabad, 1993). Further bibliographical references concerning South Asia can be found in the series edited by M. Marty and R. Scot Appleby.

See also *Journal of Historical Review* (United States); and *Revue d'histoire revisioniste* (France, specializing in Holocaust denial).

Among the ideological organs of the extreme Right in Europe are the following: *Eléments* (New Right) (Paris); *Nouvelle ecole* (Paris); *Teksten* (Belgium); *Krisis* (Paris); *Vouloir* (Belgium); *La Lettre d'information du club de l'horloge* (quarterly, Paris); *Orientations* (Belgium); *Elementi* (Italy); *Aula* (Vienna); and *Punto y coma* (Spain).

On Nazi rock, skinheads, and soccer fans, see M. Annas and R. Christoph, eds., *Neue Soundtracks für den Volksempfänger* (Berlin, 1993); G. Marshall, *Spirit of '69: A Skinhead Bible* (Dunoon, 1991); and K. Farin and E. Seidel Pialen, *Skinheads* (Munich, 1993).

Jutta Ditfurth, *Feuer in die Herzen* (Dusseldorf, 1994), describes various protofascist ecological groups from a left-wing "Green" point of view; D. Beiersdorfer et al., *Fussball und Rassismus* (Hamburg, 1994), analyzes the European soccer scene and its links with neofascist groups. A general survey of the development of Green parties in Europe, some gravitating to the left and others to the right, is provided by D. Richardson and C. Rootes, eds., *The Green Challenge* (London, 1994). Richard Herzinger and Hannes Stein, *Endzeit-Propheten oder Die Offensive der Antiwestler* (Hamburg 1995), is a systematic critique of anti-democratic, anti-Western trends among ideologues formerly belonging to the left.

Index